iPhone®

FOR

DUMMIES®

4TH EDITION

iPhone®

FOR

DUMMIES®

4TH EDITION

by Edward C. Baig
USA Today Personal Tech columnist

and

Bob LeVitus
Houston Chronicle "Dr. Mac" columnist

WILEY

Wiley Publishing, Inc.

iPhone® For Dummies®, 4th Edition

Published by
Wiley Publishing, Inc.
111 River Street
Hoboken, NJ 07030-5774

www.wiley.com

Copyright © 2010 by Wiley Publishing, Inc., Indianapolis, Indiana

Published by Wiley Publishing, Inc., Indianapolis, Indiana

Published simultaneously in Canada

For general information on our other products and services, please contact our Customer Care Department within the U.S. at 877-762-2974, outside the U.S. at 317-572-3993, or fax 317-572-4002.

For technical support, please visit www.wiley.com/techsupport.

Wiley also publishes its books in a variety of electronic formats. Some content that appears in print may not be available in electronic books.

Library of Congress Control Number: 2010932438

ISBN: 978-0-470-87870-5

Manufactured in the United States of America

10 9 8 7 6 5 4 3 2

WILEY

About the Authors

Edward C. Baig writes the weekly Personal Technology column in *USA TODAY* and is cohost of the weekly *USA TODAY*'s Talking Tech podcast with Jefferson Graham. Ed is also the author of *Macs For Dummies,* 10th Edition, and cowriter (with Bob LeVitus) of *iPad For Dummies.* Before joining *USA TODAY* as a columnist and reporter in 1999, Ed spent six years at *Business Week,* where he wrote and edited stories about consumer tech, personal finance, collectibles, travel, and wine tasting, among other topics. He received the Medill School of Journalism 1999 Financial Writers and Editors Award for contributions to the "*Business Week* Investor Guide to Online Investing." That followed a three-year stint at *U.S. News & World Report,* where Ed was the lead tech writer for the News You Can Use section but also dabbled in numerous other subjects.

Ed began his journalist career at *Fortune* magazine, gaining the best basic training imaginable during his early years as a fact checker and contributor to the Fortune 500. Through the dozen years he worked at the magazine, Ed covered leisure-time industries, penned features on the lucrative "dating" market and the effect of religion on corporate managers, and was heavily involved in the Most Admired Companies project. Ed also started *Fortune*'s Products to Watch column, a venue for low- and high-tech items.

Bob LeVitus, often referred to as "Dr. Mac," has written or cowritten nearly 60 popular computer books, including *iPad For Dummies, Incredible iPhone Apps For Dummies, Mac OS X Snow Leopard For Dummies,* and *Microsoft Office 2008 for Mac For Dummies* for Wiley Publishing, Inc.; *Stupid Mac Tricks* and *Dr. Macintosh* for Addison-Wesley; and *The Little iTunes Book,* 3rd Edition, and *The Little iDVD Book,* 2nd Edition, for Peachpit Press. His books have sold more than one million copies worldwide. Bob has penned the popular Dr. Mac column for the *Houston Chronicle* for the past 14 years and has been published in pretty much every magazine that ever used the word *Mac* in its title. His achievements have been documented in major media around the world. (Yes, that was Bob juggling a keyboard in *USA TODAY* a few years back!)

Bob is known for his expertise, trademark humorous style, and ability to translate techie jargon into usable and fun advice for regular folks. Bob is also a prolific public speaker, presenting more than 100 Macworld Expo training sessions in the United States. and abroad, keynote addresses in three countries, and Macintosh training seminars in many U.S. cities.

Dedications

I dedicate this book to my beautiful and amazingly supportive wife, Janie, for making me a better person every day I am with her. And to my incredible kids: my adorable little girl, Sydney (one of her first words was "iPod"), my little boy, Sammy (who is all smiles from the moment he wakes up in the morning), and, of course, my canine "son," Eddie. They all got their hands (or paws) on the iPhone at one time or another — and gave me a valuable perspective of the device through youthful eyes. I am madly in love with you all.

— Ed Baig

As always, this book is dedicated to my incredible wife, Lisa, who taught me almost everything I know about almost everything, except computers, and has put up with me for more than 25 years. And to my two terrific children, Allison and Jacob, who love their iPhones almost as much as I love them (my kids, not my iPhone).

— Bob LeVitus

Authors' Acknowledgments

Special thanks to everyone at Apple who helped us turn this book around so quickly: Katie Cotton, Natalie Kerris, Steve Dowling, Greg (Joz) Joswiak, John Richey, Keri Walker, Teresa Brewer, Natalie Harrison, Monica Sarkar, Tom Neumayr, Jennifer Bowcock, Janette Barrios, and everyone else. We couldn't have done it without you. We apologize if we missed anybody.

Big-time thanks to the gang at Wiley: Bob "I need it yesterday" Woerner, Jodi "I'm calm now, really" Jensen, Susan "who said you could eat?" Pink, Andy "The Boss" Cummings, Barry "Still no humorous nickname" Pruett, and our technical editor, Dennis R. Cohen, who also has no humorous nickname but did a rocking job in record time, as always. We also want to thank our invaluable proofreader, Debbye Butler, who did a tremendous job. Debbye patriotically stood (or sat) at the ready over the Fourth of July weekend waiting for us to deliver our files. Editorial assistant Amanda Graham also deserves our thanks. She handled a bevy of last-minute tasks with panache. Finally, thanks to everyone at Wiley we don't know by name. If you helped with this project in any way, you have our everlasting thanks.

Bob adds: Thanks also to super-agent Carole "Still the Swifty Lazar of Tech Agentry" Jelen, for deal-making beyond the call of duty, yet again. You've been my agent for more than 20 years and you're *still* the best. And thanks also to my family and friends for putting up with me throughout my hibernation during this book's gestation. Finally, thanks to Saccone's for killer New Jersey–style thin-crust pizza, The Iron Works, and Black's for BBQ beyond compare, Chuy's for burritos as big as yo' face, Torchy's Tacos for the most unusual and tasty tacos ever, Mighty Fine for good, cheap, tasty burgers, and Diet Vanilla Coke Zero and Diet Red Bull because they're the breakfast of champions (and tech writers).

Ed adds: Thanks to my agent Matt Wagner for again turning me into a *For Dummies* author. It is a privilege to be working with a first-class guy and true professional. I'd also like to thank Jim Henderson, Geri Tucker, Nancy Blair, and the rest of my *USA TODAY* friends and colleagues (in and out of the Money section) for your enormous support and encouragement. Most of all, thanks to my loving family for understanding my nightly (and weekend) disappearances as we raced to get this project completed on time.

And finally, thanks to you, gentle reader, for buying our book.

Publisher's Acknowledgments

We're proud of this book; please send us your comments at http://dummies.custhelp.com. For other comments, please contact our Customer Care Department within the U.S. at 877-762-2974, outside the U.S. at 317-572-3993, or fax 317-572-4002.

Some of the people who helped bring this book to market include the following:

Acquisitions and Editorial

Project Editor: Susan Pink

Acquisitions Editor: Bob Woerner

Copy Editor: Susan Pink
(Previous Edition: Becky Whitney, Susan Pink)

Technical Editor: Dennis Cohen

Editorial Manager: Jodi Jensen

Editorial Assistant: Amanda Graham

Sr. Editorial Assistant: Cherie Case

Cartoons: Rich Tennant
(www.the5thwave.com)

Composition Services

Project Coordinator: Patrick Redmond

Layout and Graphics: Samantha K. Cherolis, Joyce Haughey, Kelly Kijovsky

Proofreaders: Debbye Butler, Dwight Ramsey

Indexer: Steve Rath

Publishing and Editorial for Technology Dummies

Richard Swadley, Vice President and Executive Group Publisher

Andy Cummings, Vice President and Publisher

Mary Bednarek, Executive Acquisitions Director

Mary C. Corder, Editorial Director

Publishing for Consumer Dummies

Diane Graves Steele, Vice President and Publisher

Composition Services

Debbie Stailey, Director of Composition Services

Contents at a Glance

Table of Contents

Introduction

*P*recious few products ever come close to generating the kind of buzz seen with the iPhone. Its messianic arrival received front-page treatment in newspapers and top billing on network and cable TV shows. People lined up days in advance just to ensure landing one of the first units. Years from now, people will insist, "I was one of them."

But we trust you didn't pick up this book to read yet another account about how the iPhone launch was an epochal event. We trust you *did* buy the book to find out how to get the very most out of your remarkable device. Our goal is to deliver that information in a light and breezy fashion. We expect you to have fun using your iPhone. We equally hope you have fun spending time with us.

About This Book

Let's get one thing out of the way right from the get-go. We think you're pretty darn smart for buying a *For Dummies* book. That says to us that you have the confidence and intelligence to know what you don't know. The *For Dummies* franchise is built around the core notion that all of us feel insecure about certain topics when tackling them for the first time, especially when those topics have to do with technology.

As with most Apple products, the iPhone is beautifully designed and intuitive to use. And though our editors may not want us to reveal this dirty little secret (especially on the first page, for goodness sake), the truth is you'll get pretty far just by exploring the iPhone's many functions and features on your own, without the help of this (or any other) book.

Okay, now that we spilled the beans, let's tell you why you shouldn't run back to the bookstore and request a refund. This book is chock-full of useful tips, advice, and other nuggets that should make your iPhone experience all the more pleasurable. So keep this book nearby and consult it often.

Conventions Used in This Book

First, we want to tell you how we go about our business. *iPhone For Dummies,* 4th Edition, makes generous use of numbered steps, bullet lists, and pictures. Web addresses are shown in a special monofont typeface, `like this`.

We also include a few sidebars with information that is not required reading (not that any of this book is) but that we hope will provide a richer understanding of certain subjects. Overall, we aim to keep technical jargon to a minimum, under the guiding principle that with rare exceptions you need not know what any of it really means.

How This Book Is Organized

Here's something we imagine you've never heard before: Most books have a beginning, a middle, and an end, and you do well to adhere to that linear structure — unless you're one of those knuckleheads out to ruin it for the rest of us by revealing that the butler did it.

Fortunately, there is no ending to spoil in a *For Dummies* book. So although you may want to digest this book from start to finish — and we hope you do — we won't penalize you for skipping ahead or jumping around. Having said that, we organized *iPhone For Dummies,* 4th Edition, in an order that we think makes the most sense, as follows.

Part I: Getting to Know Your iPhone

In the introductory chapters of Part I, you tour the iPhone inside and out, find out how to activate the phone with Apple's partner in the United States, AT&T, and get hands-on (or, more precisely, fingers-on) experience with the iPhone's unique virtual multitouch display.

Part II: The Mobile iPhone

The iPhone has *phone* in its name for a reason. Part II is mostly about all the ways you can make and receive calls on the device — even video calls, where two (or more) people can see each other. But you also discover how to exchange text messages and play with the Calendar, Clock, Calculator, and Voice Memo apps.

Part III: The Multimedia iPhone

Part III is where the fun truly begins. This is the iPhone as an iPod, a camera, and yes, even a camcorder, meaning that music, videos, movies, pictures, and other diversions come to life.

Part IV: The Internet iPhone

Part IV covers the mobile Internet. You master the Safari browser, e-mail, maps, and more. We discuss the faster 3G, or third-generation, wireless network that the latest iPhone can tap into. And speaking of maps, your iPhone has the capability to locate your whereabouts through GPS (in the case of the iPhone 3G, 3GS, and 4) and other location-tracking methods.

Part V: The Undiscovered iPhone

In Part V, you find out how to apply your preferences through the iPhone's internal settings, how to find and obtain new apps at the iTunes App Store, and discover where to go for troubleshooting assistance if your iPhone should misbehave.

Part VI: The Part of Tens

The Part of Tens: Otherwise known as the *For Dummies* answer to David Letterman. The lists presented in Part VI steer you to some of our favorite iPhone apps as well as some very handy tips and shortcuts.

Icons Used in This Book

Little round pictures (icons) appear in the left margins throughout this book. Consider these icons miniature road signs, telling you something extra about the topic at hand or hammering a point home.

Here's what the four icons used in this book look like and mean.

These are the juicy morsels, shortcuts, and recommendations that might make the task at hand faster or easier.

This icon emphasizes the stuff we think you ought to retain. You may even jot down a note to yourself in the iPhone.

Put on your propeller beanie hat and pocket protector; this text includes the truly geeky stuff. You can safely ignore this material, but we wouldn't have bothered to write it if it weren't interesting or informative.

You wouldn't intentionally run a stop sign, would you? In the same fashion, ignoring warnings may be hazardous to your iPhone and (by extension) your wallet. There, you now know how these warning icons work, for you have just received your very first warning!

Where to Go from Here

Where to turn to next? Why straight to Chapter 1, of course (without passing Go).

In all seriousness, we wrote this book for you, so please let us know what you think. If we screwed up, confused you, left something out, or — heaven forbid — made you angry, drop us a note. And if we hit you with one pun too many, it helps to know that as well.

Because writers are people too (believe it or not), we also encourage positive feedback if you think it's warranted. So kindly send e-mail to Ed at `baig dummies@aol.com` and to Bob at `iPhoneLeVitus@boblevitus.com`. We'll do our best to respond to reasonably polite e-mail in a timely fashion.

Most of all, we want to thank you for buying our book. Please enjoy it along with your new iPhone.

Note: At the time we wrote this book, all the information it contained was accurate for the original iPhone, the iPhone 3G, 3GS, and 4, and the latest versions of iTunes and the iPhone OS (operating system), known as iOS 4. Apple is likely to introduce a new iPhone model or new versions of the operating system and iTunes between book editions. If you've bought a new iPhone or your version of iTunes looks a little different, be sure to check out what Apple has to say at `www.apple.com/iphone`. You'll no doubt find updates on the company's latest releases.

Part I
Getting to Know Your iPhone

*Y*ou have to crawl before you walk, so consider this part basic training for crawling. The three chapters that make up Part I serve as a gentle introduction to your iPhone.

We start out nice and easy in Chapter 1, with a big-picture overview, even letting you know what's in the box (if you haven't already peeked). Then we examine just some of the cool things your iPhone can do. We finish things off with a quick-and-dirty tour of the hardware and the software, so that you'll know where things are when you need them.

Next, after you're somewhat familiar with where things are and what they do, we move right along to a bunch of useful iPhone skills, such as turning the darn thing on and off (which is very important) and locking and unlocking your phone (which is also very important). Chapter 2 ends with useful tips and tricks to help you master iPhone's unique multitouch interface so that you can use it effectively and efficiently.

Then, in Chapter 3, we explore the process of synchronization and how to get data — contacts, appointments, movies, songs, podcasts, and such — from your computer into your iPhone, quickly and painlessly.

Unveiling the iPhone

Congratulations. You've selected one of the most incredible handheld devices we've ever seen. Of course, the iPhone is one heck of a wireless telephone, but it's actually *four* handheld devices in one. At least it's four devices right out of the box. With iPhone apps, your iPhone becomes a PDA, an e-book reader, a handheld gaming device, a memory jogger, an exercise assistant, and ever so much more. We discuss optional apps — how to obtain, install, and delete them — throughout the book and particularly in Chapter 14.

For now, we focus on the four awesome handheld devices your iPhone is the day you take it out of the box. In addition to being a killer cell phone, the iPhone is a gorgeous widescreen video iPod, a decent 2-megapixel digital camera (original iPhone and iPhone 3G) or a 3- or 5-megapixel camera/camcorder (iPhone 3GS and 4, respectively), as well as the smallest, most powerful Internet communications device yet.

In this chapter, we offer a gentle introduction to all four devices that make up your iPhone, plus overviews of its revolutionary hardware and software features.

The Big Picture

The iPhone has many best-of-class features, but perhaps its most unusual feature is the lack of a physical keyboard or stylus. Instead, it has a 3½-inch super-high-resolution touchscreen (326 pixels per inch for iPhone 4; 160 pixels per inch for other models) that you operate using a pointing device you're already intimately familiar with: your finger.

What's in the box

Somehow we think you've already opened the elegant box that the iPhone came in. But if you didn't, here's what you can expect to find inside:

- **Stereo headset:** Use this headset for music, videos and, yes, phone calls. The headset contains a built-in microphone for making yourself heard during phone calls.

- **Dock connector–to–USB cable:** Use this handy cable to sync or charge your iPhone. You can plug the USB connector into your PC or Macintosh to sync or into the included USB power adapter. By the way, if you prefer to have your iPhone standing up on your desk while you charge or sync it, as we do, check out one of the optional charging/syncing docks available from Apple and others.

- **USB power adapter:** Use this adapter to recharge your iPhone from a standard AC power outlet.

- **Some Apple logo decals:** Of course.

- **Cleaning cloth:** Expect to get smudges on the iPhone. Use the cloth to wipe it clean. We'd steer clear of Lemon Pledge. Note that the iPhone 4 doesn't come with a cleaning cloth; you can always use a clean t-shirt.

- ***Finger Tips* pamphlet:** You'll find handy tips from Apple on using the new object of your affection.

- ***iPhone 4: Important Product Information Guide* pamphlet:** Well, it must be important because it says so right on the cover. You'll find basic safety warnings, a bunch of legalese, warranty information, and info on how to dispose of or recycle the iPhone. *What! We're getting rid of it already?* A few other pieces of advice: Don't drop the iPhone if you can help it, keep the thing dry, and — as with all cell phones — give full attention to the road while driving.

- **SIM eject tool:** Alas, iPhone 4 users have no SIM eject tool; they'll have to use a straightened paper clip or something. All previous iPhone models included this handy tool used to eject your SIM card when necessary. (See Chapter 15 for more on the SIM eject tool and bent paper clips.)

- **iPhone:** You were starting to worry. Yes, the iPhone itself is also in the box.

And what a display it is. We venture that you've never seen a more beautiful screen on a handheld device in your life.

Another feature that knocked our socks off was the iPhone's built-in sensors. An accelerometer detects when you rotate the device from portrait to landscape mode and adjusts what's on the display accordingly. A proximity sensor detects when the iPhone gets near your face, so it can turn off the display to save power and prevent accidental touches by your cheek. A light sensor adjusts the display's brightness in response to the current ambient lighting situation. (Let's see your Blackberry do *that!*) The iPhone 4 even has a gyroscope for advanced motion sensing, and the iPhone 3GS and 4 have GPS that knows where in the world you are.

In this section, we take a brief look at some of the iPhone's features, broken down by product category.

The iPhone as a phone and digital camera/camcorder

On the phone side, the iPhone synchronizes with the contacts and calendars on your Mac or PC. It includes a full-featured QWERTY soft, or virtual, keyboard, which makes typing text easier than ever before — for some folks. Granted, the virtual keyboard takes a bit of time to get used to. But we think that many of you eventually will be whizzing along at a much faster pace than you thought possible on a mobile keyboard of this type.

The 2-megapixel (iPhone and iPhone 3G), 3-megapixel (iPhone 3GS), or 5-megapixel (iPhone 4) digital camera is accompanied by a decent photo management app, so taking and managing digital photos (and videos on iPhone 3GS and 4) is a pleasure rather than the nightmare it can be on other phones. Plus, you can automatically synchronize iPhone photos and videos with the digital photo library on your Mac or PC. Okay, we still wish the iPhone camera took better photos and shot better video. But models prior to iPhone 4 are still much better than most other phone cameras, and the iPhone 4 camera is perhaps the best phone camera we've seen to date.

Finally, one of our favorite phone accoutrements is visual voicemail. (Try saying that three times fast.) This feature lets you see a list of voicemail messages and choose which ones to listen to or delete without being forced to deal with every message in your voice mailbox in sequential order. Now, *that's* handy!

Those are merely a few of the iPhone's excellent telephony features. Because we still have many more chapters to go, we'll put the phone (and camera) coverage on hold for now (pun intended).

The iPhone as an iPod

We agree with Steve Jobs on this one: The iPhone is a better iPod than almost any that Apple has ever made. (Okay, we can quibble about the iPod Touch and the iPad, as well as wanting more storage.) You can enjoy all your existing iPod content — music, audiobooks, audio and video podcasts, music videos, television shows, and movies — on the iPhone's gorgeous high-resolution color display, which is bigger, brighter, and richer than any iPod display that came before it.

Bottom line: If you can get the content — be it video, audio, or whatever — into iTunes on your Mac or PC, you can synchronize it and watch or listen to it on your iPhone.

The iPhone as an Internet communications device

But wait — there's more! Not only is the iPhone a great phone and a stellar iPod, but it's also a full-featured Internet communications device with — we're about to drop a bit of industry jargon on you — a rich HTML e-mail client that's compatible with most POP and IMAP mail services, with support for Microsoft Exchange ActiveSync. (For more on this topic, see Chapter 11.) Also on board is a world-class Web browser (Safari) that, unlike on most other phones, makes Web surfing fun and easy.

Another cool Internet feature is Maps, a killer mapping app based on Google Maps. By using GPS (3G, 3GS, or 4 hardware only) or triangulation (on the original iPhone), Maps can determine your location, let you view maps and satellite imagery, and obtain driving directions and traffic information regardless of where in the United States you happen to be. You can also find businesses such as gas stations, pizza restaurants, hospitals, and Apple stores with just a few taps. And the Compass app (3GS and 4 only) not only displays your current GPS coordinates, but also orients Maps to show the direction you're facing. Let's see your Nokia do that!

You might also enjoy using Stocks, a built-in app that delivers near real-time stock quotes and charts any time and any place, or Weather, another built-in app that obtains and displays the weather forecast for as many cities as you like.

The Internet experience on an iPhone is far superior to the Internet experience on any other handheld device we've seen, except the iPad. (Technically, we'd call the iPad a "two-hand-held device," because it's difficult to hold in one hand for more than a few minutes. But we digress.)

Technical specifications

One last thing before we proceed. Here's a list of everything you need before you can actually *use* your iPhone:

- An original iPhone or iPhone 3G, 3GS, or 4
- In the United States, a wireless contract with AT&T (formerly Cingular)
- An iTunes Store account
- Internet access (required) — broadband wireless Internet access recommended

Plus you need *one* of the following:

- A Mac with a USB 2.0 port; Mac OS X version 10.5.8 or later; and iTunes 9.2 or later
- A PC with a USB 2.0 port; Windows 7, Windows Vista, or Windows XP Home or Professional with Service Pack 3 or later; and iTunes 9.2 or later

A Quick Tour Outside

The iPhone is a harmonious combination of hardware and software. In this section, we take a brief look at what's on the outside. In the next section, we peek at the software.

On the top

On the top of your iPhone, you'll find the headset jack, a microphone (iPhone 4 only), the SIM card tray (iPhone 3 and 3GS only), and the sleep/wake button, as shown in Figure 1-1. We describe these elements more fully in the following list:

- **Headset jack:** The headset jack lets you plug in the included iPhone headset, which looks a lot like white iPod earbuds. Unlike the iPod earbuds, however, the iPhone headset has a microphone so that you can talk as well as listen.

  The headset jack on the *original* iPhone is recessed, so most third-party earphones (such as those made by Shure, Etymotic, and Future Sonics) won't work with it. However, from companies such as Belkin, you can buy an adapter (starting at around $11) that enables you to use just about any brand or style of earphones you like with your iPhone. Fortunately, Apple listened to customers. The iPhone 3G, 3GS, and 4 don't have a recessed headset jack and don't require an adapter.

- **Microphone (iPhone 4 only):** Used for FaceTime calls and noise suppression during phone calls.

- **SIM card tray (iPhone 3G/3GS only):** The SIM card tray is where you remove or replace the SIM card inside your iPhone. (The SIM card tray is on the side in the iPhone 4.)

  A SIM (Subscriber Identity Module) card is a removable smart card used to identify mobile phones. It allows users to change phones by moving the SIM card from one phone to another.

- **Sleep/wake button:** This button is used to lock or unlock your iPhone and to turn your iPhone on or off. When your iPhone is locked, you can still receive calls and text messages, but nothing happens if you touch its screen. When your iPhone is turned off, all incoming calls go directly to voicemail.

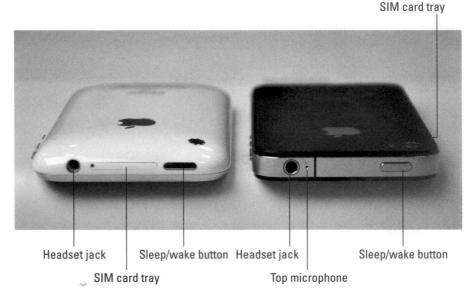

SIM card tray

Headset jack   Sleep/wake button   Headset jack   Sleep/wake button

SIM card tray   Top microphone

Figure 1-1: The top side of the iPhone 3G and iPhone 3GS (left) and the iPhone 4 (right).

On the bottom

On the bottom of your iPhone, you'll find the speaker, dock connector, and microphone, as shown in Figure 1-2:

- ✔ **Speaker:** The speaker is used by the iPhone's built-in speakerphone and plays audio — music or video soundtracks — if no headset is plugged in. It also plays the ringtone you hear when you receive a call.

- ✔ **Dock connector:** The dock connector has two purposes. One, you can use it to recharge your iPhone's battery. Simply connect one end of the included dock connector–to–USB cable to the dock connector and the other end to the USB power adapter. Two, you can use the dock connector to synchronize. Connect one end of the same cable to the dock connector and the other end to a USB port on your Mac or PC.

- ✔ **Microphone:** The microphone lets callers hear your voice when you're not using a headset.

   The iPhone 4 has two microphones. The top one is used for FaceTime calls and also works with the main mic (located on the bottom) to suppress unwanted and distracting background sounds on phone calls using dual-mic noise suppression technology.

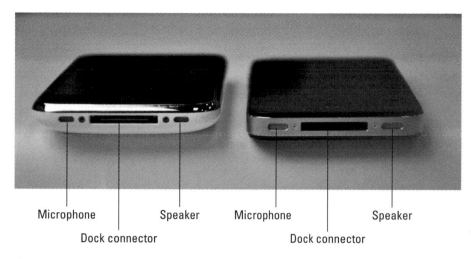

Microphone   Speaker   Microphone   Speaker

Dock connector   Dock connector

Figure 1-2: The bottom side of the iPhone 3G and iPhone 3GS (left) and the iPhone 4 (right).

On the sides and front

On the front of your iPhone, you'll find the following (labeled in Figure 1-3):

- ✓ **Ring/silent switch:** This switch, which is on the left side of your iPhone, lets you quickly switch between ring mode and silent mode. When the switch is set to ring mode — the up position, with no orange dot — your iPhone plays all sounds through the speaker on the bottom. When the switch is set to silent mode — the down position, with an orange dot visible on the switch — your iPhone doesn't make a sound when you receive a call or when an alert pops up on the screen.

  The only exceptions to silent mode are alarms you set in the built-in Clock app, which do sound regardless of the ring/silent switch setting, iPod audio, and selecting sounds such as ringtones and alert sounds in the Settings app.

  If your phone is set to ring mode and you want to silence it quickly, press the sleep/wake button on the top of the iPhone or press one of the volume buttons.

- ✓ **Volume buttons:** Two volume buttons are just below the ring/silent switch. The upper button increases the volume; the lower one decreases it. You use the volume buttons to raise or lower the loudness of the ringer, alerts, sound effects, songs, and movies. And during phone calls, the buttons adjust the voice loudness of the person you're speaking with, regardless of whether you're listening through the receiver, the speakerphone, or a headset.

✔ **SIM card tray (iPhone 4 only):** The SIM card tray is where you remove or replace the SIM card inside your iPhone. On the iPhone 4, the SIM card tray is on the right side.

✔ **Camera (iPhone 4 only):** The camera on the front of the iPhone 4 is tuned for FaceTime, so it has just the right field of view and focal length to focus on your face at arm's length, to present you in the best possible light.

✔ **Receiver:** The receiver is the speaker that the iPhone uses for telephone calls. It naturally sits close to your ear whenever you hold your iPhone in the "talking on the phone" position.

You should be the only one who hears sound coming from the receiver. If you have the volume set above about 50 percent and you're in a location with little or no background noise, someone standing nearby may be able to hear the sound, too. So be careful.

If you require privacy during phone calls, use the included Apple headset (or an optional Bluetooth headset — as discussed in Chapter 13).

✔ **Status bar:** The status bar displays important information, as you'll discover in a page or two.

✔ **Touchscreen:** You find out how to use the iPhone's gorgeous high-resolution color touchscreen in Chapter 2. All we have to say at this time is . . . try not to drool all over it.

✔ **Home button:** No matter what you're doing, you can press the Home button at any time to display the Home screen, which is the screen shown in Figure 1-3.

✔ **App buttons:** Each button on the Home screen launches an included iPhone app or one you've acquired from the App Store.

Volume buttons

Ring/silent switch   Touchscreen

Front camera   App button

Receiver   Status bar

Home button

SIM card tray

Figure 1-3: The front of the iPhone 4 is a study in elegant simplicity.

The Utilities button is the sole exception. This button is a folder containing four app buttons: Clock, Calculator, Compass, and Voice Memos. The Utilities button appears only on iPhones with iOS 4 preinstalled. If you upgraded your iPhone to iOS 4, those four apps are where they were before the upgrade, not contained in a Utilities folder.

You read more about apps and folders later in this chapter and throughout the rest of the book.

On the back

On the back of your iPhone is the camera lens. It's the little circle in the top-left corner. The iPhone 4 also has a little LED next to the camera lens that's used as a flash for still photos and as a floodlight for videos. For more on using the camera and shooting videos, see Chapters 8 and 9, respectively.

Status bar

The status bar, which is at the top of every Home screen and displayed by many (if not most) apps, displays tiny icons that provide a variety of information about the current state of your iPhone:

- **Cell signal:** The cell-signal icon tells you whether you're within range of your wireless telephone carrier's cellular network and therefore can make and receive calls. The more bars you see (five is the highest), the stronger the cellular signal. If you're out of range, the bars are replaced with the words *No service*. And if your iPhone is looking for a cellular signal, the bars are replaced with *Searching*.

  If you have only one or two bars, try moving around a little bit. Even walking just a few feet can sometimes mean the difference between no service and three or four bars.

- **Airplane mode:** You're allowed to use your iPod on a plane after the captain gives the word. But you can't use your cell phone except when the plane is in the gate area before takeoff or after landing. Fortunately, your iPhone offers an airplane mode, which turns off all wireless features of your iPhone — the cellular, 3G, GPRS (General Packet Radio Service), and EDGE networks, Wi-Fi, and Bluetooth — and makes it possible to enjoy music or video during your flight.

- **3G:** This icon informs you that your high-speed 3G data network from your wireless carrier (that's AT&T in the United States) is available and your iPhone can connect to the Internet via 3G.

- **GPRS:** This icon says that your wireless carrier's GPRS data network is available and your iPhone can use it to connect to the Internet.

- **EDGE:** This icon tells you that your wireless carrier's EDGE network is available and you can use it to connect to the Internet.

✔ **Wi-Fi:** If you see the Wi-Fi icon, your iPhone is connected to the Internet over a Wi-Fi network. The more semicircular lines you see (up to three), the stronger the Wi-Fi signal. If you have only one or two semicircles of Wi-Fi strength, try moving around a bit. If you don't see the Wi-Fi icon in the status bar, Internet access is not currently available.

Wireless (that is, cellular) carriers may offer one of three data networks. The fastest is a 3G data network, which, as you probably guessed, is available only on the iPhone 3G, iPhone 3GS, and iPhone 4. The device first looks for a 3G network and then, if it can't find one, looks for a slower EDGE or GPRS data network.

Wi-Fi networks, however, are even faster than any cellular data network — 3G, EDGE, or GPRS. So all iPhones will connect to a Wi-Fi network if one is available, even if a 3G, GPRS, or EDGE network is also available.

Last but not least, if you *don't* see one of these icons — 3G, GPRS, EDGE, or Wi-Fi — you don't currently have Internet access.

✔ **Network activity:** This icon tells you that some network activity is occurring, such as over-the-air synchronization, sending or receiving e-mail, or loading a Web page. Some third-party apps also use this icon to indicate network or other activity.

✔ **Call forwarding:** When you see this icon, call forwarding is enabled on your iPhone.

✔ **VPN:** This icon shows that your iPhone is currently connected to a virtual private network (VPN).

✔ **Lock:** This icon tells you when your iPhone is locked. See Chapter 2 for information on locking and unlocking your iPhone.

✔ **Play:** This icon informs you that a song is currently playing. You find out more about playing songs in Chapter 7.

✔ **Portrait orientation:** When this icon is displayed, the iPhone is in portrait orientation mode, but not locked in that mode. (See next entry.)

✔ **Portrait orientation lock (iPhone 3GS and 4 only):** This icon means that the iPhone screen is locked in portrait orientation. To lock your screen in portrait orientation, double-press the Home button, flick the dock (at the bottom of the screen) from left to right, and then tap the portrait orientation button.

✔ **Alarm:** This icon tells you that you've set one or more alarms in the Clock app.

✔ **Location Services:** Tells you that some application is using Location Services, a topic we describe in Chapter 12.

✔ **Bluetooth:** This icon indicates the current state of your iPhone's Bluetooth connection. If the icon is blue, Bluetooth is on and a device (such as a wireless headset or car kit) is connected. If the icon is gray, Bluetooth is turned on but no device is connected. If you don't see a Bluetooth icon at all, Bluetooth is turned off. Chapter 13 goes into more detail about Bluetooth.

✔ **Battery:** This icon reflects the level of your battery's charge. The icon is completely filled with green when your battery is fully charged, and then empties as your battery becomes depleted. You'll see a lightning bolt inside the icon when your iPhone is recharging.

✔ **TTY:** This icon informs you that your iPhone is set up to work with a teletype (TTY) machine, which is used by those who are hearing- or speech-impaired. You need an optional Apple iPhone TTY Adapter (suggested retail price $19) to connect your iPhone to a TTY machine.

Home Sweet Home Screen

The Home screen offers a bevy of icons, each representing a different built-in app or function. Because the rest of the book covers each and every one of these babies in full and loving detail, we merely provide brief descriptions here.

To get to your Home screen, press the Home button. If your iPhone is asleep when you press, the unlock screen appears. Once unlocked, you'll see whichever page of icons was on the screen when it went to sleep. If that happens to have been the Home screen, you're golden. If it wasn't, merely press the Home button again to summon your iPhone's Home screen.

Three steps let you rearrange icons on your iPhone:

1. **Press and hold any icon until all of the icons begin to jiggle.**

2. **Drag the icons around until you're happy with their positions.**

3. **Press the Home button to save your arrangement and stop the jiggling.**

If you haven't rearranged your icons, you'll see the following apps on your Home screen, starting at the top left:

✔ **Messages:** The Messages app lets you exchange text (SMS) and multimedia (MMS) messages with almost any other cell phone user, as described in Chapter 5. We've used a lot of mobile phones in our day, and this app is as good as it gets.

✔ **Calendar:** No matter what calendar program you prefer on your PC or Mac (as long as it's iCal or Microsoft Entourage, Outlook, or Exchange), you can synchronize events and alerts between your computer and your iPhone. Create an event on one and it's automatically synchronized with the other the next time they're connected. Neat stuff.

✔ **Photos:** This app is the iPhone's terrific photo manager. You can view pictures that you took with the iPhone's built-in camera or transferred from your computer. You can zoom in or out, create slideshows, e-mail photos to friends, and much more. Other phones may let you take pictures; the iPhone lets you enjoy them in many ways.

✔ **Camera:** Use this app when you want to shoot a picture with the iPhone's 2-megapixel (iPhone and iPhone 3G), 3-megapixel (iPhone 3GS), or 5-megapixel (iPhone 4) camera. Ditto if you want to shoot video on the 3GS or 4 models.

✔ **YouTube:** This app lets you watch videos from the popular YouTube Web site. You can search for a particular video or browse through thousands of offerings. It's a great way to waste a lot of time.

✔ **Stocks:** This app lets you monitor your favorite stocks, which are updated in near-real time.

✔ **Maps:** This app is among our favorites. View street maps or satellite imagery of locations around the globe, or ask for driving, walking, or public transportation directions, traffic conditions, or even the location of a nearby pizza joint.

✔ **Weather:** This app monitors the six-day weather forecast for as many cities as you like.

✔ **Notes:** This program lets you type notes while you're out and about. You can send the notes to yourself or anyone else through e-mail or just save them on your iPhone until you need them.

✔ **Utilities:** The Utilities icon is a folder that contains four utility apps:

- **Clock:** This program lets you see the current time in as many cities as you like, set one or more alarms for yourself, and use your iPhone as a stopwatch or a countdown timer.

- **Calculator:** The Calculator app lets you perform addition, subtraction, multiplication, and division. Period.

- **Compass (iPhone 3GS and 4 only):** The Compass app is kind of like having a magnetic needle compass inside your iPhone, but better.

- **Voice Memos:** This handy little app turns your iPhone into a convenient handheld recording device.

Again, note that the Utilities folder appears only on iPhones with iOS 4 pre-installed. iPhones that were upgraded to iOS 4 won't have a Utilities folder.

✔ **iTunes:** Tap here to access the iTunes Store, where you can browse, preview, and purchase songs, albums, movies, and more.

- **App Store:** This icon enables you to connect to and search the iTunes App Store for iPhone apps you can purchase or download for free over a Wi-Fi or cellular data network connection.

- **Settings:** Use this app to adjust your iPhone's settings. If you're a Mac user, think System Preferences; if you're a Windows person, think Control Panel.

- **Phone:** Tap this app icon to use the iPhone as a phone. What a concept!

- **Mail:** This app lets you send and receive e-mail with most POP3 and IMAP e-mail systems and, if you work for a company that grants permission, Microsoft Exchange accounts, too.

- **Safari:** Safari is your Web browser. If you're a Mac user, you know that already; if you're a Windows user who hasn't already discovered the wonderful Safari for Windows, think Internet Explorer on steroids.

- **iPod:** This icon unleashes all the power of a video iPod right on your phone.

- **Contacts:** Last but not least, this app stores information about your contacts, which can be synced with MobileMe, Mac OS X Address Book, Yahoo! Address Book, Google Contacts, Windows Address Book, Outlook Express, Microsoft Outlook, or Microsoft Exchange.

  You won't find the Contacts app on your Home screen — it's on the second screen of apps (which you find out about in Chapter 2) and in the iPhone app as well. If you just can't wait to see it, swipe your finger across the screen from right to left and it will appear.

Okay, then. Now that you and your iPhone have been properly introduced, it's time to turn it on, activate it, and actually use it. Onward!

iPhone Basic Training

*I*f you got caught up in the initial iPhone frenzy of 2007, you may have plotted for months about how to land one. After all, the iPhone quickly emerged as the ultimate fashion phone. And the chic device hosted a bevy of cool features.

To snag the very first version, you may have saved your pennies or said, "The budget be damned." Owning the hippest and most-hyped handset on the planet came at a premium cost compared with rival devices.

Today's iPhone is no less hip or cool, though you now get more bang for your buck. Apple has lowered the price — a lot. As of this writing, the cheapest iPhone for new U.S. customers starts at $99 with a two-year AT&T contract — $500 below its stratospheric launch price. The least expensive version is the iPhone 3GS model with 8GB of RAM. If you're not bargain hunting, you'll want the newer iPhone 4, $199 with 16GB of RAM or $299 for 32GB. Those are subsidized prices that in the United

©Corbis Digital Stock

States require a mandatory two-year contract with AT&T. For existing iPhone customers, the upgrade price for a new iPhone 4 model depends on how far you're into your previous contract with AT&T, how prompt you are at paying your bill, and other factors.

Activating the iPhone

Purchasers of the iPhone 4 experience a new and better activation experience than those 2007 buyers who got in on the bleeding edge. Back then, no sales-person was going to guide you through the process, whether you picked up your newly prized possession in an Apple retail store, an AT&T retail store, or on the Web. Instead, you handled activation solo, in the comfort of your home.

Unless you were among those people who encountered activation hiccups in the days soon after the phone was released in June 2007, the process of getting up to speed with the iPhone was (for the most part) dirt simple and fun — as it is with most products with an Apple pedigree. Still, there were some well-publicized issues in those days, so Apple eventually changed the protocol.

You're now supposed to activate the iPhone in the Apple, AT&T Wireless, Best Buy, RadioShack, or Wal-Mart store where you bought the thing, just as you do with other cell phones. However, if you buy your iPhone from Apple's online store, they'll ship it to you and you activate it through iTunes, just like the old days. You also choose your desired monthly bucket of voice minutes and SMS (Short Message Service) or text messages as well as your allotment of wireless data minutes right in the store.

As of this writing, AT&T offers a $15 a month DataPlus plan, with 200MB of data, roughly enough to send or receive about 1,000 e-mails without attachments and about 150 messages with attachments. You can also view about 400 Web pages, post about 50 photos on social media sites, and watch about 20 minutes of streaming video. (At least that's what AT&T estimates; we didn't count.)

If you exceed 200MB of usage, you'll receive an additional 200MB within the cycle for $15.

The DataPro plan costs $25 per month and gives you 2GB of data, enough to send or receive approximately 10,000 e-mails without attachments and 1,500 e-mails with attachments, view 4,000 Web pages, post 500 photos to social media sites, and watch 200 minutes of streaming video. If you exceed 2GB, you can get another 1GB for $10.

AT&T reports that 98 percent of smartphone customers use less than 2GB. So think long and hard about your anticipated usage before choosing a plan. It's also worth noting that these charges apply only to accessing AT&T's 3G and Edge networks and don't count when you connect via Wi-Fi in your home, office, or elsewhere.

DataPro plan customers have the option to add tethering for an additional $20 a month. *Tethering* is the capability to use the iPhone as a broadband modem for other devices you might carry, such as laptops and netbooks, but alas not Apple's own iPad tablet.

If you're already an AT&T subscriber, the salesperson will give you the option of keeping your current phone number.

It's not surprising why Apple and AT&T want you in their stores: After they get you in the door, they have the opportunity to sell you other stuff. And they can help crack down on techies who want to unlock, or "jailbreak," the iPhone to defect to a rival carrier.

The same two prerequisites for enjoying the iPhone are in place as with the original release and all other iPhones — at least for U.S. customers. First, there's the aforementioned business of becoming an AT&T (formerly Cingular) subscriber, unless you're already in the fold. You'll have to ink that new two-year term. If you're in the middle of a contract with a rival carrier, read the sidebar titled "The Great Escape: Bailing out of your wireless contract."

Second, make sure you download the latest version of iTunes software onto your PC or Mac. Apple doesn't supply the software in the box, so head to www.apple.com/itunes if you need to fetch a copy, or launch your current version of iTunes and then choose iTunes⇨Check for Updates (Mac) or Help⇨Check for Updates (Windows).

For the uninitiated, iTunes is the nifty Apple jukebox software that iPod owners and many other people use to manage music, videos, and more. iTunes is at the core of the iPhone as well because an iPod is built into the iPhone. You'll employ iTunes to synchronize a bunch of stuff on your computer and iPhone, including apps, photos, podcasts, videos, ringtones, and (of course) music.

We get into all that syncing business in Chapter 3.

Turning the iPhone On and Off

Apple has taken the time to partially charge your iPhone, so you'll get some measure of instant gratification. After taking it out of the box, press and hold the sleep/wake button on the top-right edge. (Refer to Chapter 1 for the location of all buttons.) If the phone has been activated, the famous Apple logo appears on your screen, followed a few seconds later by a stunning gray image covered by raindrops. You can find out how to redecorate this wallpaper in Chapter 13. If the phone is shipped to you from the Apple Store, you get a Connect to iTunes screen so that the device can connect with AT&T's servers and perform the activation.

The Great Escape: Bailing out of your wireless contract

Often, a wireless provider will sell a deeply discounted phone or even issue a free model, with one expensive catch. You're subject to hefty termination fees if you bail out of your (typical) two-year contract early.

The iPhone is one Cingular . . . make that AT&T . . . sensation (bad pun intended), so you'll have to wave sayonara to Sprint, Verizon, or other carriers if you want this device. But breaking a cell phone contract is not easy, and some options for doing so may not be quite the outs you had in mind: You can enlist in the military, move overseas, even die. (Sorry, but no guarantee that AT&T's coverage, 3G or otherwise, will reach the heavens.)

Fortunately, other strategies are available, although none are assured of working:

✔ **Complain loudly and often:** If you've been having problems with your existing carrier, contact the phone company and tell them how lousy your coverage is. Document your complaints in writing and be specific about spots where your calls drop out.

✔ **Keep an eye out for price hikes:** If the carrier ups rates dramatically on text messaging, say, you may have a legal out in your contract. The Consumerist.com Web site advises you to read any notices of changes to your Terms of Service that come your way. These changes may void the original agreement, and you'll have about a month to cancel your contract.

✔ **Use online matchmaking:** Sites such as www.celltradeusa.com and www.cellswapper.com are in the business of matching users who want to get out of their contracts with folks who are seeking a bargain. The person trying to ditch a contract pays a modest fee to these sites. So what's the motivation for the person who takes the contract off your hands? Those who get their phone service this way need not pay an activation fee to the carrier, and they incur no long-term commitment of their own.

✔ **Roam, roam on the range:** If you keep using your phone outside your carrier's network, it may become uneconomical for *them* to want to keep you because your phone company picks up expensive roaming charges.

To turn the device completely off, press and hold the sleep/wake button again until a red arrow appears at the top of the screen. Then drag the arrow to the right with your finger. Tap Cancel if you change your mind.

Locking the iPhone

Carrying a naked cell phone in your pocket is asking for trouble. Unless the phone has some locking mechanism, you may inadvertently dial a phone number. Try explaining to your boss why he or she got a call from you at 4 a.m.

Fortunately, Apple makes it a cinch to lock the iPhone so this scenario won't happen to you.

In fact, you don't need to do anything to lock the iPhone; it happens automatically, as long as you don't touch the screen for one minute. (You can change this duration in iPhone Settings, a topic in Chapter 13.)

Can't wait? To lock the iPhone immediately, press the sleep/wake button. To unlock it, press the sleep/wake button again. Or press the Home button on the front of the screen. Either way, the on-screen slider appears, but you can't do anything until you drag the slider to the right with your finger and then, in some cases, also enter a passcode, another topic reserved for Chapter 13.

By now, you're picking up on the idea that your fingers play an instrumental role in controlling your iPhone. We talk more about the responsibility your digits have later in this chapter.

Mastering the Multitouch Interface

Until the iPhone came along, virtually every cell phone known to mankind had a physical (typically plastic) dialing keypad, if not also a more complete QWERTY style keyboard, to bang out e-mails and text messages. The iPhone dispenses with both. Apple is once again living up to an old company advertising slogan to "Think Different."

Indeed, the iPhone removes the usual physical buttons in favor of a *multitouch display*. This display is the heart of many things you do on the iPhone, and the controls change depending on the task at hand.

Unlike other phones with touchscreens, don't bother looking for a stylus. You are meant, instead — at the risk of lifting another ancient ad slogan — to "let your fingers do the walking."

It's important to note that you have at your disposal several keyboard layouts in English, all variations on the alphabetical keyboard, the numeric and punctuation keyboard, and the more punctuation and symbols keyboard. Six keyboards are shown in Figure 2-1. The layout you see depends on the app you are working in. For instance, the keyboards in Safari differ from the keyboards in Notes.

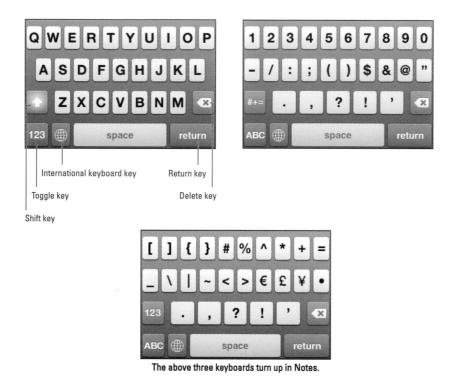

International keyboard key   Return key

Toggle key   Delete key

Shift key

The above three keyboards turn up in Notes.

These three keyboards turn up in Safari.

Figure 2-1: Six faces of the iPhone keyboard.

What's more, if you rotate the iPhone to its side, you'll get wider variations of the respective keyboards. A single example of a wide keyboard in the Notes app is shown in Figure 2-2.

Figure 2-2: Going wide on the keyboard.

Training your digits

Rice Krispies has Snap! Crackle! Pop! Apple's response for the iPhone is Tap! Flick! and Pinch! (Yikes, another ad comparison.) Oh yeah, add Drag!

Fortunately, tapping, flicking, pinching, and dragging are not challenging gestures, so you'll be mastering many of the iPhone's features in no time:

✔ **Tap:** Tapping serves multiple purposes, as will become evident throughout this book. You can tap an icon to open an app from the Home screen. Tap to start playing a song or to choose the photo album you want to look through. Sometimes you will double-tap (tapping twice in rapid succession), which has the effect of zooming in (or out) of Web pages, maps, and e-mails.

✔ **Flick:** What it sounds like. A flick of the finger on the screen lets you quickly scroll through lists of songs, e-mails, and picture thumbnails. Tap the screen to stop scrolling, or wait for the list to stop scrolling.

✔ **Pinch/spread:** Place two fingers on the edges of a Web page or picture to enlarge the images (spread your fingers apart) or make them smaller (pinch your fingers together). Pinching and spreading (or what we call *unpinching*) are easy to master and sure to wow an audience.

✔ **Drag:** Slowly press your finger against the touchscreen and then, without lifting your finger, move it. You might drag to move around a map that's too large for the iPhone's display area.

Discovering the special-use keys

The iPhone keyboard contains five keys that don't actually type a character (refer to Figure 2-1). These special-use keys follow:

- **Shift key:** Switches between uppercase and lowercase letters if you're using the alphabetical keyboard. If you're using keyboards that show only numbers and symbols, the traditional shift key is replaced by a key labeled #+= or 123. Pressing that key toggles between keyboards that have just symbols and numbers.

  To turn on Caps Lock mode and type in all caps, you first need to enable Caps Lock. You do that by tapping the Settings icon, then tapping General, and then tapping Keyboard. Tap the Enable Caps Lock item to turn it on. After the Caps Lock setting is enabled (it's disabled by default), you double-tap the shift key to turn on Caps Lock. (The shift key turns blue when Caps Lock is on.) Tap the shift key again to turn off Caps Lock. To disable Caps Lock completely, just reverse the process by turning off the Enable Caps Lock setting (tap Settings, General, Keyboard).

- **Toggle key:** Switches between the different keyboard layouts.

- **International keyboard key:** Shows up only if you've turned on an international keyboard, as explained in the sidebar titled "A keyboard for all borders," later in this chapter.

- **Delete key:** Erases the character immediately to the left of the cursor.

  If you hold down the delete key for a few seconds, it begins erasing entire words rather than individual characters.

- **Return key:** Moves the cursor to the beginning of the next line.

The incredible, intelligent, and virtual iPhone keyboard

Before you consider how to actually *use* the keyboard, we'd like to share a bit of the philosophy behind its so-called *intelligence*. Knowing what makes this keyboard smart will help you make it even smarter when you use it. The iPhone keyboard

- Has a built-in English dictionary that even includes words from today's popular culture.

- Adds your contacts to its dictionary automatically.

- Uses complex analysis algorithms to predict the word you're trying to type.

A keyboard for all borders

Apple continues to expand the iPhone's global reach by supplying international keyboard layouts for more than 50 languages. To access a keyboard that isn't customized for Americanized English, tap Settings, General, Keyboard, International Keyboards, Add New Keyboard. (Alternatively, tap Settings, General, International, Keyboards, Add New Keyboard.) Up pops the list shown in the figure included here, with custom keyboards for Russian, Slovak, Swedish, and other languages. Apple even supplies two versions of Portuguese to accommodate customers in Brazil and Portugal, and three versions of French (including keyboards geared to Canadian and Swiss users). Heck, there's even a U.K. version of English and "right-to-left" languages such as Arabic and Hebrew.

Have a multilingual household? You can select, in turn, as many international keyboards as you want. When you're working in an app that summons a keyboard, tap the international keyboard button, between the toggle and Space keys (refer to Figure 2-1), until you see the keyboard you want. Note that the Space key momentarily displays the name of the keyboard language and then translates the word *space* itself to the language of the keyboard in use. Tap again to select the next keyboard in the list of international keyboards that you turned on in Settings. If you keep cycling, you eventually come back to your original English layout. Here's an alternative method for summoning a keyboard you've enabled: Press your finger against the international keyboard key until a pop-up window displays all the keyboards that are ready for action. Slide your finger along the list until it lands on the keyboard you want to use, and then release it to select that keyboard.

You can use handwriting character recognition for simplified and traditional Chinese, as shown here. Just drag your finger in the box provided. We apologize in advance for not knowing what the displayed characters here mean. We certainly don't want to offend

✔ Suggests corrections as you type. It then offers you the suggested word just below the word you typed. When you decline a suggestion and the word you typed is *not* in the iPhone dictionary, the iPhone adds that word to its dictionary and offers it as a suggestion if you mistype a similar word in the future.

Remember to decline suggestions (by tapping the characters you typed as opposed to the suggested words that appear below what you've typed), because doing so helps your intelligent keyboard become even smarter.

✔ Reduces the number of mistakes you make as you type by intelligently and dynamically resizing the touch zones for certain keys. You can't see it, but the iPhone increases the zones for keys it predicts might come next and decreases the zones for keys that are unlikely or impossible to come next.

Navigating beyond the Home screen

The Home screen, which we discuss in Chapter 1, more than likely won't end up being the only screenful of icons on your phone. After you start adding apps from the iTunes App Store (see Chapter 14), you'll likely have multiple screens.

Initially, you see three tiny dots above the Phone, Mail, Safari, and iPod icons. Each dot denotes an additional screen, containing up to 16 additional icons for apps or folders of apps. The leftmost dot, which is dimmed (and on close inspection shaped like a tiny magnifying glass), denotes the Search screen, which you access by flicking from left to right across the middle of the screen or by tapping directly on the dot. The second dot, which is all-white, represents the Home screen, or the screen you're currently viewing. The next dot to the right is the first additional screen in which you can park icons. You get to it by flicking right to left or tapping on the dot. You can have 11 screens in all; as you add screens, you add dots.

You must be precise when tapping a dot, or you'll open one of the app or folder icons instead of switching screens.

The four icons in the last row — Phone, Mail, Safari, and iPod — are in a part of the screen known as the *dock.* When you switch from screen to screen as just described, these icons remain on the screen.

You can easily move icons within a screen or from screen to screen. Simply press and hold any icon until all the icons on the screen begin to jiggle. Then drag the icon you want to park elsewhere to its new location. The other icons on the screen kindly step aside to make room. To move an icon to an entirely new screen, drag it to the right or left edge of the screen. When you're satisfied with the new layout, press the Home button to stop the jiggling.

Press the Home button to jump back to the first screenful of icons or the Home screen. Pressing a second time brings you to a handy Spotlight search feature, which we address at the end of this chapter, in the "Search" section.

If you press two times in rapid succession, you won't jump to the first Home screen or Spotlight Search screen. Instead, the multitasking tray (described in the "Multitasking" section, later in this chapter) appears. So remember to pause briefly between presses if you want to jump to the Home or Spotlight Search screens and press twice in rapid succession to invoke multitasking.

Finger-typing on the virtual keyboards

Apple's multitouch interface just might be considered a stroke of genius. And it just might as equally drive you nuts, at least initially.

If you're patient and trusting, you'll get the hang of finger-typing in a week or so. (We've become quite good at it by now.) You have to use the virtual keyboard that appears when you tap a text field to enter notes, compose text messages, type the names of new contacts, and so forth.

Apple's own recommendation — with which we concur — is to start typing with just your index finger before graduating to two thumbs.

As we've noted, Apple has built a lot of intelligence into its virtual keyboard, so it can correct typing mistakes on the fly and take a stab at predicting what you're about to type next. The keyboard isn't exactly Nostradamus, but it does a pretty good job in coming up with the words you have in mind.

As you press your finger against a letter or number on the screen, the individual key you press gets bigger and practically jumps off the screen, as shown in Figure 2-3. That way, you know that you struck the correct letter or number.

Sending a message to an overseas pal? Keep your finger pressed against a letter, and a row of keys showing variations on the character for foreign alphabets pops up, as shown in Figure 2-4. Then you can add the appropriate accent mark. Just slide your finger until you reach the key with the relevant accent mark, and press.

Meanwhile, if you press and hold the .com key on a Safari keyboard, it offers you the choice of .com, .net, .edu, .us, or .org. Pretty slick stuff.

If you enabled any international keyboards, you'll see more choices when you hold down the .com key. For example, if you enabled a French keyboard, pressing and holding .com will also give you options for .eu and .fr.

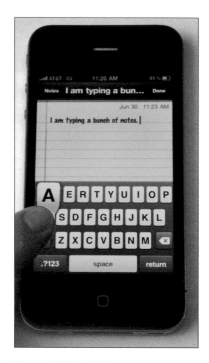

Figure 2-3: The ABCs of virtual typing.

Figure 2-4: Accenting your letters.

Alas, typing mistakes are common at first. Say that you meant to type a sentence in the Notes app that reads, "I am typing a bunch of notes." But because of the way your fingers struck the virtual keys, you actually entered "I am typing a bunch of *npyrs*." Fortunately, Apple knows that the *o* you meant to press is next to the *p* that showed up on the keyboard, just as *t* and *y* and the *e* and the *r* are side-by-side. So the software determines that *notes* was indeed the word you had in mind and places it in red under the suspect word, as shown in Figure 2-5. To accept the suggested word, merely tap the Space key. And if for some reason you actually did mean to type *npyrs* instead, tap the suggested word (*notes* in this example) to decline it.

Because Apple knows what you're up to, the virtual keyboard is customized for the task at hand. If you're entering a Web address, the keyboard inside the Safari Web browser (Chapter 10) includes dedicated period, forward slash, and (the aforementioned) .com keys but no Space key.

If you're using the Notes app (Chapter 5), the keyboard does have a Space key. And if you're composing an e-mail message, a dedicated @ key pops up on the keyboard.

When you're typing notes or sending e-mail and want to type a number, symbol, or punctuation mark, tap the 123 key to bring up an alternative virtual keyboard. Tap the ABC key to return to the first keyboard. It's not hard to get used to, but some may find this extra step irritating.

See Chapter 18 for a slick trick (the slide) that avoids the extra step involved in moving between the 123 and ABC keys.

As mentioned, you can rotate the iPhone so that its keyboard changes to a wider landscape mode in certain apps, most recently, Mail, Messages, and Notes. The feature was already present in Safari. The keys are slightly larger in landscape mode, a potential boon to those who do a lot of typing or have largish fingers.

Editing mistakes

It's a good idea to type with abandon and not get hung up over mistyped characters. The self-correcting keyboard will fix many errors. That said, plenty of typos will likely turn up, especially in the beginning, and you'll have to make corrections manually.

A neat trick for doing so is to hold your finger against the screen to bring up the magnifying glass shown in Figure 2-6. Use it to position the pointer to the spot where you need to make the correction.

Figure 2-5: When the keyboard bails you out.

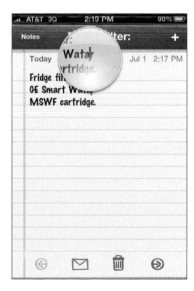

Figure 2-6: Magnifying errors.

Fingers or thumbs?

Should you use your fingers or thumbs to type? The answer is: both. It seems somewhat easier to hold the iPhone in your nondominant hand (that is, your left hand if you're right-handed or vice versa) and type with the index finger of your dominant hand, especially when you're starting out with the iPhone. And that's what we suggest you try first.

When you get the hang of typing with one index finger, try to speed things up by using both hands. You can type two-handed in two ways:

✔ Set the iPhone on a sturdy surface (such as a desk or table) and tap with both index fingers. You can't easily use this technique when you're standing up with no stable surface at the proper height.

✔ Cup the iPhone with both hands and type with both thumbs. This technique has the advantage of being possible in almost any situation, with or without a sturdy surface. The downside is that your thumbs are bigger than your other fingers, so typing accurately with them takes more practice — and if you have larger-than-average thumbs, well, you're flirting with trouble.

Which technique is better? Don't ask us — try both ways and use the method that feels the most comfortable or lets you type with the best accuracy. Better still, master both techniques and use whichever is more appropriate at the time.

Cutting, copying, pasting, and replacing

Being able to copy and paste text (or images) from one place on a computer to another has seemingly been a divine right since Moses, but getting to this Promised Land on the iPhone took awhile. Apple added Copy and Paste (and Cut) as part of OS 3.0. In its own inimitable way, Apple brought pizzazz to this long-requested feature. And with iOS 4, Apple has provided another helpful remedy for correcting errors. It's a new Replace pop-up option that appears when you double-tap a word.

On the iPhone, you might want to copy text or images from the Web, and paste them into an e-mail, text, a message, or a note. Or you might want to copy a bunch of pictures or a video into an e-mail.

Here's how to exploit the feature. Say you're in the Notes app, jotting down ideas that you want to copy into an e-mail message. Double-tap a word to select it, and then drag the blue grab points or handles to select a larger block of text (see Figure 2-7). (You can use the handles to contract selected text too.) After you've selected the text, tap Copy. (If you want to delete the text block, tap Cut instead.)

Now open the Mail program (Chapter 11) and start composing a message. When you decide where to insert the text you just copied, tap the cursor.

Up pop commands to Select, Select All, and Paste, as shown in Figure 2-8. Tap Paste to paste the text into the message.

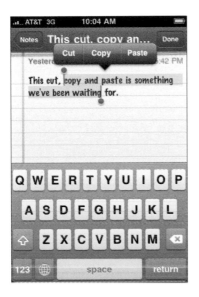

Figure 2-7: Drag the grab points to select text.

Figure 2-8: Tap Paste to make text appear from nowhere.

Here's the pizzazz part. If you make a mistake while you are cutting, pasting, replacing, or typing, shake the iPhone. It undoes the last edit.

Say you notice a typo in what you had previously entered. In Figure 2-9, for example, we inadvertently typed *their* instead of *there*. By tapping Replace, you can easily make a fix. Upon doing so, the iPhone serves up a few suggested replacement words. If the word you have in mind as a substitute is, um, there, tap it and the iPhone automatically makes the switch.

Voice dialing

Several cell phones of recent vintage let you dial a name or number by voice. Bark out "Call Mom" or "Dial 212-555-1212" and such handsets oblige. Although some third-party apps added voice dialing to the iPhone, Apple didn't get around to it until OS 3.0, as part of the feature known as Voice Control.

As you see in Chapter 7, Apple took voice controls a step beyond dialing by number or finding people in your address book. You can also issue voice commands to control music in the iPod.

Figure 2-9: Tap Replace and then tap a substitute word to make a switch.

You have two ways to summon the Voice Control feature:

- ✔ Press and hold the Home button until the Voice Control screen shown in Figure 2-10 appears. It has wavy lines that move as you speak. Scrolling in the background are some of the commands you can say out loud ("Play Artist," "Previous Track," and so on). Don't blurt out anything until you hear a quick double-beep. The iPhone will repeat the command it thinks it heard.

- ✔ Press and hold the center button on the wired headset. Once again, wait for an audible cue and then tell the iPhone what you have in mind.

Voice Control works quite nicely with the wired headset included with your iPhone. It works also with some Bluetooth headsets and car kits. If you use a wireless headset that's not supported, you'll have to hold the phone up to your lips if you want it to respond to voice commands.

Figure 2-10: Tell the iPhone to dial the phone or play a song.

You definitely want to wait for voice confirmation after you've spoken. In our experience, Voice Control isn't perfect, especially in a noisy environment. So if you're dialing a name or number, make sure the iPhone is indeed calling the person you had in mind. There's no telling what kind of trouble you might get into otherwise.

Multitasking

iOS 4 adds a bevy of important features, of which the long-overdue multitasking feature is arguably the most significant. *Multitasking* simply lets you run numerous apps in the background simultaneously or easily switch from one app to another. For example, music from a third-party app such as Slacker can play in the background while you surf the Web, peek at pictures, or check e-mail. Before multitasking hit the iPhone, Slacker would shut itself down the moment you started performing tasks in another app. (Previously, Apple did let you multitask by, for example, playing audio in the background with its iTunes app. But multitasking was limited to Apple's own apps, not those produced by outside developers.)

But that's not all. If you use an Internet voice-calling app such as Skype, you'll be able to receive notification of an incoming call even if you haven't launched the Skype app. The multitasking feature also lets a navigation app employing GPS update your position while you're listening to an Internet radio app such as Pandora. From time to time, the navigation app will pipe in with turn-by-turn directions, lowering the volume of the music so you can hear the instructions.

And if you're uploading images to a photo Web site and the process is taking longer than you'd like, you can switch to another app, confident that the images will continue to upload behind the scenes. We've also been able to leave voice notes in the Evernote app while checking out a Web page.

Multitasking couldn't be easier. Double-press the Home button, and a tray appears at the bottom of the screen, as shown in Figure 2-11. The tray holds icons for the most recently used apps. Scroll to the right to see more apps (see Figure 2-11, right). Tap the app you want to switch to: The app remembers where you left off.

Apple insists that multitasking will not drain the iPhone battery or exhaust system resources. The iPhone conserves power and resources by putting apps in a state of suspended animation. But as we just mentioned, you can wake them up instantly and return to what you were doing.

To remove an app from the tray holding icons of the most recently used apps — and thus remove the app from those in the multitasking rotation — press and hold your finger against any app until they all start to wiggle. Then tap the red circle with the white line that appears inside the app you want to remove. Poof, it's gone.

Figure 2-11: Scroll the tray to see the apps you've recently used.

Multitasking works only on the iPhone 3GS and iPhone 4 models, and presumably any future models. Older iPhones don't have the resources to handle the feature.

Note that multitasking on the iPhone doesn't work quite the same way as multitasking on a PC or a Mac. You can't display more than one window on the screen at a time — given the size of the iPhone screen, you'd have trouble viewing multiple windows anyway.

Moreover, there's some philosophical debate whether this feature is multitasking, or fast task switching, or some combination. Rather than getting bogged down in the semantics, we're just glad that multitasking, or whatever it is, has finally arrived.

Organizing Icons into Folders

Finding the single app you want to use among apps spread out over 11 screens is a daunting task. But Apple felt your pain, and with iOS 4, the company introduced a handy organization tool called Folders. The Folders feature enables you to create folder icons, each holding up to a dozen apps. As Figure 2-12 shows, you might create folders for Social apps, Photography, Travel, and any number of other categories.

To create a folder, press your finger against an icon until all the icons on the screen jiggle. Decide which apps you want to move to a folder, and drag the icon for the first app on top of the second app. The two apps now share living quarters inside a newly created folder, as shown in Figure 2-13. Apple names the folder according to the category of apps inside the folder, but you can easily change the folder name by tapping the X in the bar where the folder name appears and substituting a new name.

To launch an app that's inside a folder, tap that folder's icon and then tap the icon for the app that you want to open.

You can drag apps into and out of any folder as long as there's room for them — remember that you can have no more than 12 apps in a folder. But your iPhone can have as many as 180 folders, with a total of 2,160 apps.

If you drag all the apps outside the folder, it automatically disappears.

Figure 2-12: Keeping apps in their place through Folders.

Figure 2-13: Dragging one app on top of another to create a folder.

Searching

Using the Safari browser (see Chapter 10), you can search the Web via Google, Yahoo!, or Microsoft Bing. But you can also search for people and programs across your iPhone or within specific apps. We show you how to search within apps in the various chapters dedicated to Mail, Contacts, Calendar, Notes, and iPod.

Searching across the iPhone, meanwhile, is based on the Spotlight feature familiar to Mac owners. To access Spotlight, flick to the left of the main Home screen (or as mentioned earlier in this chapter, press the Home button from the Home screen).

In the bar at the top of the screen that slides into view, enter your search query using the virtual keyboard. The iPhone starts spitting out results the moment you type a single character, and the list narrows as you type additional characters.

The results are pretty darn thorough. Say you entered *Bell* as your search term, as shown in Figure 2-14. Contacts whose names have Bell in them will show up, along with folks who work for companies named Bell. If your iTunes library has the song "One Last Bell to Answer" or music performed by violinist Joshua Bell, those will show up, too. Same goes for a third-party iPhone app called The Bell. Tap any listing to jump to the contact, ditty, or app you're searching for.

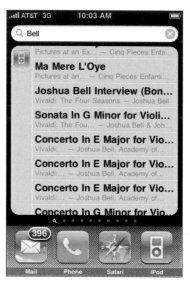

Figure 2-14: Putting the spotlight on search.

If you don't find what you're looking for, you can take your search into cyberspace. At the very bottom of the search results that popped up are two additional options, Search Web and Search Wikipedia. Tap the latter to fire up Safari and visit the vast online Wikipedia encyclopedia. The search term you entered *(Bell)* is already selected. If you tap Search Web instead, Safari brings you to a Google search page, prepopulated with the search term you selected.

You have some control over the type of search that Spotlight conducts. From the Home page, tap Settings, General, Spotlight Search. Make sure there's a check mark next to each app on the iPhone that you'd like searched automatically. By default, all the options — Contacts, Applications, Music, Podcasts, Video, Audiobooks, Notes, Mail, Calendar, and Messages — are selected. Tap to remove the check mark from any app that you don't want automatically included in your search.

There — you've survived basic training. Now the real fun is about to begin.

3

Synchronicity: Getting Stuff to and from Your iPhone

In This Chapter

▶ Starting your first sync

▶ Disconnecting during a sync

▶ Synchronizing contacts, calendars, e-mail accounts, and bookmarks

▶ Synchronizing ringtones, music, podcasts, video, photos, and applications

---

After you pass basic training (in Chapter 2), the next thing you're likely to want to do is get some or all of the following into your iPhone: contacts, appointments, events, mail settings, bookmarks, ringtones, music, movies, TV shows, podcasts, books, courseware, photos, documents, and applications.

We have good news and . . . more good news. The good news is that you can easily copy any or all of those items from your computer to your iPhone. And the more good news is that after you do that, you can synchronize your contacts, appointments, and events so they're kept up-to-date automatically in both places — on your computer and on your iPhone — whenever you make a change in one place or the other. So when you add or change an appointment, an event, or a contact on your iPhone, that information automatically appears on your computer the next time your iPhone and computer communicate.

©iStockphoto.com/ronen

This communication between your iPhone and computer is called *syncing* (short for synchronizing). Don't worry: Syncing is easy, and we walk you through the entire process in this chapter.

The information in this chapter is based on iTunes version 9.2 and iOS (formerly iPhone OS) version 4.0, which were the latest and greatest when these words were written. If your screens don't look like ours, upgrade to iTunes 9.2 and iOS 4.0 (or higher). By the way, both upgrades are free and offer significant advantages over their predecessors.

We regret to say that if, for some reason, you can't upgrade to iOS 4 or greater and iTunes 9.2 or greater, you should consider getting a newer phone or computer. Why? If you have an original, first-generation iPhone, you can't install iOS 4. If you're running a very old version of Mac OS X or Windows, you may not be able to install iTunes 9.2. And the new iPhone 4 won't run any version of iOS before version 4.

Starting to Sync

Synchronizing your iPhone with your computer is a lot like syncing an iPod with your computer. If you're an iPod user, the process will be a piece of cake. But syncing isn't difficult even for those who've never used an iPod or iTunes. Follow these steps:

1. **Start by connecting your iPhone to your computer with the USB cable that came with your iPhone.**

   When you connect your iPhone to your computer, iTunes should launch automatically. If it doesn't, chances are you plugged the cable into a USB port on your keyboard, monitor, or hub. Try plugging it into one of the USB ports on your computer instead. Why? Because USB ports on your computer supply more power to a connected device than other USB ports or most hubs.

   If iTunes still doesn't launch automatically, try launching it manually.

   One last thing: If you've taken any photos with your iPhone since the last time you synced it, your photo management software (iPhoto, Image Capture, or Aperture on the Mac; Adobe Photoshop Elements on the PC) will launch and ask whether you want to import the photos from your phone. (You find out all about this in the "Photos" section, later in the chapter.)

2. **Select your iPhone in the iTunes source list.**

   You see the Set Up Your iPhone pane, as shown in Figure 3-1. If you've already set up and named your iPhone, you can skip Steps 3 and 4a and start with Step 4b.

   If you don't see an iPhone in the source list, and you're sure it's connected to a USB port on your computer (not the keyboard, monitor, or hub), restart your computer.

iPhone selected in source list

Figure 3-1: This is the first thing you see in iTunes.

3. Name your iPhone.

We've named this one *BobLiPhone*.

4a. Decide whether you want iTunes to automatically synchronize your iPhone and your contacts, calendars, bookmarks, notes, e-mail accounts, and applications.

- If that's what you want, select the check box next to the option titled Automatically Sync Contacts, Calendars, Bookmarks, Notes, and Email Accounts to make a check mark appear, and select the check box next to the option titled Automatically Sync Applications. Then click the Done button and continue with the "Synchronizing Your Media" section, later in this chapter.

- If you want to synchronize manually, make sure both check boxes are deselected (refer to Figure 3-1), and click Done. The "Synchronizing Your Data" section tells you all about how to configure your contacts, calendars, bookmarks, notes, e-mail accounts, and applications manually.

We've chosen to not click either check box so that we can show you how to manually set up each type of sync in the upcoming sections.

4b. Click the Summary tab near the top of the window, as shown in Figure 3-2.

If you don't see a Summary tab, make sure your iPhone is still selected in the source list.

Summary tab

Figure 3-2: The Summary pane is pretty painless.

5. **If you want iTunes to launch automatically and sync your iPhone whenever you connect it to your computer, click to put a check mark in the Open iTunes When This iPhone Is Connected check box (in the Options area).**

If the Prevent iPods, iPhones, and iPads from Syncing Automatically option in the Devices pane of iTunes Preferences (iTunes➪Preferences on a Mac; Edit➪Preferences on a PC) is enabled (checked), the Open iTunes When This iPhone Is Connected option in the Summary tab will appear dimmed and be unavailable.

Your choice in Step 5 is not set in stone. If you select the Open iTunes When This iPhone Is Connected check box, you can still prevent your iPhone from syncing automatically in several ways:

- **Way #1:** After you connect the iPhone to your computer, click the Summary tab in iTunes and deselect the Open iTunes When This iPhone Is Connected check box. Removing the check mark prevents iTunes from opening automatically when you connect the iPhone. If you use this method, you can still start a sync manually by clicking the Sync button.

- **Way #2:** Launch iTunes *before* you connect your iPhone to your computer. Then press and hold Command+Option (Mac) or Shift+Ctrl (PC) and connect your iPhone. Keep pressing the keys until you see your iPhone appear in the iTunes source list. This method prevents your iPhone from syncing automatically without changing any settings.

6. **If you want to sync only items that have check marks to the left of their names in your iTunes library, select the Sync Only Checked Songs and Videos check box.**

7. **If you want iTunes to automatically create smaller audio files (so you can fit more music on your iPhone), select the Convert Higher Bit Rate Songs to 128kbps AAC check box.**

Songs you purchase from the iTunes store are encoded as AAC (Advanced Audio Coding) files with a bit rate of 256kbps. The songs sound fantastic but the files are relatively large — roughly 2MB per minute of music. Converting them to AAC files with a bit rate of 128kbps reduces the file size by nearly 50 percent with little degradation in the audio quality. Most people can't distinguish between AAC files ripped at 128kbps and ones ripped at 256kbps. Unless you have awesome ears or a fabulous sound system (or both), you probably won't notice much (if any) difference. But enabling this option will let you have roughly twice as many songs on your iPhone. Bob claims to have pretty good ears (he's a musician and record producer in his copious spare time), and even he enables this option.

8. **If you want to turn off automatic syncing in just the Music and Video panes, select the Manually Manage Music and Videos check box.**

9. **If you want to password-protect your iPhone backups (your iPhone creates a backup of its contents automatically every time you sync), select the Encrypt iPhone Backup check box.**

And, of course, if you decide not to select the Open iTunes When This iPhone Is Connected check box, you can synchronize manually by clicking the Sync button in the bottom-right corner of the window.

By the way, if you've changed any sync settings since the last time you synchronized, the Sync button will instead say Apply.

Disconnecting the iPhone

When the iPhone is syncing with your computer, its screen says "Sync in Progress" and iTunes displays a message that says that it's syncing with your iPhone. After the sync is finished, iTunes displays a message that the iPhone sync is complete and it's okay to disconnect your iPhone.

If you disconnect your iPhone before a sync is completed, all or part of the sync may fail.

To cancel a sync so that you can safely disconnect your iPhone, drag the slider on the iPhone (the one that says Slide to Cancel) during the sync.

If you get a call while you're syncing, the sync is safely cancelled so that you can disconnect your iPhone and answer the call. After you're finished with the call, just reconnect your iPhone to restart the sync.

Synchronizing Your Data

Did you choose to set up data synchronization manually (by not selecting the Automatically Sync Contacts, Calendars, Bookmarks, Notes, and Email Accounts check box or the Automatically Sync Applications check box in the Set Up Your iPhone pane shown in Figure 3-1)? If you did, your next order of business is to tell iTunes what data you want to synchronize between your iPhone and your computer. You do this by clicking the Info tab, which is to the right of the Summary tab.

The Info pane has five sections: Sync Address Book Contacts, Sync iCal Calendars, Sync Mail Accounts, Other, and Advanced. The following sections look at them one by one.

Sync Address Book Contacts

The Sync Address Book Contacts section of the Info pane determines how synchronization is handled for your contacts. One method is to synchronize all your contacts, as shown in Figure 3-3. Or you can synchronize any or all groups of contacts you've created in your computer's address book program; just select the appropriate check boxes in the Selected Groups list, and only those groups will be synchronized.

The iPhone syncs with the following address book programs:

 ✔ **Mac:** Address Book and other address books that sync with Address Book, such as Microsoft Entourage

 ✔ **PC:** Windows Contacts and Microsoft Outlook

 ✔ **Mac and PC:** Yahoo! Address Book and Google Contacts

On a Mac, you can sync contacts with multiple applications. On a PC, you can sync contacts with only one application at a time.

Figure 3-3: Want to synchronize your contacts? This is where you set things up.

If you use Yahoo! Address Book, select the Sync Yahoo! Address Book Contacts check box, and then click the Configure button to enter your Yahoo! ID and password. If you use Google Contacts, select the Sync Google Contacts check box, and then click the Configure button to enter your Google ID and password.

Syncing will never delete a contact from your Yahoo! Address Book if it has a Messenger ID, even if you delete that contact on the iPhone or on your computer.

To delete a contact that has a Messenger ID, log in to your Yahoo! account with a Web browser and delete the contact in your Yahoo! Address Book.

If you sync with your employer's Microsoft Exchange calendar and contacts, all your personal contacts and calendars will be wiped out.

Sync iCal Calendars

The Sync iCal Calendars section of the Info pane determines how synchronization is handled for your appointments and events. You can synchronize all your calendars, as shown in Figure 3-4, or any or all individual calendars you've created in your computer's calendar program. Just select the appropriate check boxes.

Figure 3-4: Set up sync for your calendar events here.

The iPhone syncs with the following calendar programs:

- **Mac:** iCal, plus any tasks or events that currently sync with iCal on your Mac, such as events and tasks in Microsoft Entourage
- **PC:** Microsoft Outlook 2003, 2007, or 2010

On a Mac, you can sync calendars with multiple applications. On a PC, you can sync calendars with only one application at a time.

Sync Mail Accounts

You can sync account settings for your e-mail accounts in the Sync Mail Accounts section of the Info pane. You can synchronize all your e-mail accounts (if you have more than one) or individual accounts, as shown in Figure 3-5. Just select the appropriate check boxes.

Figure 3-5: Transfer e-mail account settings to your iPhone here.

The iPhone syncs with the following mail programs:

- **Mac:** Mail and Microsoft Entourage
- **PC:** Microsoft Outlook 2003, 2007, or 2010 and Microsoft Outlook Express

E-mail account settings are synchronized only one way: from your computer to your iPhone. If you make changes to any e-mail account settings on your iPhone, the changes will *not* be synchronized back to the e-mail account on your computer. Trust us, this is a very good feature and we're glad Apple did it this way.

By the way, the password for your e-mail account may or may not be saved on your computer. If you sync an e-mail account and the iPhone asks for a password when you send or receive mail, do this: On the Home screen, tap Settings, Mail, Contacts, Calendars. Tap your e-mail account's name, and then type your password in the appropriate field.

Other

The Other section of the Info pane has only two options. Select the Sync Safari Bookmarks check box if you want to sync the bookmarks on your computer with bookmarks on your iPhone. The iPhone can sync bookmarks with the following Web browsers:

- **Mac:** Safari
- **PC:** Microsoft Internet Explorer and Safari

Select the second option, the Sync Notes check box, to sync notes in the Notes app on your iPhone with Notes in Apple Mail on a Mac or Microsoft Outlook on a PC. To sync notes on a Mac, you must have Mac OS X 10.5.7 or later installed.

Advanced

Every so often, the contacts, calendars, mail accounts, or bookmarks on your iPhone get so screwed up that the easiest way to fix things is to erase that information on your iPhone and replace it with information from your computer.

If that's the case, just click to select the appropriate check boxes in the Advanced section of the Info pane, as shown in Figure 3-6. Then the next time you sync, that information on your iPhone will be replaced with information from your computer.

Because the Advanced section is at the bottom of the Info pane and you have to scroll down to see it, it's easy to forget that it's there. Although you probably won't need to use this feature very often (if ever), you'll be happy you remembered that it's there if you do need it.

Figure 3-6: Replace the information on your iPhone with the information on your computer.

Synchronizing Your Media

If you chose to let iTunes manage synchronizing your data automatically, welcome back. This section looks at how you get your media — your ringtones, music, movies, TV shows, podcasts, video, iTunes U courses, books, and photos — from your computer to your iPhone.

Sharp-eyed readers may notice that we aren't covering iPhone apps in this chapter. Apps are so darn cool that we've given them an entire chapter, namely Chapter 14. In that chapter, you discover how to find, sync, rearrange, review, and delete apps, and much, much more.

Ringtones, music, podcasts, iTunes U courses, books, and video (but not photos) are synced only one way: from your computer to your iPhone. If you delete any of these items on your iPhone, they will not be deleted from your computer the next time you sync. If you purchase or download items directly to your iPhone using the iTunes app or App Store app, those items (that is, songs, ringtones, podcasts, video, iTunes U courses, and books) are synced back to your computer automatically the next time you sync.

Ringtones, music, movies, and TV shows

You use the Ringtones, Music, Movies, TV Shows, Podcasts, and iTunes U panes to specify the media that you want to copy from your computer to your iPhone. To view any of these panes, make sure that your iPhone is still selected in the source list, and then click the appropriate tab near the top of the window.

Ringtones

If you have any custom ringtones in your iTunes library, select the Sync Ringtones check box in the Ringtones pane. Then you can choose either all ringtones or individual ringtones by selecting their check boxes.

Music, music videos, and voice memos

To transfer music to your iPhone, select the Sync Music check box in the Music pane. You can then select the option for Entire Music Library or Selected Playlists, Artists, and Genres. If you choose the latter, click the check boxes next to particular playlists, artists, and genres you want to transfer. You also can choose to include music videos or voice memos or both by selecting the appropriate check boxes at the top of the pane (see Figure 3-7).

Figure 3-7: Use the Music pane to copy music, music videos, and voice memos from your computer to your iPhone.

If you choose Entire Music Library and have more songs in your iTunes library than storage space on your iPhone — more than about 7GB on an 8GB iPhone, 15GB on a 16GB iPhone, or 31GB on a 32GB iPhone — you'll see one or both of the error messages shown in Figure 3-8 when you try to sync. To avoid these errors, select playlists, artists, and genres that total less than 7, 15, or 31 gigabytes, respectively.

Figure 3-8: If you have more music than your iPhone has room for, this is what you'll see when you sync.

How much space did I use?

If you're interested in knowing how much free space is available on your iPhone, look near the bottom of the iTunes window while your iPhone is selected in the source list. You'll see a chart that shows the contents of your iPhone, color-coded for your convenience. As you can see in the figure (which shows three different charts), this 32GB iPhone 4 has 5.45GB of free space.

If you click once on the chart, it will display the number of items in each category, as shown in the middle chart in the figure. And if you click it again, it will display how long it will take to listen to all your audio or watch all your video, as shown in the bottom chart. Click again and the display returns to gigabytes and megabytes, as shown in the top chart.

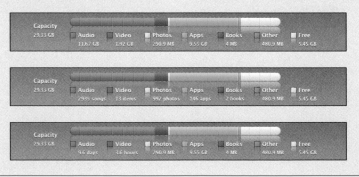

Finally, if you select the Automatically Fill Free Space with Songs check box, iTunes fills any free space on your iPhone with music.

Music, podcasts, and video are notorious for using massive amounts of storage space on your iPhone. If you try to sync too much media, you'll see lots of error messages like the ones in Figure 3-8. Forewarned is forearmed.

Movies

To transfer movies to your iPhone, select the Sync Movies check box and then choose an option for movies you want to include automatically from the pop-up menu, as shown in Figure 3-9. If you choose an option other than All, you can optionally select individual movies and playlists by checking the boxes in appropriate sections.

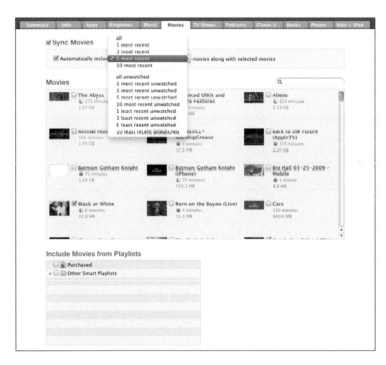

Figure 3-9: Your choices in the Movies pane determine which movies are copied to your iPhone.

TV shows

The procedure for syncing TV shows is slightly different from the procedure for syncing movies. First, select the Sync TV Shows check box to enable TV show syncing. Then choose how many episodes to include and whether you want all shows or only selected shows from the two pop-up menus, as shown in Figure 3-10. If you want to also include individual episodes or episodes on playlists, select the appropriate check boxes in the Shows, Episodes, and Include Episodes from Playlists sections of the TV Shows pane.

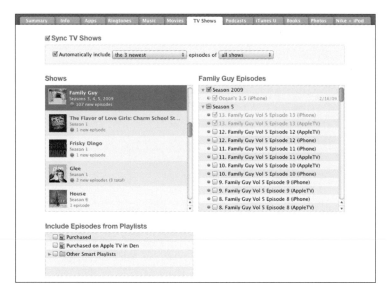

Figure 3-10: The TV Shows pane determines how TV shows are synced with your iPhone.

Podcasts, iTunes U, and Books

You can also sync podcasts, educational content from iTunes U, two types of books — e-books for reading and audiobooks for listening — and photos.

Podcasts

To transfer podcasts to your iPhone, select the Sync Podcasts check box in the Podcasts pane. Then you can automatically include however many podcasts you want by making selections from the two pop-up menus, as shown in Figure 3-11. If you have podcast episodes on playlists, you can include them by selecting the appropriate check box in the Include Episodes from Playlists section.

Figure 3-11: The Podcasts pane determines which podcasts are copied to your iPhone.

iTunes U

To sync educational content from iTunes U, first select the Sync iTunes U check box to enable iTunes U syncing. Then choose how many episodes to include and whether you want all collections or only selected collections from the two pop-up menus. If you want to also include individual items or items on playlists, select the appropriate check boxes in the Items section and Include Items from Playlists section of the iTunes U pane.

Books

By now we're sure you know the drill: You can sync all your eBooks or audio-books or just sync selected titles by choosing the appropriate buttons and check boxes in the Books pane.

To sync eBooks, you need the free iBooks app from the App Store. For more information on apps and the App Store, read Chapter 14.

Photos

Syncing photos is a little different from syncing other media because your iPhone has a built-in camera — two cameras, actually — and you may want to copy pictures or videos you take with the iPhone to your computer, as well as copy pictures stored on your computer to your iPhone.

The iPhone syncs photos and videos, too, with the following programs:

- **Mac:** Aperture or iPhoto version 4.03 or later
- **PC:** Adobe Photoshop Elements 3.0 or later

You can also sync photos with any folder on your computer that contains images.

In the Photos pane, select the Sync Photos From check box, and then choose an application or folder from the pop-up menu (which says Aperture in Figure 3-12).

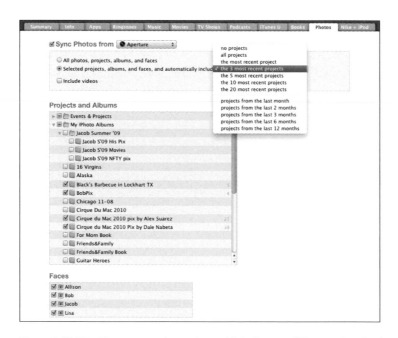

Figure 3-12: The Photos pane determines which photos will be synchronized with your iPhone.

If you choose an application that supports photo albums (such as Aperture and iPhoto), projects (Aperture), events (iPhoto), facial recognition (Aperture and iPhoto), or any combination thereof, you can automatically include recent projects (Aperture), events (iPhoto) or faces (Aperture and iPhoto) by making a selection from the same pop-up menu (refer to Figure 3-12).

If you're using iPhoto, you can also type a word or phrase in the search field (an oval with a magnifying glass) to search for a specific event or events. We're using Aperture in Figure 3-12, which is why you don't see the search field.

If you choose a folder full of images, you can create subfolders inside it that will appear as albums on your iPhone. But if you choose an application that doesn't support albums or events, or a single folder full of images with no subfolders, you have to transfer all or nothing.

Because we selected Aperture in the Sync Photos From menu, and Aperture 3 (the version installed on our Mac) supports projects and faces in addition to albums and photos, we have the option of syncing any combination of photos, projects, albums, and faces.

If you've taken any photos with your iPhone since the last time you synced it, the appropriate program launches (or the appropriate folder is selected), and you have the option of downloading the pictures to your computer.

Part II
The Mobile iPhone

The 5th Wave — By Rich Tennant

"In fact, it does come with a compass."

Your iPhone is first and foremost a mobile phone, so in this part we explore how to use typical mobile phone features, starting with all the neat ways to make an outgoing phone call. You also find out how to answer or ignore the calls that come in and discover iPhone's clever visual voicemail feature, which lets you take in messages on your terms, rather than in the order in which the messages arrived on the phone. You also figure out how to juggle calls, merge calls, and select a ringtone. And, if you're lucky enough to own an iPhone 3GS or 4, you see how easy it is to make calls with Voice Control.

After you master all the calling and listening stuff, you're ready to become a whiz at sending and retrieving SMS and MMS messages. As journalists, we especially appreciate what comes next: finding out how to become a champion note-taker.

We close this part by investigating all those C-word programs — namely, Calendar, Calculator, and Clock — plus a V-word program called Voice Memos. These handy applications enable you to stay on top of your appointments, solve arithmetic problems on the fly (with one or two nifty calculators), show up for appointments on time — thanks to a built-in alarm clock — and record memos (or lectures, or anything you can hear, really).

4

Understanding the Phone-damentals

*Y*ou may well have bought an iPhone for its spectacular photo viewer, marvelous widescreen iPod, and the best darn pocket-sized Internet browser you've ever come across. Not to mention its overall coolness.

For most of us, though, cool goes only so far. The iPhone's most critical mission is the one from which its name is derived — it is first and foremost a cell phone. And no matter how capable it is at all those other things, when push comes to shove, you had best be able to make and receive phone calls.

©PhotoDisc, Inc.

That puts a lot of responsibility in the hands of AT&T, the iPhone's exclusive wireless carrier in the United States. As with any cell phone, the strength of the wireless signal depends a great deal on your location and the robustness of the carrier's network.

As noted in Chapter 1, the cell-signal status icon at the upper-left corner of the screen can clue you in on what your phone-calling experience may be like. Simply put, more bars supposedly equate to a better experience. What you hope to avoid are those two dreaded words: *No Service.* Cell coverage aside, this chapter is devoted to all the nifty ways you can handle wireless calls on an iPhone.

And when we say *nifty,* we mean nifty. If you have an iPhone 4 and a good Wi-Fi connection and are gabbing with someone else who has an iPhone 4 and decent Wi-Fi, the two of you can *see* each other. That's right: video calling, through a remarkable feature called FaceTime. The promise of video calling has been around since LBJ occupied the White House. Despite various efforts to bring video calling or video chat to computers and certain other mobile handsets, video calling has never really gone Main Street.

We're betting that with FaceTime, Apple is going to change that. Don't take our word for it; give FaceTime a try. Sorry, but we're going to leave you hanging until the end of the chapter to figure out how to do that. (Trust us, giving FaceTime a whirl isn't hard.)

In the meantime, we present more conventional but no less important ways to make and receive calls on your iPhone. Somewhere, Alexander Graham Bell is beaming.

Making a Call

Start by tapping the Phone icon on the Home screen. You can then make calls by tapping any of the icons that show up at the bottom of the screen: Favorites, Recents, Contacts, Keypad, or Voicemail, in that order. The iPhone 3GS and the iPhone 4 have one more way of calling, by using the aptly named Voice Control feature to dial a name or phone number by voice. Let's take these options one by one.

Contacts

If you read the chapter on syncing (Chapter 3), you know how to get the snail-mail addresses, e-mail addresses, and (most relevant for this chapter) phone numbers that reside on your PC or Mac into the iPhone. Assuming that you went through that drill already, all those addresses and phone numbers are hanging out in one place. Their not-so-secret hiding place is revealed when you tap the Contacts icon in the Phone app or the Contacts icon on one of the Home screen pages.

Here's how to make those contacts work to your benefit:

1. **In the Phone app, tap Contacts.**

2. **Flick your finger so the list of contacts on the screen scrolls rapidly up or down, loosely reminiscent of the spinning Lucky 7s (or other pictures) on a Las Vegas slot machine.**

   Think of the payout on a One-Armed Bandit with that kind of power.

   Alternatively, you can move your fingers along the alphabet on the right edge of the Contacts list or tap one of the letters to jump to names that begin with that letter, easier said than done given how tiny those letters are.

   You can find a list of potential matches also by starting to type the name of a contact in the search field. Or type the name of the place your contact works. You may have to flick to get the search field into view. Another way to find people is by using Spotlight (refer to Chapter 2).

3. **When you're at or near the appropriate contact name, stop the scrolling by tapping the screen.**

   Note that when you tap to stop the scrolling, that tap doesn't select an item in the list. This may seem counterintuitive the first few times you try it, but we got used to it and now we really like it this way.

   Tap the status bar of the tiny magnifying glass on the upper-right corner to automatically scroll to the top of the list and bring the search field into view. Doing so is useful if you're really popular (or influential) and have a whole bunch of names among your contacts.

4. **Tap the name of the person you want to call.**

   As shown in Figure 4-1, you can see a bunch of fields with the individual's phone numbers, physical and e-mail addresses, and possibly even a mug shot. You may have to scroll down to see more contact info.

   If the person has more than one phone number, the hardest decision you must make is choosing which number to call.

5. **Tap the phone number, and the iPhone initiates the call.**

If you lumped your contacts into Groups on your computer, reflecting, say, different departments in your company, friends from work, friends from school, and so on, you can tap the Groups button on the upper-left side of the screen labeled All Contacts to access these groups.

Your own iPhone phone number, lest you forget it, appears at the top of the Contacts list, provided you arrived in Contacts through the Phone app.

You can also initiate text messages and e-mails from within Contacts. Those topics are discussed in greater depth in Chapters 5 and 11, respectively.

Favorites

Favorites is where you can keep a list of the people and numbers you dial most often. Consider Favorites the iPhone equivalent of speed-dialing. Merely tap the person's name in Favorites, and your iPhone calls the person.

TIP

You can set up as many favorites as you need for a person. So, for example, you may create separate Favorites listings for your spouse's office phone number and cell number.

Setting up Favorites is a breeze. When looking at one of your contacts, you may have noticed the Add to Favorites button. When you tap this button, all the phone numbers you have for that person pop up. Tap the number you want to make into a favorite and it turns up on the list.

If any of your chosen folks happen to fall out of favor, you can easily kick them off the Favorites roster. Here's how:

1. **Tap the Edit button in the upper-left corner of the screen.**

   You'll notice that a red circle with a horizontal white line appears to the left of each name in the list.

2. **Tap the circle next to the A-lister getting the heave-ho.**

   The horizontal white line is now vertical and a red Delete button appears to the right of the name, as shown in Figure 4-2.

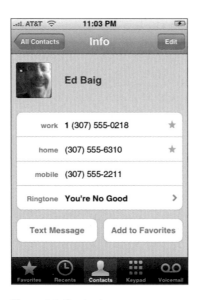

Figure 4-1: Contact me.

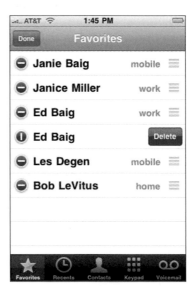

Figure 4-2: I don't like you anymore.

3. **Tap Delete.**

> The person (or one of his or her given phone numbers) is no longer afforded the privilege of being in your iPhone inner circle.

Booting someone off the Favorites list does not remove that person from the main Contacts list.

You can rearrange the order in which your favorites are displayed. Tap Edit, and then, to the right of the person you want to move, press your finger against the symbol that looks like three short horizontal lines stacked on top of one another. Drag that symbol to the place on the list where you want your favorite contact to appear. Tap Done when the listings are as you like them.

You can designate new favorites from the Favorites feature by tapping the + symbol at the upper-right corner of the screen. Doing so brings you back to Contacts. From there, select the appropriate person and number. A star appears next to any contact's number chosen as a favorite.

Recents

Tapping the Recents icon displays the iPhone call log. The Recents feature houses logs of all the, well, *recent* calls made or received, as well as calls you missed.

Here's a tricky concept: Tap All to show all the recent calls and Missed to show just those you missed. Under the All list, completed calls and missed calls that have been returned by tapping the red entry are shown in black, and missed calls that haven't been returned in this fashion are in red, along with a descriptor of the phone you were calling or received a call from (home, mobile, and so on).

By tapping the small blue circle with the right-pointing arrow next to an item in the list, you can find out the time calls were made or missed, as well as any known info about the caller from your Contacts information.

To return a call, just tap anywhere on the name.

If one of the calls you missed came from someone who isn't already in your Contacts, you can add him or her. Tap the right-pointing arrow, and then tap the Create New Contact button. If the person is among your Contacts but has a new number, tap the Add to Existing Contact button. When the list gets too long, tap Clear to clean it up.

Tap Share Contact to share a contact with a friend, family member, or colleague. You have the option to send that person an e-mail or MMS (text message). The contact info is already embedded in the message that you send.

Keypad

From time to time, of course, you have to dial the number of a person or company who hasn't earned a spot in your Contacts. That's when you'll want to tap the Keypad icon to bring up the large keys of the virtual touchtone keypad you see in Figure 4-3. Just tap the appropriate keys and tap Call.

To add this number to your address book, tap the + silhouette key (that's a + and the silhouette of a person) on the keypad and tap either Create New Contact or Add to Existing Contact.

You can use the iPhone's keypad also to remotely check your voicemail at work or home.

Come to think of it, what a perfect segue into the next section. It's on one of our favorite iPhone features, visual voicemail.

Visual voicemail

How often have you had to listen to four or five (or more) voicemail messages before getting to the message you really want, or need, to hear? As shown in Figure 4-4, the iPhone's clever visual voicemail presents a list of your voicemail messages in the order in which calls were received. But you need not listen to those messages in order.

How do you even know you have voicemail? There are a couple ways:

- ✔ A red circle showing the number of pending messages awaiting your attention appears above the Phone icon on the Home screen or above the Voicemail icon from within the Phone app.
- ✔ You may also see a message on the iPhone display that says something like, *New voicemail from Ed (or Bob)*.

Whatever draws you in, tap that Voicemail icon to display the list of voicemails. You see the caller's phone number, assuming this info is known through CallerID, and in some cases, his or her name. Or you see the word *Unknown*.

Figure 4-3: A virtually familiar way to dial.

Figure 4-4: Visual voicemail in action.

The beauty of all this, of course, is that you can ignore (or at least put off listening to) certain messages. We are not in the advice-giving business on what calls you can safely avoid; disregard messages from the IRS or your parole officer at your own risk, okay?

A blue dot next to a name or number signifies that you haven't heard the message yet.

To play back a voicemail, tap the name or number in question. Then tap the tiny play/pause button that shows up to the left. Tap once more to pause the message; tap again to resume. Tap the Speaker button if you want to hear the message through the iPhone's speakerphone.

Tap the blue arrow next to a caller's name or number to bring up any contact info on the person or to add the caller to your Contacts.

The tiny playhead along the scrubber bar (refer to Figure 4-4) shows you the length of the message and how much of the message you've heard. If you hate when callers ramble on forever, you can drag the playhead to rapidly advance through a message. Perhaps more importantly, if you miss something, you can replay that segment.

Returning a call is as simple as tapping the green Call Back button. If the caller's number is unknown, the Call Back button appears dimmed. And you can delete a voicemail by pressing Delete.

If you have no phone service, you'll see a message that says *Visual Voicemail is currently unavailable.*

You can listen to your iPhone voicemail from another phone. Just dial your iPhone number and, while the greeting plays, enter your voicemail password. You can set up such a password from the Home screen by tapping Settings, and then tapping Phone, Change Voicemail Password. You'll be asked to enter your current voicemail password, if you have one. If one doesn't exist yet, tap Done. If it does exist, enter it and then tap Done. You'll then be asked to type the new password and tap Done, twice.

The globetrotting iPhone

Apple has managed to cram a bunch of radios into the latest iPhone. It has four GSM/Edge radios (850, 900, 1,800, 1,900 MHz), four UMTS/HSDPAHSUPA radios, plus radios for Bluetooth, Wi-Fi, and GPS. And here's a bit of trivia: Apple has built antennas into the stainless steel band on the edge of the iPhone 4. Actually those antennas were anything but trivial in the days following the iPhone 4's launch. Some people who gripped the lower-left corner of the device in such a way as to make contact with the notch in that location actually lost reception.

We don't want you to break into a sweat about any of this information. Know that all we're really talking about is a 3G, or third-generation phone network that you can use to make calls (and do more) while traveling abroad. (So-called 4G or fourth-generation networks are being deployed, but the iPhone doesn't tap into 4G — yet.) You'll have to have AT&T turn on something called *international roaming* (unless, of course, you live in a foreign land and have a local carrier). Contact AT&T for the latest rates. Go to www.wireless.att.com/learn/international for details.

If you're calling the United States while overseas, you can take advantage of International Assist. This feature automatically adds the proper prefix to U.S. numbers dialed from abroad. Tap Settings, Phone, International Assist. Make sure you see the blue On button instead of the white Off button.

Although iPhone started out as a United States–only proposition, Apple has now launched versions in dozens of countries.

Recording a greeting

You have two choices when it comes to the voicemail greeting your callers will hear. You can accept a generic greeting with your phone number by default. Or you can create a custom greeting in your own voice as follows:

1. **In the voicemail app, tap the Greeting button.**

2. **Tap Custom.**

3. **Tap Record and start dictating a clever, deserving-of-being-on-the-iPhone voicemail greeting.**

4. **When you have finished recording, tap Stop.**

5. **Review the greeting by pressing Play.**

6. **If the greeting is worthy, tap Save. If not, tap Cancel and start over at Step 1.**

Voice dialing

If you have a 3GS phone or an iPhone 4, you can make a call hands-free, just by opening your mouth.

To summon Voice Control (refer to Chapter 2), press and hold the Home button or press and hold the center button on the wired headset with the remote and microphone supplied with the iPhone.

Wait for the tone and speak clearly, especially if you're in a noisy environment. You can dial by number, as in "Dial 202-555-1212." You can dial a name, as in "Call Bob LeVitus" or "Dial Ed Baig." Or you can be a tad more specific as in "Dial Bob LeVitus mobile" or "Call Ed Baig home." Before actually dialing the phone, an automated female voice repeats what she thinks she heard.

If the person you're calling has multiple phone numbers and you fail to specify which one, the female voice will prompt you, "Ed Baig, home, mobile, or work?" Tell her which one it is, or say "Cancel" if you decide not to call.

When the Voice Control screen appears, let go of the Home button before speaking a command. Otherwise, your thumb may cover the microphone, making it more difficult for the iPhone to understand your intent.

Voice Control need not be in Americanized English. From the Home screen, tap Settings, General, International, Voice Control. Then choose one of several language options in the list. Choices include Australian English and English as spoken in the U.K.

Receiving a Call

It's wonderful to have numerous options for making a call. But what are your choices when somebody calls you? The answer depends on whether you are willing to take the call or not.

Accepting the call

To accept a call, you have three options:

- ✔ Tap Answer and greet the caller in whatever language makes sense.
- ✔ If the phone is locked, drag the slider to the right.
- ✔ If you are donning the stereo earbuds that come with the iPhone, tap the microphone button. Microphone adapters for standard headsets may also work.

Actually, you have a fourth option if you wear a wireless Bluetooth headset or use a car speakerphone. Click the Answer button on your headset or speakerphone (refer to the manual if the process isn't intuitive). For more on Bluetooth, read Chapter 13.

If you're listening to music in your iPhone's iPod when a call comes in, the song stops playing and you have to decide whether to take the call. If you do take the call, the music resumes from where you left off after the conversation ends.

Rejecting the call

We're going to assume that you're not a cold-hearted person out to break a caller's heart. Rather, we assume that you are a busy person who will call back at a more convenient time.

Keeping that positive spin in mind, here are three ways to reject a call on the spot and send the call to voicemail:

- ✔ Tap Decline. Couldn't be easier than that.
- ✔ Press the sleep/wake button twice in rapid succession. (The button is on the top of the device.)
- ✔ Using the supplied headset, press and hold the microphone button for a couple of seconds, and then let go. Two beeps let you know that the call was indeed rejected.

iTunes and ringtones

When Apple first launched iPhone in June 2007, we were disappointed that we couldn't use snippets of music from our iTunes library for ringtones. A few months in, Apple let iPhone owners turn some of the songs they've purchased (or will buy) into custom ringtones. You must fork over 99 cents for songs that are already in your iTunes library on your computer or pay $1.29 for a new song from the iTunes Store online (which lets you also get full use of the track on your PC or Mac).

The ringtone-ready music in your own iTunes collection (on the computer) is designated by a little bell symbol. Clicking that symbol displays a ringtone editor that resembles Apple's GarageBand music-editing software. Drag the editor over the portion of the song you want to use as your ringtone — up to 30 seconds' worth.

You can choose to have the ringtone fade in or out by selecting the appropriate boxes in the editor. Click Preview to make sure you're happy with the result, and click Buy when you're satisfied.Connect the iPhone to your computer to synchronize the ringtone.

You can also create custom ringtones in GarageBand and through such third-party utilities as iToner. Head to Chapter 18 for more details on GarageBandringtoning. (We love coining new verbs.)

You can purchase and download ringtones wirelessly from your phone via the iTunes Store. From the Home screen, tap iTunes and then tap Ringtones. You can find ringtones by genre, by top tens (in a given musical category), and by poring through selections featured in the store.

Sometimes you're perfectly willing to take a call but you need to silence the ringer or turn off the vibration, lest the people sitting near you in the movie theater or corporate boardroom cast an evil eye your way. To do so, press the sleep/wake button a single time, or press one of the volume buttons. You'll still have the opportunity to answer.

Choosing ringtones

At the time this book was written, Apple included 25 ringtones in the iPhone, ranging from the sound of crickets to an old car horn. Read the "iTunes and ringtones" sidebar to figure out how to create your own custom ringtones.

To choose a ringtone, follow these steps:

1. **From the Home screen, tap Settings.**
2. **Tap Sounds.**
3. **Tap Ringtone to access the list of available ringtones.**

4. **Flick your finger to move up or down the list.**

5. **Tap any of the ringtones to hear what it will sound like.**

   A check mark appears next to the ringtone you've just listened to, as shown in Figure 4-5. If need be, adjust the volume slider in Sounds.

6. **If you're not pleased, try another.**

   If you're satisfied, you need do nothing more. Unbeknownst to you, you have just selected that ringtone.

You can easily assign specific ringtones to individual callers. From Contacts, choose the person to whom you want to designate a particular ringtone. Then tap Edit, and then tap Assign Ringtone to display the aforementioned list of ringtones. Select the one that seems most appropriate (a barking dog, say, for your father-in-law).

To change or delete the ringtone for a specific person, go back into Contacts, and then tap Edit. Either tap the right arrow to choose a new ringtone for that person or tap the red circle and Delete to remove the custom ringtone altogether.

While on a Call

You can do lots of things while talking on an iPhone, such as consulting your Calendar, taking notes, or checking the weather. Press the Home button to get to these other apps.

If you're using Wi-Fi or 3G, you can also surf the Web (through Safari) while talking on the phone. But you can't surf while you talk if your only outlet to cyberspace is the EDGE network.

Here are other things you can do while on a call:

- ✔ **Mute a call:** From the main call screen (shown in Figure 4-6), tap Mute. Now you need not mutter under your breath when the caller ticks you off. Tap Mute again to unmute the sound.

- ✔ **Tap Contacts to display the Contacts list.** This is useful if you want to look up a friend's number while you're talking to another pal.

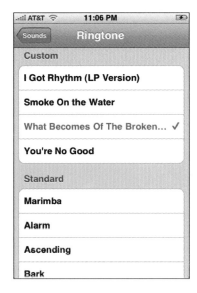

Figure 4-5: Ring my chimes: The iPhone's ringtones.

Figure 4-6: Managing calls.

✔ **Place a call on hold:** This option depends on the phone you're using. If you're on an iPhone 4, touch and hold the aforementioned Mute button. On older devices, just tap Hold. Tap Hold again to take the person off hold. You might put a caller on hold to answer another incoming call or to make a second call yourself. The next section shows you how to deal with more than one call at a time.

✔ **Tap Keypad to bring back the keypad:** This feature is useful if you have to type touchtones to access another voicemail system or respond to an automated menu system. Heaven forbid you actually get a live person when calling an insurance company or airline. But we digress. . . .

✔ **Use the speakerphone:** Tap Speaker to listen to a call through the iPhone's internal speakers without having to hold the device up to your mouth. If you've paired the iPhone with a Bluetooth device, the control is labeled Audio Source instead, as shown in Figure 4-7. Tap Audio Source and then tap Speaker (if you want the speakerphone), iPhone (if you want to hold up the phone to your ear), or the name of the Bluetooth device. A tiny speaker icon will appear next to your selection, as shown in Figure 4-8.

✔ **Make a conference call:** Read on.

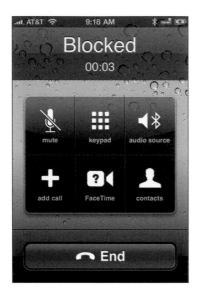

Figure 4-7: Tap Audio Source to change how you are taking the call.

Figure 4-8: The speakerphone is active.

Juggling calls

You can field a new call when you're already talking to somebody. Or ignore it (by tapping Ignore).

To take the new call while keeping the first caller on hold, tap the Hold Call + Answer button that appears, as shown in Figure 4-9. You can then toggle between calls (placing one or the other on hold) by tapping either the Swap button or the first call at the top of the screen.

If this is too much for you and that second caller is really important, tap End Call + Answer to ditch caller number one.

Conference calls

Now suppose caller number one and caller number two know each other. Or you'd like to play matchmaker so they get to know each other. Tap Merge Calls so all three of you can chitchat. At first, the phone number of each caller will scroll at the top of your screen like a rolling ticker. A few seconds later, the ticker is replaced by the word *Conference* with a circled right-pointing arrow to its immediate right.

Figure 4-9: Swapping calls.

Now let's assume you have to talk to your entire sales team at once. It may be time to initiate a full-blown conference call, which effectively takes this merge-call idea to its extreme. You can merge up to five calls at a time. In fact, creating such a conference call on the iPhone may be simpler than getting the same five people in a physical room at the same time.

Here's how you do it. Start by making a call and then placing the caller on hold as noted in the preceding "Juggling calls" section. Tap Add Call to make another call, and then tap Merge Calls to bring everyone together. Repeat this exercise to add the other calls.

Other conference call tidbits:

- ✔ iPhone is actually a two-line phone, and one of the available lines can be involved in a conference call.

- ✔ If you want to drop a call from a conference, tap Conference, and then tap the red circle with the little picture of the phone in it that appears next to the call. Tap End Call to make that caller go bye-bye.

- ✔ You can speak privately with one of the callers in a conference. Tap Conference, and then tap Private next to the caller you want to go hush-hush with. Tap Merge Calls to bring the caller back into the conference so everyone can hear him or her.

- ✔ You can add a new incoming caller to an existing conference call by tapping Hold Call + Answer followed by Merge Calls.

Seeing Is Believing with FaceTime

FaceTime video reminds us of a favorite line from The Who's rock opera *Tommy:* "See me, feel me, touch me." The "see me" (and for that matter, "see you") part arrives with FaceTime. We think a lot of people will want to see you: an old college roommate living halfway around the world; grandparents living miles away (okay, they really want to see your newborn); or an old flame in a distant location.

Fortunately, using FaceTime is as easy as making a regular call on the iPhone. Plus, FaceTime comes with at least two major benefits, *besides* the video:

- FaceTime calls don't count against your regular AT&T minutes.
- The audio quality on FaceTime calls is superior to a regular cell phone connection.

But FaceTime also has a couple of major caveats:

- Both you and the party you're talking to must have an iPhone 4. FaceTime doesn't work with older models of the iPhone or any other devices as of this writing. Apple is pushing to make FaceTime a video standard that the entire tech industry can embrace, allowing you to someday (and maybe even by the time you read this) make FaceTime calls from iPhone 4 to other handsets and computers, perhaps machines compatible with the iChat video feature on Macs.
- Both you and the caller at the other end have to access Wi-Fi. The quality of the experience depends on a solid connection.

If you meet the requirements, here's how to make FaceTime happen:

1. **The first time you make a FaceTime call, dial the person's regular iPhone number as usual, using any of the methods we describe in this chapter.**

2. **Once a regular call is established and you've broached the subject of going video, you can tap the FaceTime button shown in Figure 4-10.**

   A few seconds later, the other person gets the option to Decline or Accept the FaceTime invitation by tapping the red button or the green button, respectively, as shown in Figure 4-11. If the answer is Accept, you'll need to wait a few seconds before you can see the other person.

When someone requests FaceTime with you, you'll appreciate being able to politely decline a FaceTime call. Cool as it can be to see and be seen, ask yourself if you really want to be seen, say, when you just got out of bed.

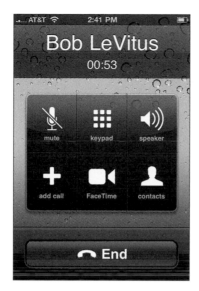

Figure 4-10: Tap FaceTime to literally watch what happens.

Figure 4-11: Say yes to see me.

Although your initial FaceTime call likely involves AT&T, your next call doesn't have to because the connection is via Wi-Fi once FaceTime commences. Search for any FaceTime calls you previously made by tapping an entry for that call in Recents. The iPhone knows to take the call straight to video, though of course the person you're talking to has to accept the invitation each time.

You can do FaceTime also by tapping a pal's listings in Contacts.

So what is a FaceTime call like? In our experience, first-time reactions were gleeful. Not only are you seeing the other person, but the quality of the video is also typically good. You also see your own mug in a small picture-in-picture (PiP) window (as shown in Figure 4-12), which you can drag to a corner of the screen. The PiP image represents what the other person sees, so it's a good way of knowing, short of the other person telling you, if your face has dropped out of the frame.

You can use FaceTime in portrait or landscape mode. You might find it easier to bring another person into a scene in landscape mode.

Mute audio   End call   Switch cameras

Recipient sees this PiP

Figure 4-12: Bob can see Ed and Ed can see Bob.

Apple says the front camera has been fine-tuned for FaceTime usage, which in photography-speak means the camera has the proper field of view and focal length. But at times, you'll want to employ the iPhone's main camera on the rear to best show off your surroundings and give the caller an idea of where you are.

To toggle between the front and main cameras, tap the icon at the bottom-right corner of the screen (refer to Figure 4-12).

If you want to mute a FaceTime video call, tap the microphone icon with the slash running through it. The caller can continue to see you but not hear you.

Although many FaceTime calls commence with a regular AT&T call, you can't go from FaceTime to an audio-only call without hanging up and redialing. Similarly, if you drop a FaceTime call because of a Wi-Fi hiccup or some other problem, you'll have to redial via FaceTime or AT&T, depending on whether you want the call to be video or only audio.

To block all FaceTime calls, tap Settings from the Home screen, tap Phone, and make sure FaceTime is off. If you can't find the FaceTime button or wonder why you're not getting FaceTime calls, go back into Settings and make sure this option is turned on.

If you want to momentarily check out another iPhone app while on a FaceTime call, press the Home button and then tap the icon for the app you have in mind. At this point, you can still talk over FaceTime, but you'll no longer see the person. Tap the green bar at the top of the screen to bring the person back in front of you.

And there you have it. That's FaceTime, arguably the coolest new feature in the iPhone.

You can do even more things with iPhone the phone, as you find out in Chapter 13. Meanwhile, we recommend that you read the next chapter to figure out how to become a whiz at text messaging

5

Texting 1, 2, 3:
Messages and Notes

*1*f this is your first experience with an intelligent virtual keyboard, it will probably feel awkward in the beginning. Within a few days, however, many iPhone users report that they not only have become comfortable using the virtual keyboard but also have become proficient virtual typists as well.

By the time you finish this chapter, we think you'll feel comfortable and proficient, too. You discover all about using the virtual keyboard in Chapter 2. In this chapter, we focus on two iPhone apps that use text — namely, Messages and Notes.

Messaging

The Messages app lets you exchange short text messages with any cell phone that supports the SMS protocol. You can also send and receive MMS messages, which lets you exchange pictures, contacts, videos, ringtones, other audio recordings, and locations with any cell phone that supports the MMS protocol.

TECHNICAL STUFF SMS is the acronym for the Short Message Service protocol; MMS is the acronym for the Multimedia Messaging Service protocol. Most phones sold today support one or both protocols.

MMS support is built into iPhone OS 3.0 and higher and works with iPhone 3G, 3GS, and 4 (but not the first-generation iPhone).

Typing text on a cell phone with a 12-key numeric keypad is an unnatural act, which is why many people have never sent a single SMS or MMS message. The iPhone will change that. The intelligent virtual keyboard makes it easy to compose short text messages, and the big, bright, high-resolution screen makes it a pleasure to read them.

But before we get to the part where you send or receive messages, let's go over some messaging basics:

- **Both sender and receiver need SMS- or MMS-enabled mobile phones.** Your iPhone qualifies, as does almost any mobile phone made in the past few years. Keep in mind that if you send messages to folks with a phone that doesn't support SMS or MMS or who choose not to pay extra for messaging services, those folks will never get your message or even know you sent a message.

- **Some phones (not the iPhone, of course) limit SMS messages to 160 characters.** If you try to send a longer message to one of these phones, your message may be truncated or split into multiple shorter messages. The point is that it's a good idea to keep SMS messages brief.

In iOS 4 and higher, the Messages app can count characters for you. To enable the option (it's off by default), tap the Settings icon on your Home screen, then tap the Messages icon and enable Character Count. You'll see the number of characters you've typed so far, then a slash, and then the number 160 (the character limit on some mobile phones, as just described) directly above the Send button.

- **AT&T iPhone data plans do not include SMS or MMS messages.** Individual SMS text messages currently cost 20¢ each unless you subscribe to one of the optional SMS text message plans, which start at $5 per month for 200 messages. MMS is available from AT&T at no additional cost to customers with an SMS text-messaging bundle.

Each individual message in a conversation counts against this total, even if it's only a one-word reply such as "OK," or "CUL8R" (which is teenager-speak for "see you later").

- **You can usually increase the number of messages in your plan for a few more dollars a month.** This is almost always less expensive than paying for them à la carte.

- **You can send or receive messages only over your wireless carrier's network (which is AT&T in the United States).** In other words, SMS or MMS messages can't be sent or received over a Wi-Fi connection.

Okay, now that we have that out of the way, let's start with how to send messages.

You send me: Sending SMS text messages

Tap the Messages icon on the Home screen to launch the Messages app, and then tap the little pencil-and-paper icon in the top-right corner of the screen to start a new text message.

At this point, the To field is active and awaiting your input. You can do three things at this point:

- ✐ If the recipient isn't in your Contacts list, type his or her cell phone number.

- ✐ If the recipient *is* in your Contacts list, type the first few letters of the name. A list of matching contacts appears. Scroll through it if necessary and tap the name of the contact.

  The more letters you type, the shorter the list becomes. And, after you've tapped the name of a contact, you can begin typing another name so you can send this message to multiple recipients at once.

- ✐ Tap the blue + icon on the right side of the To field to select a name from your Contacts list.

There's a fourth option if you want to compose the message first and address it later. Tap inside the text-entry field (the oval-shaped area just above the keyboard and to the left of the Send button) to activate it, and then type your message. When you've finished typing, tap the To field and use one of the preceding techniques to address your message.

When you've finished addressing and composing, tap the Send button to send your message on its merry way. And that's all there is to it.

Being a golden receiver: Receiving SMS text messages

First things first. If you want to hear an alert sound when you receive a message, tap the Settings icon on your Home screen, tap Sounds, tap the New Text Message item, and then tap one of the available sounds. You can audition the sounds by tapping them.

You hear the sounds when you audition them in the Settings app, even if you have the ring/silent switch set to Silent. After you exit the Settings app, however, you *won't* hear a sound when a message arrives if the ring/silent switch is set to Silent.

If you *don't* want to hear an alert when a message arrives, instead of tapping one of the listed sounds, tap the first item in the list: None.

If you receive a message when your phone is asleep, all or part of the text message and the name of the sender appear on the Unlock screen when you wake your phone.

If your phone is awake and unlocked when a message arrives, all or part of the message and the name of the sender appear on the screen in front of whatever's already there, along with Close and Reply buttons. At the same time, the Messages icon on the Home screen displays the number of unread messages. You can see all of this in Figure 5-1.

To read or reply to the message, tap Reply.

To read or reply to a message after you've tapped the Close button, tap the Messages icon. If a message other than the one you're interested in appears on the screen when you launch the Messages app, tap Messages in the top-left corner of the screen, and then tap the recipient's name; that person's messages appear on the screen.

To reply to the message on the screen, tap the text-entry field to the left of the Send button, and the keyboard appears. Type your reply and then tap Send.

Your conversation is saved as a series of text bubbles. Your messages appear on the right side of the screen in green bubbles; the other person's messages appear on the left in gray bubbles, as shown in Figure 5-2.

You can delete a conversation in two ways:

✔ **If you're viewing the conversation:** Tap the Edit button at the top-right of the conversation screen and a circle appears to the left of each text bubble. Tap a text bubble and a red check mark appears in the circle. When you've added a red check mark to all the text bubbles you want to delete, tap the red Delete button at the bottom-left of the screen. Or, to delete the entire conversation in one fell swoop, tap the Clear All button in the top-left corner of the screen.

If you want to forward all or part of a conversation to another mobile phone user (as an SMS or MMS message), follow the same procedure (that is, tap the Edit button, then tap the text bubbles you want to forward so the red check mark appears in a circle to their left). Now, instead of tapping the red Delete button at the bottom-left of the screen, tap the blue Forward button at the bottom-right of the screen. The contents of the text bubbles with check marks will be copied to a new text message; specify a recipient and then tap Send.

✐ **If you're viewing the list of text messages:** Tap the Edit button at the top-left of the Messages list, tap the red – icon that appears to the left of the person's name, and then tap the Delete button that appears to the right of the name.

Number of new messages

Sender's name   Message   What they said   What you said

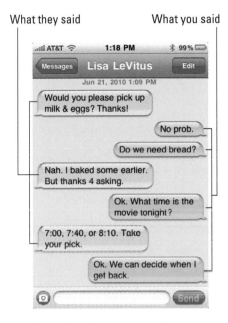

Figure 5-1: When a message arrives and your iPhone is awake.

Figure 5-2: This is what an SMS conversation looks like.

MMS: Like SMS with media

To send a picture or video (iPhone 3GS or 4 only) in a message, follow the instructions for sending a text message and then tap the camera icon to the left of the text-entry field at the bottom of the screen. You'll then have the option of using an existing picture or video or taking a new one. You can also add text to photos or videos. When you're finished, tap the Send button.

If you *receive* a picture or video in a message, it appears in a bubble just like text. Tap it to see it full-screen.

Tap the icon in the lower-left corner (as shown in the margin) for additional options. If you don't see the icon, tap the picture or video once and the icon will magically appear.

Smart messaging tricks

Here are some more things you can do with messages:

- ✔ To search your messages for a word or phrase, type the word or phrase in the Search field at the top of the Messages screen.

- ✔ To use a Bluetooth keyboard for typing (iPhone 3GS and 4 only) instead of the on-screen keyboard, follow the instructions in Chapter 13 to pair your Bluetooth keyboard with your iPhone.

  The Apple Wireless Keyboard ($69) works great with the iPhone 3GS or 4 and all iPads.

- ✔ To send a message to someone in your Favorites or Recents list, tap the Phone icon on the Home screen, and then tap Favorites or Recents, respectively. Tap the blue > icon to the right of a name or number, and then scroll down and tap Text Message at the bottom of the Info screen.

- ✔ To call or e-mail someone to whom you've sent an SMS or MMS message, tap the Messages icon on the Home screen, and then tap the person's name in the Messages list. Tap the Call button at the top of the conversation to call the person, or tap the Contact Info button and then tap an e-mail address to send an e-mail.

  You can use the preceding technique only if the contact has an e-mail address.

- ✔ Did you send someone an SMS or MMS text message? Receive one from someone? You can add the person to your Contacts list by tapping the person's name or phone number in the Text Messages list and then tapping the Add to Contacts button. If the person is already in your Contacts list, the Add to Contacts button doesn't appear, so don't bother looking for it.

- ✔ If an SMS or MMS message includes a URL, tap it to open that Web page in Safari.

- ✔ If an SMS or MMS message includes a phone number, tap it to call that number.

- ✔ If an SMS or MMS message includes an e-mail address, tap it to open a pre-addressed e-mail message in Mail.

- ✔ If an SMS or MMS message includes a street address, tap it to see a map in Maps.

And that's all there is to it. You are now an official SMS or MMS text message maven.

Take Note of Notes

Notes is an app that creates text notes that you can save or send through e-mail. To create a note, first tap the Notes icon on the Home screen, and then tap the + button in the top-right corner to start a new note. The virtual keyboard appears. Type the note. When you're finished, tap the Done button in the top-right corner to save the note. (The Done button appears only when the virtual keyboard is on-screen, however, so you can't see it in Figure 5-3.)

After a note is saved, you can do the following:

- Tap the left or right arrow button at the bottom of the screen to read the previous or next note, respectively.

- Tap the letter icon at the bottom of the screen to e-mail the note using the Mail app (see Chapter 11 for more about Mail).

- Tap the trash can icon at the bottom of the screen to delete the note.

- Tap the Notes button at the top-left corner of the screen, and you see a list of all your notes, as shown in Figure 5-4. Then just tap a note to open it for viewing or editing.

Figure 5-3: The Notes app revealed.

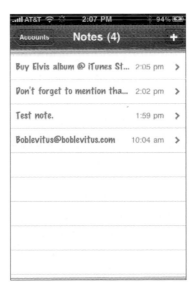

Figure 5-4: The list of notes in the Notes app.

We'd be remiss if we didn't remind you that as long as you're running iPhone OS 3.0 or later, you can sync notes with your computer (see Chapter 3). And if you're running iOS 4 and have enabled note syncing for more than one account (tap Settings and then tap Mail, Contacts, Calendars), you'll see an Accounts button at the top of the Notes list screen (refer to Figure 5-4). Tap Accounts and you can choose to display all your notes or only notes associated with a particular account.

An *account,* as mentioned to in the preceding paragraph, refers to a Microsoft Exchange, MobileMe, Gmail, Yahoo!, AOL, or other account that offers a notes feature.

And that's all she, er we, wrote. You now know everything there is to know about creating and managing notes with Notes

6

Calendars and Calculators and Clocks (Voice, Too) — Oh, My

*T*he iPhone is a smartphone. And, as a smart device, it can remind you of appointments, tell you the time where you live (or halfway around the world), and even help you perform arithmetic.

Over the next few pages, we look at four of the iPhone's core — if, frankly, unsexy — apps. Indeed, we'd venture to say that no one bought an iPhone because of its calendar, calculator, clock, or voice recorder. Just the same, it's awfully handy having these programs around.

©Robert Pierce

Working with the Calendar

The Calendar program lets you keep on top of your appointments and events (birthdays, anniversaries, and the like). You open it by tapping the Calendar icon on the Home screen. The icon is smart in its own right because it changes daily; the day of the week and date are displayed.

You have three main ways to peek at your calendar: List, Day, and Month views. Choosing one is as simple as tapping on the List, Day, or Month button at the bottom of the Calendar screen. From each view, you can always return to the current day by tapping the Today button.

Take a closer look in the following sections.

List view

List view, shown in Figure 6-1, isn't complicated. As its name indicates, List view presents current and future appointments in list format. You can drag the list up or down with your finger or flick to rapidly scroll through the list. List view compensates for the lack of Week-at-a-Glance view, though Apple certainly could add such a feature eventually, as it did on the iPhone's cousin, the iPad tablet.

The iPhone can display the color-coding you assigned in iCal. Cool, huh?

If you're a Mac user who uses iCal, you can create multiple calendars and choose which ones to sync with your phone (as described in Chapter 3). What's more, you can choose to display any or all of your calendars. You can also sync calendars with Microsoft Entourage on a Mac or Microsoft Outlook 2003, 2007 or 2010 on a PC.

Be careful: To-do items created in iCal aren't synced and don't appear on your iPhone.

Day view

Day view, shown in Figure 6-2, reveals the appointments of a given 24-hour period (though you have to scroll up or down to see an entire day's worth of entries).

Month view

By now, you're getting the hang of these different views. When your iPhone is in Month view, you can see appointments from January to December. In this monthly calendar view, a dot appears on any day that has appointments or events scheduled. Tap that day to see the list of activities the dot represents. The list of activities is just below the month in Month view, as shown in Figure 6-3.

Figure 6-1: List view.

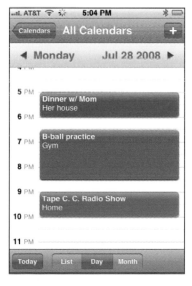

Figure 6-2: Day view.

Figure 6-3: Month view.

Adding Calendar Entries

In Chapter 3, you discover pretty much everything there is to know about syncing your iPhone, including syncing calendar entries from your Windows machine (using the likes of Microsoft Outlook) or Mac (using iCal or Microsoft Entourage).

Of course, in plenty of situations, you enter appointments on the fly. Adding appointments directly to the iPhone is easy:

1. **Tap the Calendar icon at the top of the screen, and then tap the List, Day, or Month button.**

2. **Tap the + button in the upper-right corner of the screen.**

   The + button appears whether you're in List, Day, or Month view. Tapping it displays the Add Event screen, shown in Figure 6-4.

3. **Tap the Title/Location field and finger-type as much (or as little) information as you feel is necessary.**

   Tapping displays the virtual keyboard.

4. **Tap Done.**

5. **If your calendar entry has a start time or end time (or both):**

   a. **Tap the Starts/Ends field.**

   b. **In the bottom half of the screen that appears (see Figure 6-5), choose the time the event starts and then the time it ends.**

   Use your finger to roll separate wheels for the date, hour, and minute (in 5-minute intervals) and to specify AM or PM. It's a little like manipulating one of those combination bicycle locks or an old-fashioned date stamp used with an inkpad.

   c. **Tap Done when you're finished.**

6. **If you are entering an all-day milestone (such as a birthday), tap the All-Day button so that On (rather than Off) is showing. Then tap Done.**

   Because the time isn't relevant for an all-day entry, note that the bottom half of the screen now has wheels for just the month, day, and year.

7. **If you're setting up a recurring entry, such as an anniversary, tap the Repeat window. Tap to indicate how often the event in question recurs, and then tap Done.**

   The options are Every Day, Every Week, Every 2 Weeks, Every Month, and Every Year.

Figure 6-4: The screen looks like this just before you add an event to your iPhone.

Figure 6-5: Controlling the Starts and Ends fields is like manipulating a bike lock.

8. If you want to set a reminder or alert for the entry, tap Alert. Next, tap a time, and then tap Done.

Alerts can be set to arrive on the actual date of an event, 2 days before, 1 day before, 2 hours before, 1 hour before, 30 minutes before, 15 minutes before, or 5 minutes before. When the appointment time rolls around, you hear a sound and see a message like the one shown in Figure 6-6.

If you're the kind of person who needs an extra nudge, set another reminder by tapping on the Second Alert field.

Figure 6-6: Alerts make it hard to forget.

9. **Tap Calendar to assign the entry to a particular calendar, and then tap the calendar you have in mind (Home or Work, for example). Then tap Done.**

10. **Tap Availability (if it's shown on your phone) to indicate whether you're busy, free, tentative, or out of office. Then tap Done.**

11. **If you want to enter notes about the appointment or event, tap Notes at the bottom of the Add Event screen. Type your note, and then tap Done.**

    A virtual keyboard pops up so that you can type those notes.

12. **Tap Done after you finish entering everything.**

Choose a default calendar by tapping Settings, tapping Mail, Contacts, Calendars, and then flicking the screen until the Calendar section appears. Tap Default Calendar and select the calendar that you want to show up regularly.

If you travel long distances for your job, you can also make events appear according to whichever time zone you selected for your calendars. In the Calendar settings, tap Time Zone Support to turn it on, and then tap Time Zone. Type the time zone location on the keyboard that appears.

When Time Zone Support is turned off, events are displayed according to the time zone of your current location.

To turn off a calendar alert, tap Settings, tap Sounds, and then making sure that the Calendar Alerts button is turned off.

If you want to modify an existing calendar entry, tap the entry, tap Edit, and then make whichever changes need to be made. To wipe out a calendar entry, tap Edit, and then tap Delete Event. You have a chance to confirm your choice by tapping either Delete Event (again) or Cancel.

Calendar entries you create on your iPhone are synchronized with the calendar you specified in the iTunes Info pane.

Letting your calendar push you around

If you work for a company that uses Microsoft Exchange ActiveSync, calendar entries and meeting invitations from coworkers can be *pushed* to your device so that they show up on the screen moments after they're entered, even if they're entered on computers at work. Setting up an account to facilitate this pushing of calendar entries to your iPhone is a breeze, although you should check with your company's tech or IT department to make sure that your employer allows it. Then follow these steps:

1. **Tap Settings, then tap Mail, Contacts, Calendars, and then tap Add Account.**

2. **From the Add Account list, shown in Figure 6-7, tap Microsoft Exchange.**

3. **Fill in the e-mail address, username, password, and description fields, and then tap Next.**

4. **If required, enter your server address on the next screen that appears.**

   The iPhone supports something called the Microsoft Autodiscovery service, which uses your name and password to automatically determine the address of the Exchange server. The rest of the fields should be filled in with the e-mail address, username, password, and description you just entered, as shown in Figure 6-8.

5. **Tap Next.**

6. **Tap the On switch for each information type that you want to synchronize using Microsoft Exchange.**

   The options are Mail, Contacts, and Calendars. You should be good to go now, although some employers may require you to add passcodes to safeguard company secrets.

Figure 6-7: Set up your account in the Add Account screen.

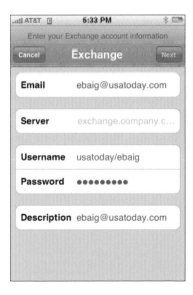

Figure 6-8: Fill in the blanks to set up your corporate account.

If you have a business-issued iPhone and it is lost or stolen — or it turns out that you're a double-agent working for a rival company — your employer's IT administrators can remotely wipe your device clean.

Only one account taking advantage of Microsoft Exchange ActiveSync can be configured to work on your iPhone.

Responding to meeting invitations

The iPhone has one more important button, the Invitations button, located just to the right of the List, Day, and Month buttons — but you see it only under certain circumstances. For instance, you see the button when the Exchange calendar syncing feature is turned on or when you have a calendar that adheres to the CalDAV Internet standard. (By the time you read this, you may also see an invitation if you use a MobileMe calendar as part of Apple's $99/year subscription service.) The Invitations button, which shows up if you have an invitation on your calendar, is represented by an arrow pointing downward into a half-rectangle. (The button is not shown in Figures 6-1, 6-2, or 6-3.)

If you have any pending invitations, tap the Invitations button now to view them, and then tap any of the items in the list to see more details.

Suppose that a meeting invitation arrives from your boss. You can see who else is attending the shindig, check scheduling conflicts, and more. Tap Accept to let the meeting organizer know you're attending, tap Decline if you have something better to do (and aren't worried about upsetting the person who signs your paycheck), or tap Maybe if you're waiting for a better offer.

You can choose to receive an alert every time someone sends you an invitation. In the Calendar settings, tap New Invitation Alerts so that the button displays On.

If you take advantage of MobileMe, you can now keep calendar entries synchronized between your iPhone and PC or Mac. When you make a scheduling change on your iPhone, it's automatically updated on your computer, and vice versa. Choose MobileMe from the Add Account screen (refer to Figure 6-7) to get started.

You find out more about configuring MobileMe when we discuss the Fetch New Data setting in Chapter 13.

Subscribing to calendars

You can subscribe to calendars that adhere to the CalDAV and iCalendar (.ics) standards, which are supported by the popular Google and Yahoo! calendars, or iCal on the Mac. Although you can read entries on the iPhone from the calendars you subscribe to, you can't create entries from the phone or edit the entries that are already present.

To subscribe to one of these calendars, tap Settings and then tap Mail, Contacts, Calendars. Next, tap Add Account, and then tap Other. You then choose either Add CalDAV Account or Add Subscribed Calendar. Next, enter the server where the iPhone can find the calendar you have in mind, and if need be, a username, a password, and an optional description.

Searching calendars

You can search calendar entries, appointments, locations for events, and so on by using Spotlight search, a topic we address in Chapter 2. You can also search for events while in the calendar List view by typing text in the Search All Calendars field at the top of the screen.

Calculate This

Quick — what's 3,467.8 times 982.3? Why, the answer is 3,406,419.94 (of course). We can solve the problem quickly thanks to the iPhone calculator, buried (until it's needed) under another of those Home screen icons.

Your handy iPhone calculator does just fine for adding, subtracting, multiplying, and dividing. Numbers and symbols (such as C for clear, and M+ for memory) are large and easy to see.

Are you thinking, "This isn't exactly the most advanced calculator I've ever used"? Well, you're right. The calculator can't handle a sine or a square root, much less more advanced functions.

Fortunately, the math whizzes at Apple were thinking right along with you. To see what they came up with, rotate the iPhone. As if by sleight of hand, your pocket calculator is now a full-fledged scientific calculator, capable of tackling dozens of complex functions. Take a gander at both calculators shown in Figure 6-9.

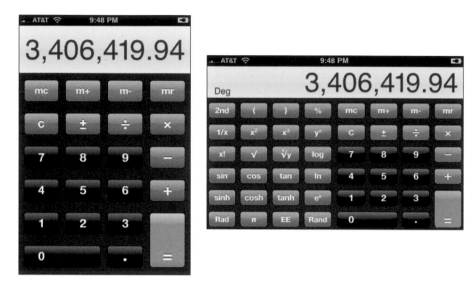

Figure 6-9: Solving simple — and more complex — mathematical problems.

Isn't it nice to know just how much smarter a smartphone can make you feel?

Punching the Clock

We hear you: "So the iPhone has a clock. Big whoop. Doesn't every cell phone have a clock?"

Well, yes, every cell phone does have a clock. But not every phone has a *world clock* that lets you display the time in multiple cities on multiple continents. And, not every cell phone has an alarm, a stopwatch, and a timer to boot.

Let's take a look at the time functions on your iPhone.

World clock

Want to know the time in Beijing or Bogota? Tapping World Clock (inside the Clock app) lets you display the time in numerous cities around the globe, as shown in Figure 6-10. When the clock face is dark, it's dark in the city you chose; if the face is white, it's light outside.

Tap the + button in the upper-right corner of the screen and use the virtual keyboard to start typing a city name. The moment you press the first letter, the iPhone displays a list of cities or countries that begin with that letter. So, as Figure 6-11 shows, typing *V* brings up both Vaduz, Liechtenstein, and Caracas, Venezuela, among myriad other possibilities. You can create clocks for as many cities as you like, though the times in only four cities appear on a single screen. To see times in other cities, scroll up or down.

To remove a city from the list, tap Edit and then tap the red circle with the white horizontal line in it to the left of the city you want to drop. Then tap Delete.

You can also rearrange the order of the cities displaying the time. Tap Edit, and then press your finger against the symbol with three horizontal lines to the right of the city you want to move up or down in the list. Then drag the city to its new spot.

Figure 6-10: What time is it in Budapest?

Figure 6-11: Clocking in around the world.

Alarm clock

Ever try to set the alarm in a hotel room? It's remarkable how complicated setting an alarm can be, on even the most inexpensive clock radio. Like almost everything else, the procedure is dirt-simple on the iPhone:

1. **Tap Clock on the Home screen to display the Clock app.**

2. **Tap the Alarm icon at the bottom of the screen.**

3. **Tap the + button in the upper-right corner of the screen.**

4. **Choose the time of the alarm by rotating the wheel in the bottom half of the screen.**

   This step is similar to the action required to set the time that an event starts or ends on your calendar.

5. **If you want the alarm to go off on other days, tap Repeat and then tell the iPhone the days you want the alarm to be repeated, as in Every Monday, Every Tuesday, Every Wednesday, and so on.**

6. **Tap Sound to choose the ringtone (see Chapter 4) that will wake you up. You can even use a custom ringtone you created.**

   Your choice is a matter of personal preference, but we can tell you that the ringtone for the appropriately named Alarm managed to wake Ed from a deep sleep.

7. **Tap Snooze to have the alarm, accompanied by a Snooze button, appear on the screen.**

   Tap the Snooze button to shut down the alarm for nine minutes.

8. **If you want to call the alarm something other than, um, Alarm, tap the Label field and use the virtual keyboard to type another descriptor.**

9. **Tap Save when the alarm settings are to your liking.**

You know that an alarm has been set and activated because of the tiny status icon (surprise, surprise — it looks like a clock) that appears in the upper-right corner of the screen.

An alarm takes precedence over any tracks you're listening to on your iPod. Songs momentarily pause when an alarm goes off and resume when you turn off the alarm (or press the Snooze button).

When your ring/silent switch is set to Silent, your iPhone doesn't ring, play alert effects, or make iPod sounds. But it *will* play alarms from the Clock app. That's good to know when you set your phone to Silent at a movie or the opera. And, although it seems obvious, if you want to *hear* an alarm, you have to make sure that the iPhone volume is turned up.

Not all phone carriers support the network time option in all locations, so an alarm may not sound at the correct time in a given area.

Stopwatch

If you're helping a loved one train for a marathon, the iPhone Stopwatch function can provide an assist. Open it by tapping Stopwatch in the Clock app.

Just tap Start to begin the count, and then tap Stop at the finish line. You can also tap a Lap button to monitor the times between laps.

Timer

Cooking a hard-boiled egg or Thanksgiving turkey? Again, the iPhone comes to the rescue. Tap Timer (in the Clock app) and then rotate the hour and minute wheels until the time you have in mind is highlighted. Tap When Timer Ends to choose the ringtone that will signify time's up.

After you set up the length of the timer, tap Start when you're ready to begin. You can watch the minutes and seconds wind down on the screen, if you have nothing better to do.

If you're doing anything else on the iPhone — admiring photos, say — you hear the ringtone and see a *Timer Done* message on the screen at the appropriate moment. Tap OK to silence the ringtone.

Voice Memos

Consider all the times you'd find it useful to have a voice recorder in your pocket — perhaps when you're attending a lecture or interviewing an important source (that's a biggie for us journalist types). Or maybe you just want to leave yourself a quickie reminder about something ("Pick up milk after work"). Well, you're in luck. Apple includes a built-in digital voice recorder.

A bunch of third-party apps add voice recording to the iPhone. Ed uses Recorder from Retronyms and Dictation from Dragon, and Bob uses iTalk Recorder from Griffin.

Making a recording

After you have that recorder in your pocket, how do you capture audio? When you tap the Voice Memos icon on the Home screen, up pops the microphone displayed in Figure 6-12. We'd tell you to talk right into that microphone, but it's mainly for show. The two real microphones on the iPhone 4 are on the top and bottom of the device (as pictured in Chapter 1).

Figure 6-12: Miked: Leaving a voice memo.

Tap the red record button in the lower-left part of the screen to start recording. You see the needle in the audio level meter move as the Voice Memo detects sounds, even when you pause a recording by tapping the red button a second time. A clock at the top of the screen indicates how long your recording session is lasting. It's that easy.

The audio meter can help you determine an ideal recording level. Apple recommends that the loudest level on the meter be between –3dB and 0dB. We recommend speaking in a normal voice. To adjust the recording level, simply move the microphone closer or farther from your mouth.

Listening to recordings

After you capture your thoughts or musings, how do you play them back?

You can start playback in a couple of ways, and both involve tapping the same button:

- ✓ **Immediately after recording the memo, tap the button to the right of the audio level meter.** A list of all your recordings pops up in chronological order, as shown in Figure 6-13, with the most recent memo on top. That memo is the one you just recorded, of course, and it automatically starts to play.

- ✓ **If you haven't just recorded something, tapping the button to the right summons the same list of all your recordings.** However, nothing plays until you tap a recording in the list and then tap the little play button that appears to the left of the date and time that the recording was made (or, alternatively, to the left of the label you assigned to the recording, as we explain in the "Adding a label to a recording" section, later in this chapter).

You can drag the playhead along the scrubber bar to move ahead to any point in the memo.

If you don't hear anything after tapping play, tap the Speaker button in the upper-left corner of the screen. Sound pumps through the built-in iPhone speaker.

Trimming recordings

Maybe the person who left the recording rambled on and on. You just want to cut to the chase, for goodness' sake. Fortunately, you can trim the audio directly on the iPhone.

Tap the right-pointing arrow next to the memo you want to trim, and then tap Trim Memo. A narrow, blue tube representing the recording appears inside a yellow bar, as shown in Figure 6-14. Drag the edges of this *audio region* to adjust the start and end points of the memo. You can preview your edit before tapping the Trim Voice Memo button by tapping the little play button.

Your edits are permanent. Make sure that you're completely satisfied with your cuts before tapping Trim Voice Memo.

Adding a label to a recording

When a memo is added to your list of recordings, it just shows up with the date and time of the recording. You see no other identifier. As memos accumulate, you may have a tough time remembering which recording was made for which purpose. You can label a recording with one of the labels Apple has supplied or, better, create a custom label.

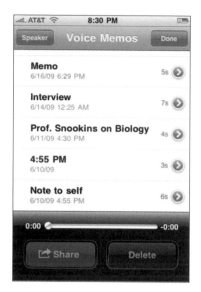

Figure 6-13: Tap the voice memo you want to play.

Figure 6-14: Trim a memo when someone says too much.

Here's how:

1. **From the list of recordings, tap the right-pointing arrow for the memo to which you want to add a label.**

   The Voice Memo information screen appears.

2. **Tap the right-pointing arrow in the box showing the date and time and the length of the video you just recorded.**

3. **Select a label from the list that appears.**

   Your choices are None, Podcast, Interview, Lecture, Idea, Meeting, Memo, and Custom.

4. **Choose Custom to type your own label (*Professor Snookins on Biology,* for example).**

   That's it. Your recording is duly identified.

Sharing memos

You may want to share with others the good professor's wacky theories. Tap Share from either the main Voice Memos list or the information screen. You then have the option to either e-mail the memo or (if your carrier permits it) send it as part of an MMS, or multimedia picture, message.

You can also sync Voice Memos to your PC or Mac by using iTunes, as described in Chapter 3.

When you have no further use for a recording, you can remove it from the Voice Memos app by tapping it in the list and then tapping the Delete button.

Part III
The Multimedia iPhone

The 5th Wave By Rich Tennant

"Okay, the view's just up ahead. Everyone switch to 'America the Beautiful' on your iPhone playlist."

*Y*our iPhone is arguably the best iPod in the world that can make and receive phone calls (with a tip of the hat to the iPad and iPod touch, the best iPods in the world that can't make and receive phone calls). So in this part, we look at the multimedia side of your phone — audio, video, and still pictures, too. There has never been a phone that was this much fun to use, and we show you how to wring the most out of every multimedia bit of it.

First we explore how to enjoy listening to music, podcasts, and audiobooks on your iPhone.

Then we move on to everything you always wanted to know about photos and iPhones: how to shoot them well, store them, sync them, and do all kinds of other interesting things with them.

We conclude this multimedia part by looking at some video, both literally and figuratively. We start with a quick segment about how to find good video for your iPhone, followed by instructions for watching video on your iPhone. Finally, we provide a delightful little ditty about shooting and sharing video with your iPhone 3GS or 4. And before we leave the video scene, you also see how to have a blast with video from the famous YouTube Web site, using iPhone's built-in YouTube application.

7

Get in Tune(s):
Audio on Your iPhone

In This Chapter

▶ Checking out your iPhone's inner iPod

▶ Bossing your tunes around

▶ Have it your way: Tailoring your audio experience

*A*s we mention elsewhere in this book, your iPhone is one of the best iPods ever — especially for working with audio and video. In this chapter, we show you how to use your iPhone for audio; in Chapter 9, we cover video.

We start with a quick tour of the iPhone's iPod app. Then we look at how to use your iPhone as an audio player. After you're nice and comfy with using it this way, we show you how to customize the listening experience so that it's just the way you like it. Then we offer a few tips to help you get the most out of using your iPhone as an audio player. Finally, we show you how to use the iTunes app to buy music, audiobooks, videos, and more, and how to download free content, such as podcasts.

We assume that you already synced your iPhone with your computer and that your iPhone contains audio content — songs, podcasts, or audiobooks. If you don't have any audio on your iPhone yet, we humbly suggest that you get some (flip to Chapter 3 and follow the instructions) before you read the rest of this chapter — or Chapter 9, for that matter.

©iStockphoto.com/HannahmariaH

Okay, now that you have some audio content on your iPhone to play with, are you ready to rock?

Introducing the iPod inside Your iPhone

To use your iPhone as an iPod, just tap the iPod icon in the lower-right corner of the Home screen. At the bottom of the screen that appears, you should see five icons: Playlists, Artists, Songs, Videos, and More.

If you don't see these icons, tap the back button in the upper-left corner of the screen (the one that looks like a little arrow pointing to the left).

Or, if you're holding your iPhone sideways (the long edges are parallel to the ground), rotate it 90 degrees so that it's upright (the short edges are parallel to the ground).

You'll understand why your iPhone's orientation matters when you read the later section "Go with the Cover (Flow)."

Playlists

Tap the Playlists icon at the bottom of the screen and a list of playlists appears. If you have no playlists on your iPhone, don't sweat it. Just know that if you had some, this is where they'd be. (Playlists let you organize songs around a particular theme or mood: opera arias, romantic ballads, British invasion — whatever. Younger folks sometimes call them *mixes.*)

Tap a playlist and you see a list of the songs it contains. If the list is longer than one screen, flick upward to scroll down. Tap a song in the list and it plays. Or, tap Shuffle at the top of the list to hear a song from that playlist (and all subsequent songs) at random.

That's all there is to selecting and playing songs from a playlist.

You find out how to create your own playlists on your iPhone a little later in this chapter.

Artistic license

Now we tell you how to find and play a song ordered by artist name rather than by playlist. Tap the Artists icon at the bottom of the screen and an alphabetical list of artists appears.

If the list is longer than one screen (which it probably is), you can, of course, flick upward to scroll down or flick downward to scroll up. But you have easier ways to find an artist.

For example, at the top of the screen, above the first artist's name, you see a search field. Tap it and type the name of the artist you want to find. Now tap the Search button to see a list of all matching artists.

Another way to find an artist is to tap one of the little letters on the right side of the screen, to jump directly to artists whose names start with that letter. In Figure 7-1, for example, that letter is *B*.

Notice that a magnifying glass appears above the *A* on the right side of the screen. Tap the magnifying glass to jump directly to the search field.

As you can see, those letters are extremely small, so unless you have tiny fingers, you may have to settle for a letter close to the one you want or else tap several times until you select the correct one.

Tap an artist's name and one of two things occurs:

- **If you have songs from more than one album by an artist in your music library:** A list of albums appears, as shown in Figure 7-2. Tap an album to see a list of the songs it contains. Or, tap the first item in the list of albums — All Songs — to see a list of all songs on all albums by that artist.

- **If all songs in your music library by that artist are on the same album or aren't associated with a specific album:** A list of all songs by that artist appears.

Either way, just tap a song and it begins to play.

Song selection

Now we tell you how to find a song by its title and play it. Tap the Songs icon at the bottom of the screen and a list of songs appears.

You find songs the same ways you find artists: Flick upward or downward to scroll; use the search field at the top of the list; or tap a little letter on the right side of the screen.

If you're not sure which song you want to listen to, try this: Tap the shuffle button at the top of the list between the search field and the first song title. Your iPhone will now play songs from your music library at random.

You can also find songs (or artists, for that matter) by typing their names in a Spotlight search, as we mention in Chapter 2.

Magnifying glass

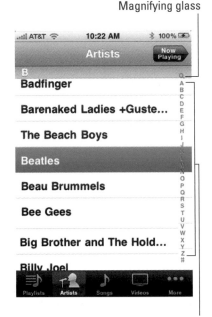

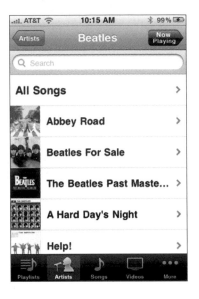

Little letters

Figure 7-1: Tap the *B* on the right side of the screen to jump to artists with names that begin with a *B*.

Figure 7-2: A list of albums will appear when you tap the artist's name.

Taking Control of Your Tunes

Now that you have the basics down, take a look at some other things you can do when your iPhone is in its iPod mode.

Go with the (Cover) Flow

Finding tracks by playlist, artist, or song is cool, but finding them with Cover Flow is even cooler. Cover Flow lets you browse your music collection by its album artwork. To use Cover Flow, turn your iPhone sideways (long edges parallel to the ground). As long as you aren't browsing or viewing video (and, of course, you tapped the iPod icon on the Home screen so that your iPhone behaves like an iPod), Cover Flow fills the screen, as shown in Figure 7-3.

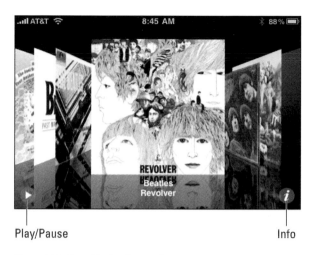

Play/Pause   Info

Figure 7-3: Go with the Cover Flow.

Flipping through your cover art in Cover Flow is simple. All you have to do is drag or flick your finger left or right on the screen and the covers go flying by. Flick or drag quickly and the covers whiz by; flick or drag slowly and the covers move leisurely. Or, tap a particular cover on the left or right of the current (centered) cover and that cover jumps to the center.

Try it — you'll like it! Here's how to put Cover Flow to work for you:

- **To see tracks (songs) on an album:** Tap the cover when it's centered or tap the info button (the little *i*) in the lower-right corner of the screen. The track list appears.

- **To play a track:** Tap its name in the list. If the list is long, scroll by dragging or flicking up and down on it.

- **To go back to Cover Flow:** Tap the title bar at the top of the track list or tap the little *i* button again.

- **To play or pause the current song:** Tap the play/pause button in the lower-left corner.

If no cover art exists for an album in your collection, the iPhone displays a plain-looking cover decorated with a single musical note. The name of the album appears below this generic cover.

And that, friends, is all there is to the iPhone's cool Cover Flow mode.

Flow's not here right now

As you saw earlier in this chapter, when you hold your iPhone vertically (the short edges are parallel to the ground) and tap the Playlists, Artists, or Songs button, you see a list rather than Cover Flow.

Along the same lines, when you're listening to music, the controls you see are different depending on which way you hold your iPhone. When you hold your iPhone vertically, as shown in Figure 7-4, you see controls that don't appear when you hold your iPhone sideways. Furthermore, the controls you see when viewing the Playlists, Artists, or Songs lists are slightly different from the controls you see when a song is playing.

Figure 7-4: Hold your iPhone vertically when you play a track and you see these controls.

Here's another cool side effect of holding your iPhone vertically: If you add lyrics to a song in iTunes on your computer (by selecting the song, choosing File⇨Get Info, and then pasting or typing the lyrics into the Lyrics tab in the Info window), the lyrics are displayed along with the cover art.

Here's how to use the controls that appear when the iPhone is vertical:

✐ **Back button:** Tap to return to whichever list you used last — Playlists, Artists, or Songs.

✐ **Switch to track list button:** Tap to switch to a list of tracks.

If you don't see the repeat button, the scrubber bar, and the shuffle button, tap the album cover once to make them appear.

✐ **Repeat button:** Tap once to repeat songs in the current album or list. The button turns blue. Tap it again to play the current song repeatedly; the blue button displays the number 1 when it's in this mode. Tap the button again to turn off this feature. The button goes back to its original gray color.

✐ **Scrubber bar:** Drag the little dot (the playhead) along the scrubber bar to skip to any point within the song.

✐ **Genius button:** Tap once and a Genius playlist appears with 25 songs that iTunes thinks will go great with the song that's playing.

The less popular the song, artist, or genre, the more likely the so-called Genius will choke on it. When that happens, you see an alert asking you to try again because this song doesn't have enough related songs to create a Genius playlist.

At the top of the Genius playlist, you find three buttons:

• **New:** Select a different song to use as the basis for a Genius playlist.

• **Refresh:** See a list of 25 different songs that "go great with" the song you're listening to.

• **Save:** Save this Genius playlist so that you can listen to it whenever you like.

If you like the Genius feature, you can also create a new Genius playlist by tapping the Playlists button at the bottom of the screen and then tapping Genius, which is the first item on the list of playlists.

✔ **Shuffle button:** Tap once to shuffle songs and play them in random order. The button turns blue when shuffling is enabled. Tap it again to play songs in order again. The button goes back to its original color — gray.

You can also shuffle tracks in any list of songs — such as playlists or albums — by tapping the word *Shuffle,* which appears at the top of the list. Regardless of whether the shuffle button has been tapped, this technique always plays songs in that list in random order. And, as you see later in this chapter, another setting, when enabled, lets you shake your iPhone from side-to-side to shuffle and play a different song at random.

✔ **Restart/previous track/rewind button:** Tap once to go to the beginning of the track. Tap this button twice to go to the start of the preceding track in the list. Touch and hold this button to rewind the song at double speed.

✔ **Play/pause button:** Tap to play or pause the song.

✔ **Next track/fast-forward button:** Tap to skip to the next track in the list. Touch and hold this button to fast-forward through the song at double speed.

✔ **Volume control:** Drag the little dot left or right to reduce or increase the volume level.

If you're using the headset included with your iPhone, you can squeeze the mic to pause, and squeeze it again to play. You can also squeeze it twice in rapid succession to skip to the next song. Sweet!

When you tap the switch to track list button, the iPhone screen and the controls change, as shown in Figure 7-5.

Here's how to use *those* controls:

✔ **Switch to Now Playing button:** Tap to switch to the Now Playing screen for the current track (refer to Figure 7-5).

✔ **Rating bar:** Drag across the rating bar to rate the current track using zero to five stars. The track shown in Figure 7-5 has a four-star rating.

The tracks are the songs in the current list (album, playlist, or artist, for example), and the current track indicator shows you which song is now playing (or paused). Tap any song in a track list to play it.

And that, gentle reader, is all you need to know to enjoy listening to music (and podcasts and audiobooks) on your iPhone.

Current track

Switch to Now Playing

Back

Rating bar

Tracks

Figure 7-5: Tap the switch to track list button and these new controls appear.

Customizing Your Audio Experience

In this section, we cover some iPod features designed to make your listening experience more enjoyable.

Finding even more choices

If you prefer to browse your audio collection by criteria other than playlist, artist, or song, you can: Tap the More button in the lower-right corner of the screen. The More list appears. Tap a choice in the list — albums, audiobooks, compilations, composers, genres, iTunes U, or podcasts — and your audio collection is organized by your criterion.

Wait — there's more. You can swap out the Playlists, Artists, Songs, and Video buttons for ones that better suit your needs. For example, if you listen to a lot of podcasts and never watch video, you can replace the Video button with a Podcasts button.

Here's how:

1. **In the lower-right corner of the screen, tap the More button.**

2. **In the upper-left corner of the screen, tap the Edit button.**

3. **Drag any button on the screen — Albums, Audiobooks, Compilations, Composers, Genres, iTunes U, Podcasts, — to the button at the bottom of the screen that you want to replace.**

4. **(Optional) Rearrange the five buttons by dragging them to the left or right.**

5. **When you have everything just the way you like it, tap the Done button to return to the More list.**

If you replace one of the buttons this way, the item you replaced is available by tapping the More button and choosing the item in the More list.

Setting preferences

You can change a few preference settings to customize your iPhone-as-an-iPod experience.

Play all songs at the same volume level

The iTunes Sound Check option automatically adjusts the level of songs so that they play at the same volume relative to each other. That way, one song never blasts out your ears even if the recording level is much louder than that of the song before or after it. To tell the iPhone to use these volume settings, you first have to turn on the feature in iTunes on your computer. Here's how to do that:

1. **Choose iTunes⇨Preferences (Mac) or Edit⇨Preferences (PC).**

2. **Click the Playback tab.**

3. **Select the Sound Check check box to enable it.**

Now you need to tell the iPhone to use the Sound Check settings from iTunes. Here's how to do *that:*

1. **On the iPhone's Home screen, tap the Settings icon.**

2. **In the list of settings, tap iPod.**

3. **Tap Sound Check to turn it on.**

Choose an equalizer setting

An *equalizer* increases or decreases the relative levels of specific frequencies to enhance the sound you hear. Some equalizer settings emphasize the bass (low end) notes in a song; other equalizer settings make the higher frequencies more apparent. The iPhone has more than a dozen equalizer presets, with names such as Acoustic, Bass Booster, Bass Reducer, Dance, Electronic, Pop, and Rock. Each one is ostensibly tailored to a specific type of music.

The way to find out whether you prefer using equalization is to listen to music while trying out different settings. To do that, first start listening to a song you like. Then, while the song is playing, follow these steps:

1. **Press the Home button on the front of your iPhone.**

2. **On the Home screen, tap the Settings icon.**

3. **In the list of settings, tap iPod.**

4. **In the list of iPod settings, tap EQ.**

5. **Tap different EQ presets (Pop, Rock, R&B, or Dance, for example), and listen carefully to the way they change how the song sounds.**

6. **When you find an equalizer preset that you think sounds good, press the Home button and you're finished.**

If you don't like any of the presets, tap Off at the top of the EQ list to turn off the equalizer.

According to Apple's iPhone battery information page (www.apple.com/batteries/iphone.html), applying an equalizer setting to song playback on your iPhone can decrease battery life. So you need to decide which is more important to you: using equalization or maximizing battery life.

Set a volume limit for music (and videos)

You can instruct your iPhone to limit the loudest listening level for audio or video. To do so, here's the drill:

1. **On the Home screen, tap the Settings icon.**

2. **In the list of settings, tap iPod.**

3. **In the list of iPod settings, tap Volume Limit.**

4. **Drag the slider to adjust the maximum volume level to your liking.**

5. **(Optional) Tap Lock Volume Limit to assign a four-digit passcode to the setting so that others can't easily change it.**

The Volume Limit setting limits the volume of only music and videos. It doesn't apply to podcasts or audiobooks. And, although the setting works with any headset, headphones, or speakers plugged into the headset jack on your iPhone, it doesn't affect sound played on your iPhone's internal speaker.

Enable the Shake to Shuffle option

Shake to Shuffle does just what its name implies — shakes your iPhone to listen to a different song selected at random. To enable this setting, here's what to do:

1. **On the Home screen, tap the Settings icon.**

2. **In the list of settings, tap iPod.**

3. **Tap the Shake to Shuffle button to turn the feature on or off.**

From shake to shuffle — how can you not love that feature?

Make a playlist on your iPhone

Of course you can make playlists in iTunes and sync them with your iPhone, but you can also create playlists on your iPhone when you're out and about. Here's how:

1. **In the lower-right corner of the Home screen, tap the iPod icon.**

2. **At the bottom of the screen, tap the Playlists button.**

3. **Tap the second item in the list: Add Playlist.**

4. **Type a name for your new playlist, and then tap Save.**

   An alphabetical list of all songs on your iPhone appears. A little + appears to the right of each song.

5. **Tap the + next to a song name to add the song to your playlist.**

   To add all these songs to your playlist, tap the + next to the first item in the list: Add All Songs.

6. **In the upper-right corner, tap the Done button.**

If you create a playlist on your iPhone and then sync it with your computer, that playlist is saved both on the iPhone and in iTunes on your computer.

The playlists remain until you delete them from iTunes. To do that, select the playlist's name in the source list and then press Delete or Backspace.

You can also edit playlists on your iPhone. To do so, tap the Playlists button at the bottom of the screen, and then tap the playlist you want to edit. Three buttons appear near the top of the screen — Edit, Clear, and Delete — with the songs in the playlist listed below them.

Tap Clear to remove all the songs from this playlist; tap Delete to delete this playlist from your iPhone; or tap Edit to do any (or all) of the following:

✓ **To move a song up or down in the playlist:** A little icon with three gray bars appears to the right of each song. Drag the icon up to move the song higher in the list or drag down to move the song lower in the list.

✓ **To add more songs to the playlist:** Tap the + button in the upper-left corner.

✓ **To delete a song from the playlist:** Tap the – sign to the left of the song name. Note that deleting a song from the playlist doesn't remove the song from your iPhone.

When you finish editing, tap the Done button near the top of the screen. And that's all there is to creating and managing playlists on your iPhone.

Set a sleep timer

If you like to fall asleep with music playing but don't want to leave your iPhone playing music all night long, you can turn on its sleep timer.

Here's how:

1. **On the Home screen, tap the Utilities folder button.**

   If you don't have a Utilities folder, go on to Step 2.

2. **Tap the Clock button.**

3. **In the lower-right corner, tap the Timer icon.**

4. **Set the number of hours and minutes you want the iPhone-as-an-iPod to play, and then tap the When Timer Ends button.**

5. **Tap the first item in the list: Sleep iPod.**

   If you don't see the Sleep iPod item, don't be alarmed (semi-clever word-play intended). You're simply looking at the middle (or the end) of the list of available alert sounds. To scroll to the top of the list, flick down-ward on the list a few times or tap the clock in the middle of the status bar at the top of the screen. The list of sounds will scroll to the top and the elusive Sleep iPod item will appear.

6. **In the upper-right corner, tap the Set button.**

7. **Tap the big, green Start button.**

That's it! If you have music playing already, you're finished. If not, press the Home button, tap the iPod button, and select the music you want to listen to as you fall asleep. When the specified time period elapses, your iPod stops playing and your iPhone goes to sleep. By then, we hope you're in slumberland as well.

Use your voice to control your iPod (iPhone 3GS and 4 only)

Here's something cool: If you have an iPhone 3GS or 4, you can boss around your music by using nothing but your voice. Here are the things you can say:

- **To play an album, an artist, or a playlist:** Say "Play" and then say "album," "artist," or "playlist" and the name of the album, artist, or playlist, respectively. You can issue these voice commands at any time except when you're on a phone call or having a FaceTime video chat. In other words, you don't have to have music playing for these voice commands to work.

- **To shuffle the current playlist:** Say "Shuffle." This voice command works only if you're listening to a playlist.

- **To find out more about the song that's playing:** Ask "What's playing?" "What song is this?" "Who sings this song?" or "Who is this song by?" Again, these commands work only if you're already listening to music.

- **To use Genius to play similar songs:** Say "Genius," "Play more like this," or "Play more songs like this." If your iPhone has no Genius playlists and you say "Genius," your iPhone will politely inform you that "Genius is not available." The same thing happens if you say, "Play more like this" or "Play more songs like this," when no song is playing.

And hey, because your iPod happens to be an iPhone, you won't look stupid talking to it!

Although we found that controlling your iPod by speaking aloud works most of the time, in noisy environments the iPhone may mishear your verbal request and start playing the wrong song or artist or try to call someone on the phone. Using the wired headset helps. And syntax counts, so remember to use the exact wording in the list.

Shopping with the iTunes app

Last but certainly not least, the iTunes app lets you use your iPhone to download, buy, or rent just about anything you can download, buy, or rent with the iTunes application on your Mac or PC, including music, audiobooks, iTunes U classes, podcasts, and videos. And, if you're fortunate enough to have an iTunes gift card or gift certificate in hand, you can redeem it directly from your iPhone.

If you want to do any of those tasks, however, you must first sign in to your iTunes Store account:

1. **On the Home screen, tap the Settings icon.**

2. **Tap Store in the list of settings.**

3. **Tap Sign In.**

4. **Type your username and password, and then tap OK.**

Or, in the unlikely event that you don't have an iTunes Store account already:

1. **On the Home screen, tap the Settings icon.**

2. **Tap Store in the list of settings.**

3. **Tap Create New Account.**

4. **Follow the on-screen instructions.**

After the iTunes Store knows who you are (and, more importantly, knows your credit card number), tap the iTunes icon on your Home screen and shop until you drop.

"Smile": Taking Pictures with Your iPhone

In This Chapter

▶ Taking pictures

▶ Focusing your shot

▶ Importing your pictures

▶ Viewing and admiring pictures

▶ Creating a slideshow

▶ Adding stunts for your photos

▶ Finding pictures by face, event, and place

amera phones may outsell dedicated digital cameras nowadays, but with relatively few exceptions, camera phones are rather mediocre picture takers. Come to think of it, most mobile phones don't show off digital images all that well, either.

Of course, most mobile phones aren't iPhones.

The device you have recently purchased (or are lusting after) is a spectacular photo viewer. And though its built-in digital camera isn't the one we'd rely on for snapping pictures during an African safari or even your kid's fast-paced soccer game, the iPhone in your steady hands can produce perfectly acceptable photos.

©Corbis Digital Stock

What's more, the picture keeps getting better and better. The iPhone 4 has not one camera, but two: a 5-megapixel autofocus camera on the rear, and a VGA camera on the front. The latter is used for FaceTime video (see Chapter 4) and for taking, dare we say, rather snappy self-portraits. The iPhone 4 also has an LED flash, the first iPhone with such a built-in nicety.

Over the next few pages, you discover how best to exploit the iPhone's camera — or in the case of iPhone 4, cameras. We then move on to the real magic — making the digital photos that reside on the iPhone come alive — whether you imported them from your computer or captured them with the iPhone's camera.

Taking Your Best Shot

As with many apps on the iPhone, you find the Camera app icon on the Home screen. Unless you moved things around, the Camera app is positioned on the upper row of icons, all the way to the right and adjacent to its next of kin, the Photos icon. We tap both icons throughout this chapter.

Might as well snap an image now:

1. **On the Home screen, tap the Camera app icon.**

   This tap turns the iPhone into the rough equivalent of a Kodak Instamatic, minus the film, of course.

2. **Keep your eyes fixed on the iPhone display.**

   The first thing you notice on the screen is something resembling a closed camera shutter. But that shutter opens in about a second, revealing a window into what the camera lens sees.

3. **Aim the camera at whatever you want to shoot, using the iPhone's brilliant 3½-inch display as your viewfinder.**

   We marvel at the display throughout this book; the Camera app gives us another reason to do so.

4. **When you're satisfied with what's in the frame, tap the icon that resembles a camera at the bottom of the screen (see Figure 8-1) to snap the picture.**

   As we show you in a moment, you'll be able to change the point of focus if necessary.

If you're using the iPhone 3GS or 4 camera, make sure the switch at the bottom-right corner of the screen is set to camera mode rather than video mode. The on-screen button is under the little picture of a camera rather than the little picture of a video camera.

Be careful. The camera icon is directly above the Home button. We've seen more than one iPhone user erroneously press the Home button instead.

Tap for preview of last picture taken

Switch from still camera to
video camera (3GS and 4 only)

Camera icon

Figure 8-1: Say "Cheese."

You'll experience momentary shutter lag, so be sure to remain still. When the shutter reopens, you see the image you shot, but just for a blink. The screen again functions as a viewfinder so that you can capture your next image.

That's it: You've snapped your first iPhone picture.

5. Repeat Steps 3 and 4 to capture additional images.

If you position the iPhone sideways while snapping an image, the picture is saved in landscape mode.

In our experience, the iPhone camera button is supersensitive. We have accidentally taken a few rotten snapshots because of it. Be careful: A gentle tap is all that's required to snap an image.

If you have trouble keeping the camera steady, try this trick. Rather than tap the camera icon at the bottom of the screen (as suggested in Step 4), keep your finger pressed against the icon and *release* it only when you're ready to snap an image.

Keeping Things in Focus (3GS and 4 Only)

If you have an iPhone 3GS or 4, you can take advantage of the Tap to Focus feature. Normally, the camera on these models focuses on a subject in the center of the display, which you're reminded of when you momentarily see a square appear in the middle of the screen, as shown in Figure 8-2. But if you tap elsewhere in the frame, perhaps on the face of your kid in the background, the iPhone accordingly shifts its focus there, adjusting the exposure and the phenomenon that photographers refer to as the *white balance*. For another moment or so, you see a new, smaller square over your child's face.

Flash
(iPhone 4 only)

Front/rear camera
(iPhone 4 only)

Focus area

Camera roll

Snap shot

Zoom slider

Camera/video switch

Figure 8-2: Squaring up for a focused photo.

From the front to the rear — and back

We figure that most of the time, you'll use the main rear camera while shoot-ing pictures (or video). But you may want to capture a shot of your own pretty face to post, say, on a social networking site such as Facebook. Not a problem. Just tap the front/rear camera button at the upper-right corner of the screen (labeled in Figure 8-2) to toggle between the front and rear cam-eras on the iPhone 4. The button doesn't appear on older iPhones, which have just a single camera.

Firing up the flash

The iPhone 4 is the only model with an LED (light-emitting diode) flash — or any kind of flash — so it's the only iPhone with a flash button (labeled in Figure 8-2). Because no flash is associated with the front-facing camera, you won't see the button when you're using that camera. When the button is avail-able, tap it to change the setting to On, Off, or Auto. We suggest using the Auto setting, which lets the iPhone decide when it's a good idea to fire up the flash.

Tasty pixels and other digital camera treats

The original iPhone and the iPhone 3G are 2-megapixel digital cameras. The iPhone 3GS increases that number to 3 megapixels, and the iPhone 4 raises the ante to 5 megapixels.

If you've been shopping for a digital camera of any type, you're aware that megapixels are marketed like chocolate chips: The more of them, the better. But that may not always be true (for cameras, not cookies). Although the number of megapixels matters, so do a bevy of other factors, including lens quality and shutter lag.

Megapixels measure a camera's *resolution,* or picture sharpness, which is particularly important to folks who want to blow up prints well beyond snapshot size. For example, you probably want at least a 4-megapixel stand-alone digital camera if you hope to print decent 8-by-10-inch or larger photos. From a camera-phone perspective, 2 megapixels is barely acceptable and 3 megapixels is fairly decent. More and more these days, you find cell phones with a higher megapixel count, including the iPhone 4. (The iPhone 4 uses the same pixel

size as the 3GS, while increasing the number of megapixels.)

Most of you will be satisfied with the pictures you take with the iPhone, as long as you keep your expectations in check and don't expect to produce large images. However, the digital camera in older iPhones lacks some features found on rival camera phones — notably, a flash. And only the 3GS and 4 can shoot video. What's more, the iPhone has no advanced photo-editing features.

Despite all that, those other camera phones can't hold a candle to the iPhone when it comes to showing off images, as the rest of this chapter proves. The high-resolution 480-by-320 screen — yep, it's measured in pixels — on the iPhone 3GS boasts an impressive screen. But to see something truly stunning, check out the display on the iPhone 4. It exploits something Apple marketers call retina display, leading to the sharpest characters you've ever see on a smartphone. The backlit display boasts 960-by-640 pixels, four times as many as the 3GS.

Using the digital zoom

Apple added a digital zoom feature to the camera as part of the iOS 4 upgrade. Tap the screen to summon the zoom slider (labeled in Figure 8-2), and drag the slider to the right to get closer to a subject or to the left to zoom back out.

You may not always love the results you get when zooming in close. The iPhone has a digital zoom, not an optical zoom, and the quality distinction is enormous. Using the digital zoom, you can get closer to your subject by zooming in up to 5x. Not to sound harsh, but a subject's imperfections — and any inadequacies on the photographer's part — may come to light.

Importing Pictures

You needn't use only the iPhone's digital camera to get pictures onto the device. You can also synchronize photos from a PC or Mac by using the Photos tab on the iTunes iPhone page, which is described in Chapter 3. (We assume that you already know how to get pictures onto your computer.)

Quickie reminder: On a Mac, you can sync photos via iPhoto software version 4.03 or later and Aperture. On a PC, you can sync with Adobe Photoshop Elements 3.0 or later. Alternatively, with both computers, you can sync with any folder containing pictures.

When the iPhone is connected to your computer, click the Photos tab on the iTunes iPhone page. Then select the appropriate check boxes to specify the pictures and photos you want to synchronize. Or, choose All Photos and Albums if you have enough storage on the iPhone to accommodate them.

Syncing pictures is a two-way process, so photos captured with the iPhone's digital camera can also end up in the photo library on your computer.

Mac users: Connecting the iPhone with photos in the camera roll usually launches iPhoto in addition to iTunes.

Where Have All My Pictures Gone?

So where exactly do your pictures hang out on the iPhone? The ones you snapped on the iPhone end up in a photo album appropriately dubbed the *camera roll.* The photos you imported are readily available too (and grouped in the same albums they were on the computer). We show you not only where they are but also how to display them and share them with others — and how to dispose of the duds that don't measure up to your lofty photographic standards.

Get ready to literally get your fingers on the pics (without having to worry about smudging them). You can get to your pictures from the Photos app or the Camera app. However, in the Camera app, you can see only the pictures and videos stored on the Camera roll; in the Photos app, you can view all the pictures and videos you've imported as well.

Let's start with the procedures for the Photos app:

1. **Tap the Photos icon on the Home screen, and then tap the Camera Roll album or any other album that appears in the list of photo albums.**

Doing so displays a thumbnail of all the photos and, if you have the iPhone 3GS or iPhone 4 models, videos in the selected album, such as the one shown in Figure 8-3. (The process of shooting videos is described in the next chapter.)

2. **Browse through the thumbnail images in the album until you find the picture or video you want to display.**

   You'll know when a thumbnail represents a video rather than a still image because the thumbnail displays a tiny movie camera icon and the video length. If the thumbnail you have in mind doesn't appear on this screen, flick your finger up or down to scroll through the pictures rapidly or use a slower dragging motion to pore through the images more deliberately. Buttons at the bottom of the screen let you view photos and videos by albums, events, faces, or places, as described later in this chapter.

3. **Tap the appropriate thumbnail.**

   The picture or video you selected fills the entire screen.

4. **Tap the screen again.**

   The picture controls appear, as shown in Figure 8-4. We discuss later what they do.

5. **To make the controls disappear, tap the screen again or just wait a few seconds and they go away on their own.**

If you instead want to start from the Camera app, do the following:

1. **Tap the Camera icon on the Home screen, and then tap the camera roll button at the bottom-left corner of the display.**

   Note that the camera roll button displays a thumbnail of your last shot taken in the Camera Roll (refer to Figure 8-2).

   The shutter closes for just an instant and the last shot you took slides up onto the screen. You see the camera controls displayed in Figure 8-3. If you don't see the camera controls (they disappear after a few seconds), tap the screen again. You can drag your finger from left to right to bring up earlier shots stored in the Camera Roll.

2. **To transform the iPhone back into a picture-taker rather than a picture-viewer, make sure that the picture controls are displayed and then tap Done in the upper-right corner.**

   Note that this option is available only if you arrived at the camera roll from the Camera app. If you started in the Photos app instead, you have to back out of the app altogether by pressing the Home button. Then tap the Camera app icon on the Home screen to call the iPhone's digital camera back into duty.

Return to Albums list

Share, copy, or delete
selected photos and video

View albums

View events

View photos and
videos by subject

View photos
and videos
by location

Slideshow

Trash picture

Next picture

Previous picture

Use image as wallpaper, e-mail it, send via
MMS, assign to a contact, or sent to MobileMe

Figure 8-3: Your pictures at a glance.

Figure 8-4: Picture controls.

Admiring Pictures

Photographs are meant to be seen, of course, not buried in the digital equivalent of a shoebox. The iPhone affords you some neat ways to manipulate, view, and share your best photos.

You may already know (from the preceding section) how to find a photo and view it full-screen and display picture controls. But you can do a lot of maneuvering of your pictures without summoning those controls. Here are some options:

- **Skip ahead or view the preceding picture:** Flick your finger left or right, or tap the left- or right-arrow control.

✔ **Landscape or portrait:** The iPhone's wizardry (or, more specifically, the device's accelerometer sensor) is at work. When you turn the iPhone sideways, the picture automatically reorients itself from portrait to landscape mode, as the images in Figure 8-5 show. Pictures shot in landscape mode fill the screen when you rotate the iPhone. Rotate the device back to portrait mode and the picture readjusts accordingly.

Figure 8-5: The same picture in portrait (left) and landscape (right) modes.

✔ **Zoom:** Double-tap to zoom in on an image and make it larger. Do so again to zoom out and make it smaller. Alternatively, take your thumb and index finger and pinch to zoom in, or unpinch the photo to zoom out.

✔ **Pan and scroll:** This cool little feature is practically guaranteed to make you the life of the party. After you zoom in on a picture, drag it around the screen with your finger. Besides impressing your friends, you can bring front and center the part of the image you most care about. That lets you zoom in on Fido's adorable face as opposed to, say, the unflattering picture of the person holding the dog in his lap.

Launching Slideshows

Those of us who store a lot of photographs on computers are familiar with running slideshows of those images. It's a breeze to replicate the experience on the iPhone:

1. **Choose your camera roll or another album from the Photo Albums list.**

   To do so, tap the Photos icon from the Home screen or tap the Camera Roll button in the Camera app.

2. **Select a picture, and then tap the photo's play button .**

   If you're in the Camera app and summon the Camera Roll, you can also start a slideshow by tapping play at the bottom of the thumbnails screen.

3. **Tap the play button again to stop the slideshow.**

   Unless you've set the slideshow to repeat, as explained in the next chapter, the slideshow ends automatically.

That's it! Enjoy the show.

Special slideshow effects

You can alter the length of time each slide is shown, change the transition effects between pictures, and display images in random order.

From the Home screen, tap Settings and then scroll down and tap Photos. Then tap any of the following to make changes:

- **Play Each Slide For:** You have five choices (2 seconds, 3 seconds, 5 seconds, 10 seconds, 20 seconds). When you're finished, tap the Photos button to return to the main Settings screen for Photos.

- **Transition:** This effect is the one you see when you move from one slide to the next. Again, you have five choices (cube, dissolve, ripple, wipe across, wipe down). Why not try them all, to see what you like? Tap the Photos button when you're finished.

- **Repeat:** If this option is turned on, the slideshow continues to loop until you stop it. If it's turned off, the slideshow for your camera roll or album plays just once. The Repeat control may be counterintuitive. If Off is showing, tap it to turn on the Repeat function. If On is showing, tap it to turn off the Repeat function.

- **Shuffle:** Turning on this feature plays slides in random order. As with the Repeat feature, tap Off to turn on shuffle or tap On to turn off random playback.

Press the Home button to leave the settings and return to the Home screen.

Adding music to your slideshow

Ed loves backing up slideshows with Sinatra, Sarah Vaughan, or Gershwin, among numerous other artists. Bob loves using Beatles songs or stately classical music.

Adding music to a slideshow couldn't be easier. Just tap iPod and begin playing a song. Then return to the Photo app to start a slideshow, as described in the beginning of the earlier section "Launching Slideshows."

Deleting pictures

We told a tiny fib by intimating that photographs are meant to be seen. We should have amended that statement by saying that *some* pictures are meant to be seen. Others, well . . . you can't get rid of them fast enough. Fortunately, the iPhone makes it a cinch to bury the evidence:

1. **From the camera roll, tap the objectionable photograph.**

2. **Tap to display the picture controls, if they're not already displayed.**

3. **Tap the trash can icon.**

4. **Tap Delete Photo (or Cancel, if you change your mind).**

   The photo gets sucked into the trash can and mercifully disappears.

More (Not So) Stupid Picture Tricks

You can take advantage of the photos on the iPhone in a few more ways. In each case, you tap the picture and make sure the picture controls are displayed. Then tap the icon at the bottom left that looks like an arrow trying to escape a rectangle (see the icon in the margin) to display the five choices shown in Figure 8-6.

Here's what each choice does:

✓ **Email Photo:** Some photos are so precious that you just have to share them with family members and friends. When you tap Email Photo, the picture is automatically embedded in the body of an outgoing e-mail message. Use the virtual keyboard to enter the e-mail addresses, subject line, and any comments you want to add — you know, something profound, like "Isn't this a great looking photo?" After tapping Send to whisk picture and accompanying message on their way, you have the option to reduce the image size (small, medium, or large) or keep the actual

Figure 8-6: Look at what else I can do!

size. Consider the tradeoffs: A smaller-sized image may get through any limits imposed by your or the recipient's Internet provider or company. But if you can get the largest image through, you will give the recipient the full picture (forgive the pun) in all its glory. (Check out Chapter 11 for more info on using e-mail.)

You can also press and hold on the screen until a Copy button appears. Tap that button, and now you can paste the image into an e-mail.

✔ **MMS:** Apple and AT&T support picture messaging through what's called MMS (Multimedia Messaging Service). Tap the MMS option, and the picture is embedded in your outgoing message; you merely need to enter the phone number of the device to which you're sending the picture.

✔ **Send to MobileMe:** If you're a member of Apple's $99-a-year MobileMe online service (formerly .Mac), you can publish a photo to an album in the MobileMe Gallery. Tap Send to MobileMe, and then tap the appropriate Gallery album to which you want to add the picture. Enter the title of the photo and an optional description in the spaces provided in the Publish Photo screen that pops up. Tap Publish. Your photo is on its way to the "cloud." You also have to select an Album Setting box in the Gallery that has a strangely worded label: Adding of Photos via E-Mail or iPhone.

✔ **Assign to Contact:** If you assign a picture to someone in your Contacts list, the picture you assign pops up whenever you receive a call from that person. Tap Assign to Contact. Your list of contacts appears on the screen. Scroll through the list to find the person who matches the picture of the moment. As with the Use as Wallpaper option (described next), you can drag and resize the picture to get it just right. Then tap Set Photo.

As Chapter 4 explains, you can also assign a photo to a contact by starting out in Contacts. As a refresher, start by tapping Phone, and then tapping Contacts. From Contacts, choose the person, tap Edit, and then tap Add Photo. At that point, you can take a new picture with the iPhone's digital camera or select an existing portrait from one of your onboard picture albums.

To change the picture you assigned to a person, tap her name in the Contacts list, tap Edit, and then tap the person's thumbnail picture, which also carries the label Edit. From there, you can take another photo with the iPhone's digital camera, select another photo from one of your albums, edit the photo you're already using (by resizing and dragging it to a new position), or delete the photo you no longer want.

✔ **Use As Wallpaper:** The default background image on the iPhone when you unlock the device is a gorgeous view of the earth. Dramatic though it may be, you probably have an even better photograph to use as the iPhone's wallpaper. A picture of your spouse, your kids, or your pet, perhaps?

When you tap the Use As Wallpaper button, you see what the present image looks like as the iPhone's background picture. And, as Figure 8-7 shows, you're given the opportunity to move the picture around and resize it, through the now familiar action of dragging or pinching against the screen with your fingers. When you're satisfied with what the wallpaper will look like, tap the Set button. Options appear that let you use the photo as wallpaper for the Lock screen, the Home screen, or both. Per usual, you also have the option to tap Cancel. (You find out more about wallpaper in Chapter 13.)

 You can also share, copy or delete in bulk. From a thumbnails view of your pictures, tap the icon at the upper-right (shown in the margin). The Share, Copy, and Delete buttons appear at the bottom of the page.

Figure 8-7: Beautifying the iPhone with wallpaper.

Tap each image in the thumbnails view that you want to share, copy, or delete so that a check mark appears. As you do, the buttons display a number associated with the number of images you've selected. Tap Share, Copy, or Delete, depending on what you want to do. If you tap Share, you'll have the option to e-mail the pictures, send them via MMS, or Send to MobileMe. If you tap Delete, you get the chance to change your mind.

Places, Faces, and Events

We've already showed you how pictures on the iPhone can be organized into albums. Apple has also added iPhone support for the nifty places, faces, and events features, which are familiar to Mac owners who use iPhoto software.

Consult Chapter 3 on syncing for a refresher on getting data to and from a computer to your iPhone and back. When the iPhone is connected to a computer, you can sync up photo events (pictures taken around, birthdays, anniversaries, and so on) or faces (all the shots taken with a particular person in them). In Figure 8-8, all the pictures have Ed's mug in them. Meanwhile, as you'll soon see, the places feature is all about where pictures were taken.

The faces feature requires that you sync to the iPhone with iPhoto or Aperture on a Mac.

We think you'll be jazzed by the places feature. All the images taken with the iPhone can be geotagged with the location where they were shot. The first few times you use the iPhone's Camera app, it asks for your permission to use your current location. Similarly, third-party apps ask whether it's okay to use your location, perhaps so a friend hanging out in the same area can find you on a social networking site.

To access places, tap Places from the thumbnails view (refer to Figure 8-3). You could instead tap Events to view pictures by occasion or Faces to view all the pictures containing a particular person.

If you tap Places, a map with red pins similar to the one shown in Figure 8-9 will appear. Tap a pinhead to see how many pix were shot in that area. You can pinch or unpinch the map to zoom in or out and find pictures by town or neighborhood. We think Places is really cool and gives you a nice sense of where you've been and who you've been there with.

Before leaving this photography section, we want to steer you to the App Store, which we explore in greater depth in Chapter 14. As of this writing, hundreds of photography-related apps, many free, are available. These come from a variety of sources and range from Omer Shoor's Photogene (a $2.99 suite of photo-editing tools) to Color Splash from Pocket Pixels Inc., a $1.99 program that lets you convert photos to black-and-white while keeping certain details in color.

You have just passed Photography 101 on the iPhone. We trust that the coursework was, forgive the pun, a snap.

Figure 8-8: Facing Ed in faces.

Figure 8-9: Finding pictures by location.

9

You Oughta Be in Pictures: Video on Your iPhone

*P*icture this scene: The smell of popcorn permeates the room as you and your family congregate to watch the latest Hollywood blockbuster. A motion picture soundtrack swells up. The images on the screen are stunning. And all eyes are fixed on the iPhone.

Okay, here's the reality check. The iPhone is not going to replace a wall-sized high-definition television as the centerpiece of your home theater. But we want to emphasize that with its glorious widescreen 3½-inch display — the best we've seen on a smartphone — watching movies and other videos on the iPhone can be a cinematic delight.

As you discover later in this chapter, if you own the iPhone 3GS or 4, you can even shoot your own blockbuster footage. Let's get on with the show!

©Corbis Digital Stock

Finding Stuff to Watch

The video you'll watch on the iPhone generally falls into one of four categories:

- **Movies, TV shows, and music videos that you've downloaded directly to your iPhone or that reside in iTunes software on your PC or Mac that you synchronize with your iPhone.** (For more on synchronization, refer to Chapter 3.) You can watch these by tapping the iPod icon at the bottom of the Home screen and then tapping Videos.

  Apple's own iTunes Store features dedicated sections for purchasing episodes of TV shows (from *Curb Your Enthusiasm* to *Curious George*) and movies (such as *Avatar* or *Invictus*). The typical price as of this writing is $1.99 to $2.99 per episode for TV shows. You can also buy complete seasons of certain series; *Dexter, Season 4,* to take one example, costs $35.88. Movies generally fetch between $9.99 and $14.99, at least for features, though you'll find bargains below these, um, ticket prices.

  You can also rent some movies, typically for $2.99 or $3.99, but again sometimes for less. You'll have 30 days to begin watching a rented flick, and 24 hours to finish once you've started. Such films appear in their own Rented Movies section in the video list, which you get to by tapping iTunes and then tapping Videos. The number of days before your rental expires is displayed.

- **The boatload of video podcasts, just about all of them free, featured in the iTunes Store.** Podcasts started out as another form of Internet radio, although instead of listening to live streams, you downloaded files onto your computer or iPod to take in at your leisure. There are still lots of audio podcasts, but the focus here is on video. You can watch free episodes that cover *Sesame Street* videos, sports, investing, political shows, and much more. And you can take a seminar at Harvard, Stanford, and other prestigious institutions. Indeed, iTunes U boasts more than 250,000 free lectures from around the world, many of them videos. Better still, there's no homework and no grades.

- **Homegrown videos from the popular YouTube Internet site.** Apple obviously thinks highly of YouTube because it devoted a dedicated Home screen icon to the site. More on YouTube's special place in the iPhone later in this chapter.

- **The movies you've created in iMovie software or other software on the Mac or, for that matter, other programs on the PC.** Plus all the other videos you may have downloaded from the Internet.

You may have to prepare these videos so that they'll play on your iPhone. To do so, highlight the video in question after it resides in your iTunes library. Go to the Advanced menu in iTunes on your computer, and click Create iPod or iPhone Version.

For more on compatibility, check out the "Are we compatible?" sidebar in this chapter (but read it at your own risk).

Are we compatible?

Sidebars in this book are considered optional reading, but we secretly hope you digest every word because you may discover something, or be entertained, or both. But you can safely skip the material contained herein — no matter how much you want to curry favor with your teachers, um, authors.

Still, we present this list of video formats supported by the iPhone as a courtesy to those with geek aspirations (you know who you are). And just to point out how absurd the world of tech can sound sometimes — even from a consumer-friendly company such as Apple — we are quoting this passage from Apple's Web site verbatim.

"Video formats supported: H.264 video up to 720p, 30 frames per second, Main Profile level 3.1 with AAC-LC audio up to 160 Kbps, 48kHz, stereo audio in .m4v, .mp4, and .mov file formats; MPEG-4 video, up to 2.5 Mbps, 640 by 480 pixels, 30 frames per second, Simple Profile with AAC-LC audio up to 160 Kbps per channel, 48kHz, stereo audio in .m4v, .mp4, and .mov file

formats; Motion JPEG (M-JPEG) up to 35 Mbps, 1280 by 720 pixels, 30 frames per second, audio in ulaw, PCM stereo audio in .avi file format."

Got all that? Here's the takeaway message: The iPhone works with a whole bunch of video, but not everything you'll want to watch will make it through. And you may not know if the video will play until you try. Indeed, several Internet video standards — most notably Adobe Flash, which Apple CEO Steve Jobs has publicly denigrated — were not supported when this book was in production. And we should probably point out that some video that will play on an iPod Classic or iPod Nano might not play in the iPhone for technical reasons we won't bore you with right now. (This situation may have changed by the time you read this.)

Then again, with the appropriate utility software, you may be able to convert some non-working video to an iPhone-friendly format. If something doesn't play now, it may well in the future — because Apple has the capability to upgrade the iPhone through software.

Playing Video

Now that you know what you want to watch, here's how to watch it:

1. **On the Home screen, tap the iPod icon and then tap the Videos icon.**

   Your list of videos pops up. Videos are segregated by category — Movies, TV Shows, Music Videos, as shown in Figure 9-1 — although other categories such as Rented Movies and Podcasts may also appear. Listings are accompanied by thumbnail images and the length of the video.

2. **Flick your finger to scroll through the list, and then tap the video you want to play.**

   You may see a spinning circle for just a moment and then the video will begin. We've found that on the truly snappy iPhone 3GS and 4, the video starts playing without such a delay.

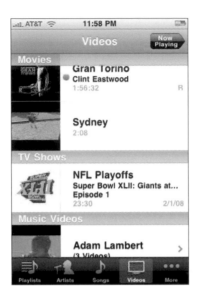

Figure 9-1: Choosing the video to watch.

3. **Turn the device to its side because the iPhone plays video only in landscape, or widescreen, mode.**

   For movies, this is a great thing. You can watch flicks as the filmmaker intended, in a cinematic *aspect ratio*.

4. **Now that the video is playing, tap the screen to display the controls shown in Figure 9-2.**

5. **Tap the controls that follow as needed:**

   - To play or pause the video, tap the play/pause button.

   - Drag the volume slider to the right to raise the volume and to the left to lower it. Alternatively, use the physical volume buttons to control the audio levels. If the video is oriented properly, the buttons will be on the bottom left of the iPhone.

   - Tap the restart/rewind button to restart the video or tap and hold the same button to rewind.

   - Tap and hold the fast-forward button to advance the video. Or skip ahead by dragging the playhead along the scrubber bar.

   - Tap the scale button to toggle between filling the entire screen with video or fitting the video to the screen. Alternatively, you can double-tap the video to go back and forth between fitting and filling the screen.

Fitting the video to the screen displays the film in its theatrical aspect ratio. But you may see black bars above or below the video (or to its sides), which some people don't like. *Filling* the entire screen with the video may crop or trim the sides or top of the picture, so you aren't seeing the complete scene that the director shot.

6. **Tap the screen again to make the controls go away (or just wait for them to go away on their own).**

7. **Tap Done when you've finished watching. (You have to summon the controls back if they're not already present.)**

You return to the iPhone's video menu screen.

To delete a video manually, swipe left or right over the video listing. Then tap the small red Delete button that materializes. To confirm your intention, tap the larger Delete button that appears.

Sometimes you want to hear a song from a music video but don't want to watch it. Instead of tapping the Videos icon to grab that selection, choose the ditty by tapping the Songs or Artists icon instead.

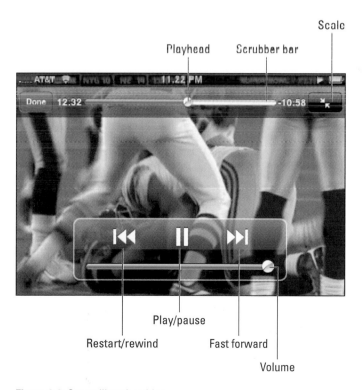

Figure 9-2: Controlling the video.

Shooting Video

The 3GS was the first iPhone to let you shoot video; the iPhone 4 joined the video party. If you bought one of these phones, read this section to get the most out of the video camera built into your handset. If you don't have one, we hope you stick with us anyway. You might own a 3GS or 4 someday — and even if you don't, we kind of like having you around.

Here's how to shoot video on a 3GS and 4 phone. Note that you can capture video in portrait or landscape mode:

1. **Tap the Camera icon on the Home screen.**

2. **Drag the little onscreen button at the bottom-right corner of the display from the camera position to the video camera position, as shown in Figure 9-3.**

3. **Tap the red record button at the bottom center to begin shooting a scene.**

   The button blinks and you see a counter timing the length of your video.

4. **When you're finished, tap the red button again to stop recording.**

   Your video is automatically saved to the camera roll, alongside any other saved videos and still pictures.

You can tap the LED flash button to shine a light while you record video. And, as with taking digital stills, you can switch from the front to the rear camera before starting to shoot video. But you can't switch from the front to back camera while you are capturing video.

The 3GS shoots VGA video at up to 30 frames-per-second. That's tech jargon for *full-motion video,* which means your video won't be herky-jerky or look like it was shot in Jell-O. It isn't high definition, but we think you'll be quite satisfied. Meanwhile, the iPhone 4 does shoot in high definition up to the 720p techie standard. Auteurs Bob and Ed have shot videos in HD that look really sweet.

Editing what you shot

We assume that you captured some really great stuff — as well as some footage that belongs on the cutting room floor. That's not a problem because you can perform simple edits right on your iPhone 3GS and iPhone 4. Just do the following:

1. **Tap a video recording to display the on-screen controls shown in Figure 9-4.**

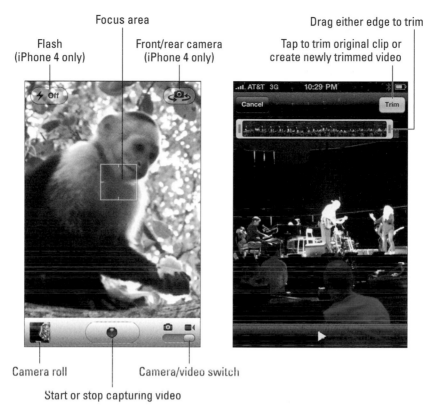

Focus area

Flash
(iPhone 4 only)

Front/rear camera
(iPhone 4 only)

Drag either edge to trim

Tap to trim original clip or
create newly trimmed video

Camera roll

Camera/video switch

Start or stop capturing video

Figure 9-3: Lights, camera, action!

Figure 9-4: Trimming video.

2. **Drag the start and end points along the timeline to select only the video you want to keep.**

   Hold your finger over the section to expand the timeline to make it easier to apply your edits. You can tap the play button to preview the edit.

3. **Tap Trim.**

4. **Decide what to do with your trimmed clip.**

   You can tap Trim Original to permanently remove scenes from the original clip. Or tap Save as New Clip to create a newly trimmed video clip; the original video is unaffected and the new clip is stored in the Camera Roll. Or tap Cancel to start over.

If you want to do more ambitious editing directly on the iPhone 4, check out iMovie for iPhone, a $4.99 app that resembles a lite version of iMovie for Mac computers.

After loading the video clips you've shot on the phone, iMovie lets you go Hollywood, within limits. Apple supplies five custom themes — Modern, Bright, Travel, Playful, and News — for adding titles and transitions to your budding masterpiece. Custom soundtracks are also available, though you can select a tune from your own music library. When you are finished editing, you can export the movie in one of three file sizes and share it via e-mail, MMS, MobileMe, or on YouTube, as discussed in the following sections.

Sharing video

Unlike other video on your iPhone, you can play back what you've just shot in portrait or landscape mode. And if the video is any good (and why wouldn't it be), you're likely going to want to share it with others. To do so, display the playback controls by tapping the screen, and then tap the icon all the way to left of the screen (the icon is shown in the margin). You can e-mail the video, include it in an MMS, send it to Apple's MobileMe service, or send it to YouTube. And speaking of YouTube, read on.

Hey You, It's YouTube

YouTube has come to define video sharing on the Internet. The wildly popular site, now owned by Google, has become so powerful that American presidential hopefuls and even politicians in other countries campaign and hold debates there. YouTube has staked a humongous claim on mainstream culture because YouTube is, well, about you and us and our pets and so on. It is the cyberdestination, as YouTube boldly proclaims, to "Broadcast Yourself."

Apple has afforded YouTube its own cherished icon on the Home screen. Many millions of videos are available on the iPhone, nearly the complete YouTube catalog.

The back catalog of YouTube videos was converted to the H.264 video-compression standard that the iPhone, iPad, and iPod Touch (and another Apple product called Apple TV) can recognize.

As with other videos, you can tap the screen when a YouTube video is playing to display video controls. Many of these controls are identical to those in Figure 9-2. But as Figure 9-5 shows, YouTube displays special controls of its own, notably for adding favorites and sending e-mail links of the video you're watching.

Favorites   E-mail

Figure 9-5: YouTube video controls.

Hunting for YouTube gems

So where exactly do YouTubers find the videos that will offer them a blissful respite from their day? By tapping any of the buttons parked at the bottom of the YouTube screen. In Figure 9-6, we show you the screen you see when you tap the first of the following buttons:

- **Featured:** Videos recommended by YouTube's own staffers.

- **Most Viewed:** What the YouTube community is watching. After tapping Most Viewed, tap All to see the most watched YouTube videos of all time. Tap Today or This Week to check out the videos most currently in vogue.

- **Search:** Tap the Search icon, and then tap the blank YouTube search field at the top of the screen. Up pops one of the iPhone's virtual keyboards. Type a search phrase and then tap the Search button to generate results. (In Figure 9-7, we typed *Steve Jobs.*)

- **Favorites:** After stumbling on a video you like, add it to your Favorites by tapping the Favorites control. You can log into your YouTube account with your username and password to save and sync these favorites.

- **More:** Tapping More leads to more buttons or icons. As in those that follow. . . .

  - **Most Recent:** Newly submitted videos.

  - **Top Rated:** The people's choice. YouTube's audience chooses the best.

- **History:** Videos you recently viewed.
- **My Videos:** The place for videos you star in.
- **Subscriptions:** YouTube channels you subscribe to.
- **Playlists:** Videos categorized into playlists.

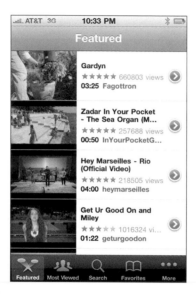

Figure 9-6: Featured presentations on YouTube.

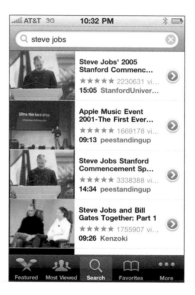

Figure 9-7: Finding Steve Jobs on YouTube.

Only four YouTube icons (besides the More button) appear at the bottom of the screen at any one time. If you'd prefer a different icon than one of the four shown — Top Rated instead of Favorites, say — you can make it one of your Fab Four icons.

To change the icons shown on that first YouTube screen, tap More and then tap Edit. Then simply drag your preferred icon (Top Rated in this example) over the one you want to relegate to the YouTube bench (Favorites in this case). You can also rearrange the order of the icons by dragging them left or right.

While the movie you've selected is downloading — and how fast it arrives depends on your network coverage from AT&T or Wi-Fi, as discussed in greater detail in Chapter 10 — you see a black-and-gray screen with video controls and the YouTube logo. This screen is shown in Figure 9-8. The controls disappear when the movie starts playing.

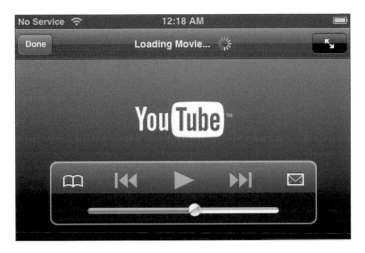

Figure 9-8: Waiting to be entertained.

Sharing YouTube videos

We were as enthralled as that harshest of critics, Simon Cowell, was by Paul Potts, the British mobile-phone worker turned opera singer. His star turn on the *American Idol*-like *Britain's Got Talent* has been immortalized on YouTube and watched by millions. Ditto for Susan Boyle. What is it about that show?

You can share a video as you are watching it by tapping the E-mail button (refer to Figure 9-5). When you do so, one of the iPhone's virtual keyboards pops up. iPhone has already filled in the e-mail Subject line with the name of the video. And the body of the message is populated with a link to the video on YouTube. All you need to do is fill in the To field with the e-mail address of the person you are sending the link to, along with any additional comments.

Alternatively, from the list of videos, tap the blue button with the right-pointing arrow to see all sorts of details on a particular video. You'll see a description of the video, the number of people who viewed it, the date it was added, and other information. From there, tap the Share button to bring up the e-mail program just described. You can also add the video to your favorites or to a playlist.

Restricting YouTube (and other) usage

If you've given an iPhone to your kid or someone who works for you, you may not want that person spending time watching YouTube videos. You want him or her to do something more productive, like homework or the quarterly budget.

That's where parental (or might we say "Mean Boss") restrictions come in. Please note that the use of this iron-fist tool can make you really unpopular.

Tap Settings, General, Restrictions. Then tap Enable Restrictions. You'll be asked to establish or enter a previously established passcode. Twice. Having done so, tap YouTube so that the Off button rather than the On button is displayed. You can also set restrictions based on movie ratings (PG or whatever).

If you made YouTube a no-no, the YouTube icon is missing in action when you return to the Home screen. Same goes for any other restricted activities. To restore YouTube or other privileges, go back into Restrictions and tap Disable Restrictions. You'll have to reenter your passcode.

You can apply restrictions also to iTunes, Safari, the App Store, Camera, FaceTime, and location settings, as you see when we delve into Settings further (see Chapter 13).

With that, let's roll the closing credits to this chapter.

Part IV
The Internet
iPhone

*T*he commercials for the iPhone used to say that it provides you with the real Internet — and, for the most part, it does. This part looks at the Internet components of your phone, starting with a chapter covering the best Web browser ever to grace a handheld device, Safari. We reveal how to take advantage of links and bookmarks and how to open multiple Web pages at the same time. We show you how to run a Web search on an iPhone. And we spend time discussing EDGE, 3G, and Wi-Fi — the wireless networks that are compatible with the device.

Then we visit the Mail program and see how easy it is to set up e-mail accounts and send and receive real honest-to-goodness e-mail messages and attachments.

Finally, we examine four superb Web-enabled applications. In Maps and in Compass, you discover your direction, determine the businesses and restaurants you'd like to visit, get driving directions and the traffic en route, and take advantage of the iPhone's capability to find you. In Weather, you get the forecast for the city you live in and those you plan on visiting. And in Stocks, you get the lowdown on how well the equities in your portfolio are performing.

Going On a Mobile Safari

"*T*he Internet in your pocket."

That's what Apple promised the iPhone would bring to the public when the product was announced in January 2007. Steve Jobs & Co. have come tantalizingly close to delivering on that pledge.

For years, the cell phone industry offered a watered-down mobile version of the Internet, but their approaches typically fell far short of what people had come to experience while sitting in front of a computer.

Apple, however, has managed for the most part to replicate the real-deal Internet with the iPhone. Web pages look like Web pages on a Windows PC or Mac, right down to swanky graphics and pictures — and at least some video.

In this chapter, you find out how to navigate through cyberspace on your iPhone.

©PhotoDisc/Getty Images

Living on the EDGE

You can't typically make or receive phone calls on a wireless phone without tapping into a cellular network. And, you can't prowl the virtual corridors of cyberspace (or send e-mail) on a mobile phone without accessing a wireless *data* network. In the United States, the iPhone works with Wi-Fi, AT&T EDGE, and AT&T 3G. (It works also with another wireless technology, *Bluetooth,* but that serves a different purpose and is addressed in Chapter 13.)

The iPhone automatically hops onto the fastest available network, which is almost always *Wi-Fi,* the friendly moniker applied to the far geekier 802.11 designation. And "eight-oh-two-dot-eleven" (as it's pronounced) is followed by a letter — typically, *b, g,* or *n.* So you see it written as 802.11b, 802.11g, and so on. The letters relate to technical standards that have to do with the speed and range you can expect from the Wi-Fi configuration. But we don't want you to lose sleep over this issue if you haven't boned up on this geeky alphabet.

For the record, because the iPhone adheres to the 802.11b, 802.11g, and 802.11n standards, you're good to go pretty much anywhere you can find Wi-Fi. These days, Internet hotspots are in lots of places: airports, colleges, coffeehouses, libraries, public parks, and elsewhere. If you have to present a password to take advantage of a hotspot because it costs money or you have to authenticate your credentials, you can enter the password by using the iPhone's virtual keyboard.

Still, Wi-Fi isn't ubiquitous yet, which leads us and, at times you, right back to EDGE or 3G. EDGE is shorthand for Enhanced Datarate for GSM Evolution (good to know only if you're on a million-dollar game show) and is based on the global GSM phone standard. And 3G stands for third generation; 3G Web sites typically download two times faster than EDGE, in our experience, and sometimes even faster. But, again, Wi-Fi downloads are even zippier.

The bottom line is this: Depending on where you live, work, or travel, you may feel like you're teetering on the EDGE in terms of acceptable Internet coverage, especially if Wi-Fi or true 3G is beyond your reach. We've used the iPhone in areas where Web pages load extremely slowly, not-so-vaguely reminiscent of dial-up telephone modems for your computer.

But the picture is indeed brightening. Wi-Fi is in more places than ever before, and the same can be said for 3G cellular. The iPhone 3GS and iPhone 4 not only load Web pages a lot faster but also manage to do so with longer-lasting batteries.

Surfin' Dude

A version of the Apple Safari Web browser is a major reason that the Net on the iPhone is very much like the Net you've come to expect on a computer. Safari for the Mac (and for Windows) is one of the best Web browsers in the computer business. In our view, Safari has no rival as a cell phone browser.

Exploring the browser

We start our cyberexpedition with a quick tour of the Safari browser. Take a gander at Figure 10-1: Not all browser controls found on a PC or Mac are present. Still, Safari on the iPhone has a familiar look and feel. We describe these controls and others throughout this chapter.

Search Google, Yahoo!, or Bing

Reload Web page

Address field

Navigation bar

Previous Web page

Next Web page

Add Bookmark/Home screen/Mail Link page

Bookmarks

Pages

Figure 10-1: The iPhone's Safari browser.

Before plunging in, we recommend a little detour. Read the "Living on the EDGE" sidebar to find out more about the wireless networks that let you surf the Web on the iPhone in the first place.

Blasting off into cyberspace

We told you how great Web pages look on the iPhone, so we bet you're eager to get going. We won't hold you back much longer.

When you tap the address field (as you will in a moment), the virtual keyboard appears. You may notice one thing about the keyboard right off the bat: Because so many Web addresses end with the suffix .com (pronounced "dot com"), the virtual keyboard has a dedicated .com key. For other common Web suffixes — .edu, .net, .us, and .org — press and hold the .com key and choose the relevant suffix.

Of equal importance, both the period (.) and the slash (/) are on the virtual keyboard because you frequently use them when you enter Web addresses.

The moment you tap a single letter, you see a list of Web addresses that match those letters. For example, if you tap the letter *s* (as we did in the example in Figure 10-2, left), you see Web listings for Si.com, Scholastic.com, and CNET Shopper, among others. Tapping *U* or *H* instead may display listings for *USA TODAY* or the *Houston Chronicle* (shameless plugs for the newspapers where Ed and Bob are columnists). Scroll to see more suggestions and the virtual keyboard slides off the screen, as shown in Figure 10-2, right.

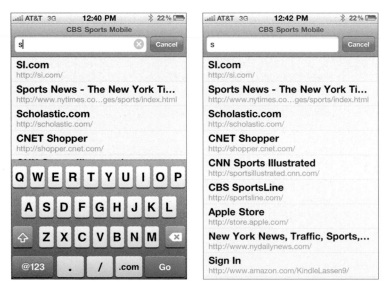

Figure 10-2: Web pages that match your search letter.

The iPhone has two ways to determine Web sites to suggest when you tap certain letters. One method is the Web sites you already bookmarked from the Safari or Internet Explorer browser on your computer (and synchronized, as described in Chapter 3). More on bookmarks later in this chapter.

The second method iPhone uses when suggesting Web sites when you tap a particular letter is to suggest sites from the History list — those cyberdestinations where you recently hung your hat. Because history repeats itself, we also tackle that topic later in this chapter.

You might as well open your first Web page now. It's a full HTML page, to borrow from techie lingo. Do the following:

1. **Tap the Safari icon at the bottom of the Home screen.**

   This icon is another member of the Fantastic Four (along with Phone, Mail, and iPod).

2. **Tap the address field (refer to Figure 10-1).**

   If you can't see the address field, tap the status bar or scroll to the top of the screen.

3. **Begin typing the Web address on the virtual keyboard that slides up from the bottom of the screen.**

   The Web address is also called the *URL* (Uniform Resource Locator, for trivia buffs).

4. **Do one of the following:**

   a. **To accept one of the bookmarked (or other) sites that show up on the list, merely tap the name.**

      Safari automatically fills in the URL in the address field and takes you where you want to go.

   b. **Keep tapping the proper keyboard characters until you enter the complete Web address for the site you have in mind, and then tap Go in the lower-right corner of the keyboard.**

      It's not necessary to type *www* at the beginning of a URL. So, if you want to visit www.theonion.com (for example), typing theonion.com or even just onion.com is sufficient to transport you to the humor site.

To erase a URL you've erroneously typed, tap the address field and then tap the circled X to the right of the field.

Even though Safari on the iPhone can render Web pages the way they're meant to be displayed on a computer, every so often you may run into a site that serves up the light, or mobile, version of the Web site, sometimes known as a WAP site. Graphics may be stripped down on these sites. Alas, the producers of these sites may be unwittingly discriminating against you for dropping in on them by using a cell phone. Never mind that the cell phone in this case is an iPhone. You have our permission to berate these site producers with letters, e-mails, and phone calls until they get with the program.

I Can See Clearly Now

If you know how to open a Web page (if you don't, read the preceding section, "Blasting off into cyberspace"), we can show you how radically simple it is to zoom in on the pages so that you can read what you want to read and see what you want to see, without enlisting a magnifying glass.

Try these neat tricks:

✏ **Double-tap the screen so that the portion of the text you want to read fills up the entire screen:** It takes just a second before the screen comes into focus. By way of example, check out Figure 10-3. It shows two views of the same *Sports Illustrated* Web page. In the first view, you see what the page looks like when you first open it. In the second one, you see how the picture takes over much more of the screen after you double-tap it. To return to the first view, double-tap the screen again.

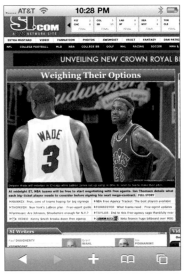

Figure 10-3: Doing a double-tap dance zooms in and out.

✔ **Pinch the page:** Sliding your thumb and index finger together and then spreading them apart (or as we like to say, *unpinching*) also zooms in and out of a page. Again, wait just a moment for the screen to come into focus.

✔ **Press down on a page and drag it in all directions, or flick through a page from top to bottom:** You're panning and scrolling, baby.

✔ **Rotate the iPhone to its side:** Watch what happens to the White House Web site, shown in Figure 10-4. It reorients from portrait to a widescreen view. The keyboard is also wider, making it a little easier to enter a new URL.

Figure 10-4: Going wide.

Opening multiple Web pages at a time

When we surf the Web on a desktop PC or laptop, we rarely go to a single Web page and call it a day. In fact, we often have multiple Web pages open at the same time. Sometimes, several pages are open because we choose to hop around the Web without closing the pages we visit. Sometimes, a link (see the next section) automatically opens a new page without shuttering the old one. (If these additional pages are advertisements, they aren't always welcome.)

Safari on the iPhone lets you open multiple pages simultaneously. Tap the Pages icon (refer to Figure 10-1), on the right side of the navigation bar at the bottom of the screen, and then tap New Page on the screen that pops up next. Tap the address field and then type a URL for your new page.

The number inside the Pages icon lets you know how many pages are open. To see the other open pages, flick your finger to the left or right, as shown in Figure 10-5, left. Tap a page to have it take over the full screen, as shown in Figure 10-5, right.

To close one of your open Web pages, tap the white X in the red circle, which appears in the upper-left corner of each open page.

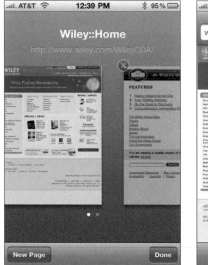 

Figure 10-5: After tapping a Web page, it appears full-screen.

Looking at lovable links

Surfing the Web would be a real drag if you had to enter a URL every time you want to navigate from one page to another. That's why bookmarks are so useful. And, it's why handy links are welcome too. Because Safari functions on the iPhone the same way browsers work on your PC or Mac, links on the iPhone behave much the same way, too.

Text links that transport you from one site to another are underlined or appear in a different color from other text on the page. Merely tap the link to go directly to that site. But tapping on some other links leads to different outcomes:

✓ **Open a map:** Tapping on a map launches the Google Maps app that is, um, addressed in Chapter 12.

✔ **Prepare an e-mail:** Tap an e-mail address and the iPhone opens the Mail program (see the next chapter) and prepopulates the To field with that address. The virtual keyboard is also summoned so that you can add other e-mail addresses and compose a Subject line and message. This shortcut doesn't work in all instances in which an e-mail appears on the Web.

✔ **Make a phone call:** Tap a phone number embedded in a Web page and the iPhone offers to dial it for you. Just tap Call to make it happen, or tap Cancel to forget the whole thing.

To see the URL for a link, press your finger against the link and keep it there. Use this method also to determine whether a picture has a link. The window that slides up from the bottom of the screen to show you the URL gives you other options. You can tap to open the page (replacing the current one). You can tap to open a link in a new page. Or you can tap to copy the URL to, say, pasting it in a note or in an outgoing e-mail.

Not every Web link cooperates with the iPhone. As of this writing, the iPhone didn't support some common Web standards — most notably sites that rely on Adobe Flash video. Given the public stance against Flash by Apple CEO Steve Jobs, this void seems unlikely to be addressed any time soon. If Apple does change its tune, it could magically distribute a software upgrade to remedy the situation. Apple is throwing its weight behind another emerging video standard called HTML5. In the meantime, if you see an incompatible link, nothing may happen — or a message may appear that you need to install a plug-in.

Book (mark) 'em, Dano

You already know how useful bookmarks are and how you can synchronize bookmarks from the browsers on your computer. It's equally simple to bookmark a Web page directly on the iPhone:

1. **Make sure that the page you want to bookmark is open, and tap the + symbol in the bottom-middle area of the screen.**

   As you see in Figure 10-6, you have the opportunity to tap Add Bookmark, Add to Home Screen, or Mail Link to This Page. Figure 10-7 shows the screen that appears when you tap Add Bookmark. The screen arrives with a default name and folder location.

2. **Decide whether to go with the default bookmark name and location:**

   • To accept the default bookmark name and default bookmark folder, tap Save, in the upper-right corner.

   • To change the default bookmark name, tap the X in the circle next to the name, and enter the new title (using the virtual keyboard). Tap Save unless you also want to change the location where the bookmark is saved.

- • To change the location, tap the > symbol in the Bookmarks field, tap the folder where you want the bookmark kept, and tap the Add Bookmark button in the upper-left corner of the screen. Then tap Save.

Figure 10-6: On your way to a bookmark or other options.

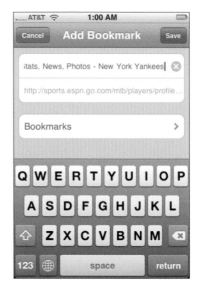

Figure 10-7: Turning into a bookie.

To open a bookmarked page after you set it up, tap the Bookmarks icon at the bottom of the screen (refer to Figure 10-1) and then tap the appropriate bookmark.

If the bookmark you have in mind is buried inside a folder, tap the folder name first, and then tap the bookmark you want.

If you tapped Add to Home Screen rather than the Add Bookmark option in Step 1 of the preceding set of steps, your iPhone adds an icon to your Home screen to let you quickly access the site. If you tapped Mail Link to This Page instead, the Mail program opens, with a link for the page in the message and the name of the site in the Subject line.

Altering bookmarks

If a bookmarked site is no longer meaningful, you can change it or get rid of it:

- ✔ To remove a bookmark (or folder), tap the bookmarks icon and then tap Edit. Tap the red circle next to the bookmark you want to toss off the list, and then tap Delete.

↙ To change a bookmark name or location, tap Edit and then tap the book-mark. The Edit Bookmark screen appears, showing the name, URL, and location of the bookmark already filled in. Tap the fields you want to change. In the Name field, tap the X in the gray circle and then use the keyboard to enter a new title. In the Location field, tap the > symbol and scroll up or down the list until you find a new home for your bookmark.

↙ To create a new folder for your bookmarks, tap Edit and then tap the New Folder button. Enter the name of the new folder and choose where to put it.

↙ To move a bookmark up or down on a list, tap Edit and then drag the three bars to the right of the bookmark's name.

Letting History repeat itself

Sometimes, you want to revisit a site that you failed to bookmark, but you can't remember the darn destination or what led you there in the first place. Good thing you can study the history books.

Safari records the pages you visit and keeps the logs on hand for several days. Tap the bookmarks icon, tap History, and then tap the day you think you hung out at the site. When you find the listing, tap it. You're about to make your triumphant return.

To clear your history so that nobody else can trace your steps — and just what is it you're hiding? — tap Clear at the bottom of the History list. Alternatively, tap Settings on the Home page, tap Safari, and then tap Clear History. In both instances, per usual, you have a chance to back out without wiping the slate clean.

Launching a mobile search mission

Most of us spend a lot of time using search engines on the Internet. And, the search engines we summon most often are Google, Yahoo!, and Microsoft Bing. So it goes on the iPhone.

Although you can certainly use the virtual keyboard to type *google.com, yahoo.com,* or *bing.com* in the Safari address field, Apple doesn't require that tedious effort. Instead, you tap into Google, Yahoo!, or Bing by using the dedi-cated search box shown in Figure 10-8. The default search engine of choice on the iPhone is Google. Yahoo! or Bing must come off the bench.

To conduct a Web search on the iPhone, tap the search field (labeled in Figure 10-1). The field expands and temporarily replaces the address bar at the top of the screen, and the virtual keyboard slides up from the bottom. Enter your search term or phrase, and then tap the Google button in the lower-right corner of the keyboard to generate pages of results. (Note that the button will read Search instead of Google if you've selected Yahoo! or

Bing as your default search engine, as described next.) New with iOS 4 are search suggestions. Start tapping out some letters and you'll start to see results. In Figure 10-8, for example, typing the letters *le* yields such suggestions as Lebron James and Lexus. Tap any search results that look promising or keep tapping out letters.

To switch the search box from Google to Yahoo! to Bing or back, tap Settings on the Home page, scroll down and tap Safari, tap Search Engine, and then tap to choose one search behemoth over the other.

As we point out in Chapter 2, you can search the Web also through Spotlight. Merely enter your search term in the Spotlight search field and then tap Search Web. Doing so will initiate a Google search, even if you've chosen Yahoo! or Bing as your search engine.

Saving Web pictures

You can capture most pictures you come across on a Web site — but be mindful of any potential copyright violations, depending on what you plan to do with the image. To copy an image from a Web site, press your finger against the image and tap the Save Image button that slides up, as shown in Figure 10-9. Saved images end up in your camera roll, from which they can be synced back to a computer. If you tap Copy instead, you can paste the image into an e-mail or as a link in a program such as Notes.

Figure 10-8: Running a Google search on the iPhone.

Figure 10-9: Hold your finger against a picture in Safari to save it to the iPhone.

Smart Safari Settings

Along with the riches galore found on the Internet are places in cyberspace where you're hassled. You might want to take pains to protect your privacy and maintain your security.

Return with us now to Settings, by tapping the Settings icon on the Home page. Now tap Safari.

You may have already discovered how to change the default search engine and clear the record of the sites you visited through Settings. Now see what else you can do:

- **Fill out forms with AutoFill:** When AutoFill is turned on, Safari can automatically fill out Web forms by using your personal contact information, usernames, and passwords, or information from other contacts in your address book.

- **Clear cookies:** We're not talking about crumbs you may have accidentally dropped on the iPhone. *Cookies* are tiny bits of information that a Web site places on the iPhone when you visit so that the site recognizes you when you return. You need not assume the worst: Most cookies are benign.

  If this concept wigs you out, you can take action: Tap Clear Cookies at the bottom of the screen and then tap it again (rather than tap Cancel). Separately, tap Accept Cookies and then tap Never. Theoretically, you will never again receive cookies on the iPhone. A good middle ground is to accept cookies only from the sites you visit. To do so, tap From Visited. You can also tap Always to accept cookies from all sites. Tap Safari to return to the main Safari settings page.

  If you don't set the iPhone to accept cookies, certain Web pages don't load properly, or sites such as Amazon or organizations you belong to will no longer recognize you when you appear at their doors.

- **Clear the cache:** The cache stores content from some Web pages so that they load faster the next time you stop by. Tap Clear Cache and then tap Clear Cache again on the next screen to (you guessed it) clear the cache.

- **Turn JavaScript on or off:** This setting is on when the blue On button is showing and off when the white Off button is showing. Programmers use JavaScript to add various kinds of functionality to Web pages, such as displaying the date and time or changing images when you access them. In the past, some security risks have also been associated with JavaScript, though none we know of that affect mobile Safari.

- **Fraud Warning:** By turning this setting on, you'll be warned when you inadvertently visit a fraudulent Web site.

- **Block pop-ups:** Pop-ups are those Web pages that show up whether you want them to or not. Often, they're annoying advertisements. But at some sites, you welcome the appearance of pop-ups, so remember to turn off blocking under such circumstances.

- **Databases:** Web developers can create apps that work without access to the Internet (thanks to what's called HTML5 offline support). So along with the app, developers can choose to store an app's data on the system so you always have the information you need. Sometimes developers store data through a cookie (or super cookie) and sometimes through a database. This is the long way of saying that the database storage preference customizes how much space a Web app can have on your machine before it asks you for permission for more space. Our best recommendation for most folks is to leave the default setting as is and not give this another moment's thought.

- **Use Developer:** Unless you happen to be a developer, don't pay much attention to this setting either. It lets you turn on and off a debug console (showing errors, warnings, tips, logs, and similar details that developers find useful).

Taming Safari is just the start of exploiting the Internet on the iPhone. In upcoming chapters, you discover how to master e-mail, maps, and more.

The E-Mail Must Get Through

hapter 5 shows you how well your iPhone sends SMS text messages. But SMS text messages aren't the iPhone's only written communication trick, not by a long shot. One of the niftiest things your iPhone can do is send and receive real, honest-to-gosh e-mail, using Mail, its modern e-mail app. It's designed not only to send and receive text e-mail messages but also to handle rich HTML e-mail messages — formatted e-mail messages complete with font and type styles and embedded graphics.

Furthermore, your iPhone can read several types of file attachments, including PDF, Microsoft Word, PowerPoint, and Excel documents, as well as stuff produced through Apple's own iWork software. Better still, all this sending and receiving of text, graphics, and documents can happen in the background so that you can surf the Web or talk to a friend while your iPhone quietly and efficiently handles your e-mail behind the scenes. And Mail is compatible with the most popular e-mail providers, including Yahoo! Mail, Gmail, AOL, and Apple's own MobileMe.

©ImageState

As you discover in this chapter, the iOS 4 upgrade brought two important improvements to the Mail app. For starters, you can access a unified inbox of all your e-mail accounts (assuming you have multiple accounts). Moreover, you can organize messages by thread, or conversation.

Prep Work: Setting Up Your Accounts

First things first. To use Mail, you need an e-mail address. If you have broadband Internet access (that is, a cable modem or DSL), you probably received one or more e-mail addresses when you signed up. If you're one of the handful of readers who doesn't already have an e-mail account, you can get one for free from Yahoo! (`http://mail.yahoo.com`), Google (`http://mail.google.com`), AOL (`http://www.aol.com`), or one of many other service providers.

Many (if not all) free e-mail providers add a small bit of advertising at the end of your outgoing messages. If you'd rather not be a billboard for your e-mail provider, either use the address(es) that came with your broadband Internet access (*yourname*@comcast.net or *yourname*@att.net, for example) or pay a few dollars a month for a premium e-mail account that doesn't tack advertising (or anything else) onto your messages. You can get a me.com e-mail account as part of Apple's $99-a-year MobileMe service (which you may be able to find at a discount at Amazon or other online vendors).

Set up your account the easy way

Chapter 3 explains the option of automatically syncing the e-mail accounts on your computer with your iPhone. If you chose that option, your e-mail accounts should be configured on your iPhone already. You may proceed directly to the later section "Darling, You Send Me (E-Mail)."

If you haven't yet chosen that option but want to set up your account the easy way now, go to Chapter 3 and read the section on syncing mail accounts with the iPhone. Then you, too, can proceed directly to the "Darling, You Send Me (E-Mail)" section.

Set up your account the less easy way

If you don't want to sync the e-mail accounts on your computer, you can set up an e-mail account on your iPhone manually. It's not quite as easy as clicking a box and syncing your iPhone, but it's not rocket science either.

If you have no e-mail accounts on your iPhone, the first time you launch Mail, you're walked through the following procedure. If you have one or more e-mail accounts on your iPhone already and want to add a new account manually, start by tapping Settings on the Home screen, and then tap Mail, Contacts, Calendars, and Add Account.

Either way, you should now be staring at the Add Account screen, shown in Figure 11-1. Proceed to one of the next two sections, depending on your e-mail account.

Setting up an e-mail account with MobileMe, Google, Yahoo!, or AOL

If your account is with Apple's own MobileMe service, Google's Gmail, Yahoo!, or AOL, tap the appropriate button on the Add Account screen now. If you're setting up company e-mail through Microsoft Exchange, skip to the "Set up corporate e-mail" section. If your account is with a provider other than the ones listed, tap the Other button and skip to the next section.

Enter your name, e-mail address, and password, as shown in Figure 11-2. The description field is usually filled in automatically with the content you have in the address field, but you can replace that text with your own description (such as Work or Personal).

Tap the Next button in the upper-right corner of the screen. Your e-mail provider will verify your credentials. If you pass muster, that's all there is to setting up your account.

Figure 11-1: Tap a button to add an account.

Figure 11-2: Just fill 'em in and tap Next, and you're ready to rock.

Setting up an account with another provider

If your e-mail account is with a provider other than MobileMe, Gmail, Yahoo!, AOL, or Microsoft Exchange, you have a bit more work ahead of you. You're going to need a bunch of information about your e-mail account that you may not know or have handy.

We suggest that you scan the following instructions, note the items you don't know, and go find the answers before you continue. To find the answers, look at the documentation you received when you signed up for your e-mail account or visit the account provider's Web site and search there.

Here's how you set up an account:

1. **On the Add Account screen, tap the Other button.**

2. **Under Mail, tap Add Mail Account. Fill in the name, address, password, and description in the appropriate fields, the same as if you were setting up a MobileMe, Gmail, Yahoo!, or AOL account. Tap Next.**

   With any luck, that's all you'll have to do, although you may have to endure a spinning cursor for awhile as the iPhone attempts to retrieve information and validate your account with your provider. Otherwise, continue with Step 3.

3. **Tap the button at the top of the screen that denotes the type of e-mail server this account uses: IMAP or POP, as shown in Figure 11-3.**

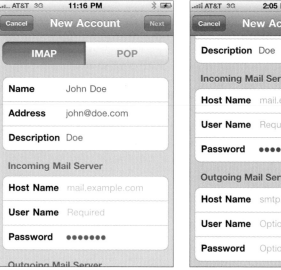

Figure 11-3: If you're not a MobileMe, Gmail, Yahoo!, or AOL user, you may have a few more fields to fill in before you can rock.

4. **Fill in the Internet host name for your incoming mail server, which should look something like mail.*providername*.com.**

5. **Fill in your username and password.**

6. **Enter the Internet host name for your outgoing mail server, which should look something like smtp.*providername*.com.**

You may have to scroll down to the bottom of the screen to see the outgoing mail server fields (refer to Figure 11-3, right).

7. **Enter your username and password in the appropriate fields.**

8. **Tap the Next button in the upper-right corner to create the account.**

Some outgoing mail servers don't need your username and password. The fields for these items on your iPhone note that they're optional. Still, we suggest that you fill them in anyway. That way, you won't have to add them later if your outgoing mail server *does* require an account name and password, which many do these days.

Set up corporate e-mail

The iPhone is friendly for business users, in large measure because it makes nice with the Microsoft Exchange servers that are a staple in large enterprises.

What's more, if your company supports something known as Microsoft Exchange ActiveSync, you can exploit push e-mail (messages are *pushed* to your iPhone automatically as opposed to being *pulled* in on a schedule) so that messages arrive pronto on the iPhone, just as they do on your other computers. (To keep everything up to date, the iPhone also supports push calendars and push contacts.) For push to work, your company must be simpatico with one of the last several iterations of Microsoft Exchange ActiveSync. Ask your company's IT or tech department if you run into an issue.

Setting up Exchange e-mail isn't particularly taxing, and the iPhone connects to Exchange right out of the box. However, you still might have to consult your employer's techie types for certain settings.

Start out by tapping the Microsoft Exchange icon on the Add Account screen. Fill in what you can: your e-mail address, username (usually as *domain\user*), and password. Or, call on your IT staff for assistance.

On the next screen, shown in Figure 11-4, enter the server address, assuming that the Microsoft Autodiscovery service didn't already find it. That address usually begins with *exchange.company.com*.

The company you work for doesn't want just anybody having access to your e-mail — heaven forbid if your phone is lost or stolen. So your bosses may insist that you change the passcode lock inside Settings on the phone. (This is different from the password for your e-mail account.) Skip over to Chapter 13 to find instructions for adding or changing a passcode. (We'll wait for you.) And, if your iPhone ends up in the wrong hands, your company can remotely wipe the contents clean.

After your corporate account is fully configured, you have to choose which information you want to synchronize through Exchange. You can choose

Mail, Contacts, and Calendars. Tap each one that you want to synchronize through Microsoft Exchange. After you select an item, you see the blue On button next to it, as shown in Figure 11-5.

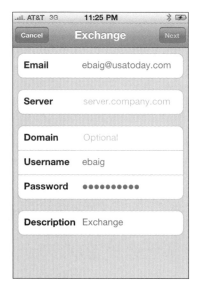

Figure 11-4: You're on your way to a corporate e-mail account.

Figure 11-5: Keeping Mail, Contacts, and Calendars in sync.

By default, the iPhone keeps e-mail synchronized for three days. To sync for a longer period, head to Settings and tap Mail, Contacts, Calendars, and then tap the Mail account using ActiveSync. Tap Mail Days to Sync, and then tap No Limit or choose another time frame (1 day, 1 week, 2 weeks, or 1 month).

If you're moonlighting at a second job, you can now configure more than one Exchange ActiveSync account on your iPhone; there used to be a limit of just one such account per phone.

See Me, Read Me, File Me, Delete Me: Working with Messages

Now that your e-mail accounts are all set up, it's time to find out how to receive and read the stuff. Fortunately, you already did most of the heavy lifting when you set up your e-mail accounts. Getting and reading your mail is a piece of cake.

You can tell when you have unread mail by looking at the Mail icon at the bottom of your Home screen. The cumulative number of unread messages across all your e-mail inboxes appears in a little red circle in the upper-right area of the icon.

Reading messages

Tap the Mail icon now to summon the Mailboxes screen shown in Figure 11-6. At the top of the Inboxes section is the All Inboxes inbox, which as its name suggests is a repository for all the messages across all your accounts. The number to the right of All Inboxes should match the number on the Mail icon in your Home page. Again, it's the cumulative tally of unread messages across all your accounts.

Below the All Inboxes listing are the inboxes for your individual e-mail accounts. The tally this time is only for the unread messages in those accounts.

Scroll down toward the bottom of the Mailboxes screen and you'll find an Accounts section with a similar listing of e-mail accounts. But if you tap on the listings here, you'll see any subfolders for each individual account (Drafts, Sent Mail, Trash, and so on), as shown in Figure 11-7.

To read your mail, tap an inbox: either All Inboxes to examine all your messages in one unified view or an individual account to check out messages from just that account.

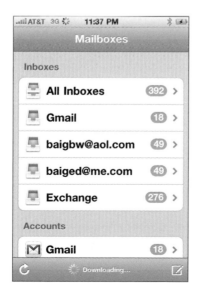

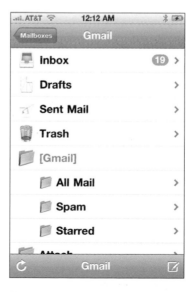

Figure 11-6: The Mailboxes screen is divided by inboxes and accounts.

Figure 11-7: Tap one of your e-mail accounts to reveal its subfolders.

If you have just a single mail account configured on your iPhone, you'll see only that one inbox on the Mailboxes screen.

When you tap a mailbox to open it, Mail fetches the most recent messages and displays the total number of unread messages at the top of the screen.

Now tap a message to read it. When a message is on the screen, buttons for managing incoming messages appear below it. These controls are addressed in the next section.

Managing messages

When a message is on your screen, you can do many tasks in addition to reading it (see Figure 11-8).

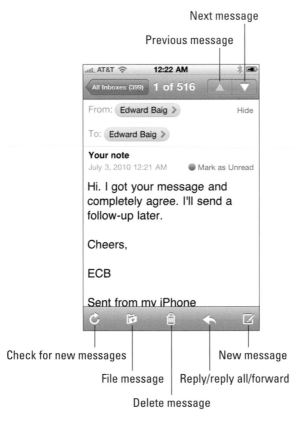

Figure 11-8: Reading and managing an e-mail message.

You can perform the following actions:

- ✔ View the next message by tapping the next message arrow at the upper-right corner of the screen (it's the downward-pointing arrow).

- ✔ View the preceding message by tapping the previous message arrow (the one pointing upward).

- ✔ Check for new messages by tapping the check for new messages icon.

- ✔ File this message in another folder by tapping the file message icon. When the list of folders appears, tap the folder where you want to file the message.

- ✔ Delete this message by tapping the delete message icon. You have to dig in the trash to retrieve the message if you tap the delete message icon by mistake. Go to Mail Settings if you want the iPhone to ask you before deleting a message.

- ✔ Reply, reply to all, or forward this message by tapping the reply/reply all/forward icon.

- ✔ Create a new e-mail message by tapping the new message icon.

You can delete e-mail messages without opening them (see Figure 11-9).

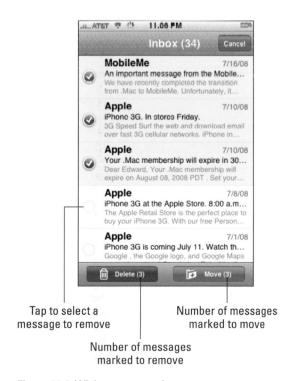

Tap to select a
message to remove

Number of messages
marked to move

Number of messages
marked to remove

Figure 11-9: Wiping out or moving messages, en masse.

Delete your messages in two ways:

✔ Swipe left or right across the message, and then tap the red Delete button that appears to the right of the message. In some e-mail accounts, notably Google's Gmail, an Archive button appears instead of Delete. Tap the button to archive the message; it is not deleted.

✔ Tap the Edit button in the upper-right corner of the screen, and tap the little circle to the left of each message you want to remove. Tapping that circle puts a check mark in it and brightens the red Delete button at the bottom of the screen. Tap that Delete button to erase all messages you selected. Deleted messages are moved to the Trash folder.

Threading messages

As part of the iOS 4 upgrade, Apple lets you *thread* messages or have Mail automatically group related missives. The beauty of this arrangement is that you can easily trace back an e-mail conversation. When you organize messages by a thread, the related messages show up as a single entry in the mailbox, with a number next to the right-pointing arrow in the entry indicating how many underlying messages are represented by the thread. So the number 4 next to Teresa's message in Figure 11-10 (left) shows that four messages constitute this particular thread; when you tap that listing, the four threaded messages appear, as shown in Figure 11-10, right.

Figure 11-10: Your e-mails are hanging together by a thread.

You have to turn on threading in Settings. From the Home screen, tap Settings, tap Mail, Contacts, Calendars, and tap Organize by Thread. Then tap the button so that it reads On, as shown in Figure 11-11. You may have to scroll down to see the Organize by Thread setting.

When you look at a message that's part of a thread, the numbers at the top of the screen tell you your location in the conversation. For example, in Figure 11-12, the note is number 3 of 4 in this thread.

Figure 11-11: To keep related messages together, turn on the Organize by Thread setting.

Figure 11-12: Reading a threaded message.

Searching e-mails

As part of Spotlight search, you can easily search through a bunch of messages to find the one you want to read right away — such as that can't-miss stock tip from your broker. Tap the status bar to scroll through the top of the inbox. You can type *stock* or whichever search term seems relevant. All matching e-mails that have already been downloaded appear. Or, by tapping in the search box itself, you can display tabs that let you narrow the search to the From, To, or Subject fields. It's too bad that (at press time, anyway) you can't run a search to find words within the body of an e-mail message.

If you're using Exchange, MobileMe, or certain IMAP-type e-mail accounts, you may even be able to search messages that are stored on the e-mail provider's servers or out in the Internet "cloud." When available, tap Continue Search on Server, as shown in Figure 11-13.

The capability to search e-mails may vary by e-mail account. In some instances, you can search only whole words; in other cases, partial words may work.

You can delete messages in bulk. In much the same way, you can move them to another folder in bulk. Tap Edit and then tap the circle to the left of each message you want to move so that a check mark appears. Tap the Move button at the bottom of the screen (refer to Figure 11-9), and tap the new folder where you want those messages to hang out.

Don't grow too attached to attachments

Your iPhone can even receive e-mail messages with attachments in a wide variety of file formats:

- **Apple Keynote:** .key
- **Apple Numbers:** .numbers
- **Apple Pages:** .pages
- **Contact information:** .vcf
- **Images:** .jpg, .tiff, .gif
- **Microsoft Excel:** .xls, .xlsx
- **Microsoft PowerPoint:** .ppt, .pptx
- **Microsoft Word:** .doc, .docx
- **Preview and Adobe Acrobat:** .pdf
- **Rich Text:** .rtf
- **Text:** .txt
- **Web pages:** .htm, .html

If the attachment is a file format not supported by the iPhone (for example, a Photoshop .psd file), you see the name of the file but you can't open it on your iPhone.

Here's how to read an attachment:

1. **Open the mail message containing the attachment.**

2. **Tap the attachment.**

   You probably need to scroll down to see the attachement, which appears at the bottom of the message. The attachment, like the one shown in Figure 11-14, downloads to your iPhone and opens automatically.

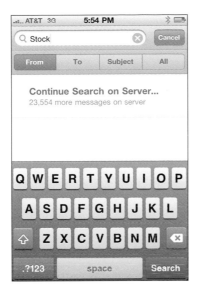

Figure 11-13: Your search doesn't end here.

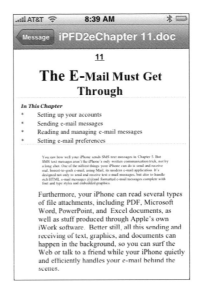

Figure 11-14: Text from a Microsoft Word file attached to an incoming e-mail message.

3. Read the attachment.

4. Tap the Message button in the upper-left corner of the screen to return to the message text.

More things you can do with messages

Wait! You can do even more with your incoming e-mail messages:

TIP

✔ To see all recipients of a message, tap the word *Details* (displayed in blue) to the right of the sender's name.

If all recipients are displayed, the word in blue is *Hide* rather than *Details*. Tap it to hide all names except the sender's.

✔ To add an e-mail recipient or sender to your contacts, tap the name or e-mail address at the top of the message and then tap either Create New Contact or Add to Existing Contact.

✔ To mark a message as unread, tap Mark As Unread, which appears near the top of each message in blue with a blue dot to its left. When you do, the message is again included in the unread message count on the Mail icon on your Home screen, and its mailbox again has a blue dot next to it in the message list for that mailbox.

✔ To zoom in and out of a message, employ the pinch and unpinch gestures, which we suspect you excel at now.

✔ To follow a link in a message, tap the link. (Links are typically displayed in blue and may be underlined, but sometimes they appear in other colors.) If the link is a URL, Safari opens and displays the Web page. If the link is a phone number, the Phone app opens and offers to dial the number. If the link is a map, Maps opens and displays the location. If the link is a day, date, or time, you can tap the item to create a Calendar Event. If the link is a shipper's tracking number, you may be able to get the status of a package. And last but not least, if the link is an e-mail address, a preaddressed blank e-mail message is created.

If the link opens Safari, Phone, or Maps and you want to return to your e-mail, press the Home button on the front of your iPhone and then tap the Mail icon.

Darling, You Send Me (E-Mail)

So now that you're a whiz at reading and organizing incoming messages, let's look at how to use your iPhone to send e-mail.

Makin' messages

Several subspecies of messages are available: pure text, text with a photo, a partially finished messages (a *draft*) that you want to save and complete later, a reply to an incoming message, and a message you want to forward to someone else. The following sections examine these subsets one at a time.

Sending an all-text message

To compose a new e-mail message, tap Mail on the Home screen to open the Mailboxes screen (refer to Figure 11-6) or whichever screen was up when you last left the app.

Now, to create a new message, follow these steps:

1. **Tap the New Message button in the lower-right corner of the screen.**

   The button appears on all the Mail screens, so don't worry if you're not at the main Mailboxes screen. A screen like the one shown in Figure 11-15 appears.

2. **Type the names or e-mail addresses of the recipients in the To field or tap the + button to the right of the To field to select a contact or contacts from your iPhone's address book.**

Figure 11-15: The New Message screen appears, ready for you to start typing the recipient's name.

3. **(Optional) Enter a name in the Cc field, Bcc field, or both fields. Or choose to send mail from a different account in the From field, as follows:**

   a. **Tap the field labeled Cc/Bcc, From.**

   Doing so breaks the single field into separate Cc, Bcc, and From fields. The Cc/Bcc label stands for *carbon copy/blind carbon copy.* Bcc enables you to include a recipient on the message that other recipients can't see has been included. It's great for those secret agent e-mails!

   b. **Tap the respective Cc or Bcc field and type the name.**

   Or, tap the + symbol that appears in those fields to add a contact.

   If you start typing an e-mail address, e-mail addresses that match what you typed appear in a list below the To or Cc field. If the correct one is in the list, tap it to use it.

   c. **Tap the From field to send the message from any of your e-mail accounts on the fly, assuming, of course, that you have more than one account and want to send mail from an account different from the one already shown.**

4. **Type a subject in the Subject field.**

   The subject is optional, but it's considered poor form to send an e-mail message without one.

5. **Type your message in the message area.**

   The message area is immediately below the Subject field.

6. **Tap the Send button in the upper-right corner of the screen.**

Your message wings its way to its recipients almost immediately. If you aren't in range of a Wi-Fi network or the AT&T EDGE or 3G data network when you tap Send, the message is sent the next time you're in range of one of these networks.

Apple includes a bunch of landscape orientation keyboards to various apps, including Mail. When you rotate the phone to its side, you can compose a new message using a wider-format virtual keyboard.

Sending a photo with a text message

Forgive the cliché, but sometimes a picture truly is worth a thousand words. When that's the case, here's how to send an e-mail message with a photo enclosed.

Tap the Photos icon on the Home screen, and then find the photo you want to send. Tap the button that looks like a little rectangle with a curved arrow springing out of it (see the icon in the margin), in the lower-left corner of the screen, and then tap the Email Photo button.

An e-mail message appears onscreen with the photo already attached. The image appears to be embedded in the body of the message, but the recipient receives the image as a regular e-mail attachment. Just address the message and type whatever text you like, as you did for an all-text message in the preceding section, and then tap the Send button. You have the option to choose a file size for your picture, among Small, Medium, or Actual Size.

Saving an e-mail message so that you can send it later

Sometimes you start an e-mail message but don't have time to finish it. When that happens, you can save it as a draft and finish it some other time.

Here's how: Start an e-mail message as described in one of the two preceding sections. When you're ready to save the message as a draft, tap the Cancel button in the upper-left corner of the screen and three buttons appear. Tap the Save Draft button if you want to save this message as a draft and complete it another time; tap the Delete Draft button to ditch your efforts; or tap Cancel to return to the message and continue crafting it to perfection.

If you tap the Delete Draft button, the message disappears immediately without a second chance. Don't tap Delete Draft unless you mean it.

To work on the message again, tap the Drafts mailbox for the account in question. All messages you saved as drafts hang out in that mailbox. Tap the one you want resume working on so that it reappears on the screen. When you're finished, tap Send to send it or Cancel to go through the drill of saving it as a draft again.

The number of drafts appears to the right of the Drafts folder, the same way that the number of unread messages appears to the right of other mail folders, such as your inbox.

Replying to or forwarding an e-mail message

When you receive a message and want to reply to it, open the message and then tap the reply/reply all/forward icon (labeled in Figure 11-8). Then tap the Reply, Reply All, or Forward button.

The Reply button creates a new e-mail message addressed to the sender of the original message. The Reply All button creates an outgoing e-mail message addressed to the sender and all other recipients of the original message. In both cases, the Subject line is retained with a *Re:* prefix added. So if the original Subject line were *iPhone Tips,* the reply's Subject line would be *Re: iPhone Tips.* You also see text from the original message in the body of your reply (whether you are replying to one person or more than one person).

Tapping the Forward button creates an unaddressed e-mail message that contains the text of the original message. Add the e-mail address(es) of the person or people you want to forward the message to, and then tap Send. In this case, rather than a *Re:* prefix, the Subject line begins with *Fwd:.* So this time the Subject line reads *Fwd: iPhone Tips.*

You can edit the Subject line of a reply or a forwarded message or edit the body text of a forwarded message the same way you would edit any other text. It's usually considered good form to leave the Subject lines alone (with the *Re:* or *Fwd:* prefix intact), but you may want to change them sometimes. Now you know that you can.

To send your reply or forwarded message, tap the Send button as usual.

Settings for sending e-mail

You can customize the mail you send and receive in lots of different ways. In this section, we explore settings for sending e-mail. Later in this chapter, we show you settings that affect the way you receive and read messages. In each instance, you start by tapping Settings on the Home screen. Then:

✔ **To hear an alert when you successfully send a message:** Tap the Sounds icon on the main Settings screen, and then turn on the Sent Mail setting. If you want to change other settings, tap the Settings button in the upper-left corner of the screen. If you're finished setting settings, press the Home button on the front of your iPhone.

The preceding paragraph is similar for all the settings we discuss in this section and later sections, so we won't repeat them again. To summarize, if you want to continue using settings, you tap whichever button appears in the upper-left corner of the screen — it might be named Settings, Mail, Accounts, or something else. The point is that the upper-left button always returns you to the preceding screen so that you can change other settings. The same concept applies to pressing the Home button on the front of your iPhone when you're finished setting a setting. That action always saves the change you just made and returns you to the Home screen.

✔ **To add a signature line, phrase, or block of text to every e-mail message you send:** Tap Settings, tap Mail, Contacts, Calendars, and then tap Signature. (You may need to scroll down to see it). The default signature is *Sent from my iPhone.* You can add text before or after it, or delete it and type something else. Your signature is now affixed to the end of all your outgoing e-mail.

✔ **To have your iPhone send you a copy of every message you send:** Tap Settings, tap Mail, Contacts, Calendars, and then turn on the Always Bcc Myself setting.

✔ **To set the default e-mail account for sending e-mail from outside the Mail app:** Tap the Settings icon on the Home screen, tap Mail, and then tap Default Account. Tap the account you want to use as the default. For example, when you want to e-mail a picture directly from the Photos app, this designated e-mail account is the one that's used. Note that this setting applies only if you have more than one e-mail account on your iPhone.

That's what you need to know about the settings that apply to sending e-mail.

Setting your message and account settings

This final discussion of Mail involves more settings that deal with your various e-mail accounts.

Checking and viewing e-mail settings

Several settings affect the way you check and view e-mail. You might want to modify some, so we describe what they do and where to find them:

✔ **To specify how often the iPhone checks for new messages:** Tap the Settings icon on the Home screen, tap Mail, Contacts, Calendars, and then tap Fetch New Data. You're entering the world of *fetching* or *pushing.* Check out Figure 11-16 to glance at your options. If your e-mail program supports push and you have it turned on (the On button is showing), fresh messages are sent to your iPhone automatically as soon as they reach the server. If you turned off push (Off is showing) or your e-mail program doesn't support it, the iPhone fetches data instead. Choices for fetching are Every 15 Minutes, Every 30 Minutes, Hourly, and Manually. Tap the one you prefer.

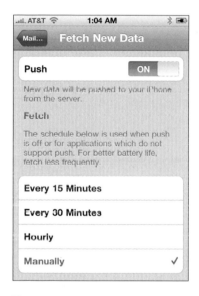

Figure 11-16: Fetch or push? Your call.

To determine these push and fetch settings for each account, tap Advanced at the bottom of the screen (it's not visible in Figure 11-15). Then tap the account in question. Push is shown as an option only if the e-mail account you tapped supports the feature.

As of this writing, Yahoo!, MobileMe, and Microsoft Exchange ActiveSync were among the awfully pushy e-mail accounts (but only in a good way).

✔ **To hear an alert sound when you receive a new message:** Tap the Sounds icon on the main Settings screen and then turn on the New Mail setting.

✔ **To set the number of recent messages that appear in your inbox:** Tap the Settings icon on the Home screen, tap Mail, Contacts, Calendars, and then tap Show. Your choices are 25, 50, 75, 100, and 200 recent messages. Tap the number you prefer.

You can see more messages in your inbox regardless of this setting by scrolling all the way to the bottom and tapping Download More.

✔ **To set the number of lines of each message to be displayed in the message list:** Tap the Settings icon on the Home screen, tap Mail, Contacts, Calendars, tap Preview, and then choose a number. Your choices are 0, 1, 2, 3, 4, and 5 lines of text. The more lines of text you display in the list, the fewer messages you can see at a time without scrolling. Think before you choose 4 or 5.

✔ **To set the font size for messages:** Tap the Settings icon on the Home screen, tap Mail, Contacts, Calendars, and then tap Minimum Font Size. Your options are Small, Medium, Large, Extra Large, and Giant. Use trial-and-error to find out which size you prefer. Select one and then read a message. If it's not just right, select a different size. Repeat until you're happy.

✔ **To specify whether the iPhone shows the To and Cc labels in message lists:** Tap the Settings icon on the Home screen, tap Mail, Contacts, Calendars, and then turn on or off the Show To/Cc Label setting.

✔ **To turn on or off the Ask before Deleting warning:** Tap the Settings icon on the Home screen, tap Mail, Contacts, Calendars, and then turn on or off the Ask before Deleting setting. If this setting is turned on, you need to tap the trash can icon at the bottom of the screen and then tap the red Delete button to confirm the deletion. When the setting is turned off, tapping the trash can icon deletes the message and you never see a red Delete button.

✔ **To specify whether the phone will automatically load remote images:** Tap Load Remote Images so that the On button is showing. If it's off, you can still manually load remote images.

Altering account settings

The last group of settings we explore in this chapter deals with your e-mail accounts. You most likely will never need most of these settings, but we'd be remiss if we didn't at least mention them briefly. So here they are, whether you need 'em or not:

✔ **To stop using an e-mail account:** Tap the Settings icon on the Home screen, tap Mail, Contacts, Calendars, and then tap the account name. Tap the switch to turn off the account.

This setting doesn't delete the account; it only hides it from view and stops it from sending or checking e-mail until you turn it on again.

- **To delete an e-mail account:** Tap the Settings icon on the Home screen, tap Mail, Contacts, Calendars, and then tap the account name. Scroll to the bottom and tap the red button that says Delete from My iPhone. You're given a chance to reconsider by tapping either Keep on My iPhone or Cancel.

The last settings are reached the same way: Tap the Settings icon on the Home screen, tap Mail, Contacts, Calendars, and then tap the name of the account you want to work with. Next, tap the Account Info button and then tap Advanced. The settings you see under Advanced and how they appear vary a little by account. This list describes some of the ones you see:

- **To specify how long until deleted messages are removed permanently from your iPhone:** Tap Advanced and then tap Remove. Your choices are Never, After One Day, After One Week, and After One Month. Tap the choice you prefer.

- **To choose whether drafts, sent messages, and deleted messages are stored on your iPhone or on your mail server:** Tap Advanced if this option is presented. Then, under the Mailbox Behaviors heading, choose various settings to determine whether you're storing such messages on the iPhone or on the server. Your options vary according to your e-mail account. If you choose to store any or all of them on the server, you can't see them unless you have an Internet connection (Wi Fi, EDGE, or 3G). If you choose to store them on your iPhone, they're always available, even if you don't have Internet access.

We strongly recommend that you not change these next two items unless you know exactly what you're doing and why. If you're having problems with sending or receiving mail, start by contacting your ISP (Internet service provider), e-mail provider, or corporate IT person or department. Then change these settings only if they tell you to.

- **To reconfigure mail server settings:** Tap Host Name, User Name, or Password in the Incoming Mail Server or Outgoing Mail Server section of the account settings screen and make your changes.

- **To adjust Use SSL, Authentication, IMAP Path Prefix, or Server Port:** Tap Advanced, and then tap the appropriate item and make the necessary changes.

And that, as they say in baseball, retires the side. You're now fully qualified to set up e-mail accounts and send and receive e-mail on your iPhone.

12

Tracking with Maps, Compass, Stocks, and Weather

In This Chapter

▶ Mapping your route with Maps

▶ Course-setting with Compass

▶ Getting quotes with Stocks

▶ Watching the weather with Weather

*1*n this chapter, we look at four of the iPhone's Internet enabled apps: Maps, Compass, Stocks, and Weather. We call them *Internet-enabled* because they display information collected over your Internet connection — whether Wi-Fi or wireless data network — in real time (or in the case of Stocks, near-real time).

Maps Are Where It's At

In the first edition of this book, we said that the Maps feature was one of the sleeper hits of our iPhone experience and an app we both use more than we expected because it's so darn handy. Since then, Maps has become better and more capable. With Maps, you can quickly and easily discover exactly where you are, find nearby restaurants and businesses, get turn-by-turn driving, walking, and public transportation instructions from any address to any other address, and see real-time traffic information for many locations.

©Corbis Digital Stock

Finding your current location with Maps

Let's start with something supremely simple yet extremely useful —
determining your current location. At the risk of sounding like self-help
gurus, here's how to find yourself: Tap the Maps icon and then tap the
little arrowhead icon in the lower-left corner.

If you have an iPhone 3G, 3GS, or 4, a pulsating blue marker indicates your
location on the map when the phone's GPS is used to find your location and
a purple arrowhead appears to the right of the current time in the status bar
(both are shown in Figure 12-1).

If GPS is not being used because you're out of the satellite's sight line or
because you're using a first-generation iPhone (which had no GPS), a somewhat larger pale blue circle shows your approximate location. Either way,
when you move around, the iPhone updates your location and adjusts the
map so the location indicator stays in the middle of the screen.

If you tap or drag the map, your iPhone continues to update your location;
but it won't recenter the marker, which means that the location indicator can
move off the screen.

Finding a person, place, or thing

To find a person, place, or thing with Maps, tap the search field at the top of
the screen to make the keyboard appear. Now type what you're looking for.
You can search for addresses, zip codes, intersections, towns, landmarks,
and businesses by category and by name, or combinations, such as *New
York, NY 10022, pizza 60645,* or *Auditorium Shores Austin TX.*

If the letters you type match names in your Contacts list, the matching contacts appear in a list below the search field. Tap a name to see a map of that
contact's location. Maps is smart about it, too; it displays only the names of
contacts that have a street address.

How does it do that?

Maps uses iPhone's Location Services to determine your approximate location using available
information from your wireless data network,
local Wi-Fi networks (if Wi-Fi is turned on),
and GPS (iPhone 3G, 3GS, and 4 only). If you're
not using Location Services, turning it off (tap
Settings, General, Location Services) will conserve your battery. Don't worry if Location

Services is turned off when you tap the arrowhead icon — you'll be prompted to turn it on.
Note that Location Services may not be available in all areas at all times. One last thing:
The purple arrowhead appears in the status
bar whenever *any* app (not just Maps) is using
Location Services and GPS to determine your
current location.

When you finish typing, tap Search. After a few seconds, a map appears. If you searched for a single location, it is marked with a single pushpin. If you searched for a category (*pizza 60645,* for example), you see multiple push-pins, one for each matching location, as shown in Figure 12-2.

Figure 12-1. A blue marker shows your location and a purple arrowhead in the status bar shows you're using GPS.

Figure 12-2: Search for *pizza 60645* and you see pushpins for all nearby pizza joints.

Views, zooms, and pans

The preceding section talks about how to find just about anything with Maps. Now here's a look at some ways you can use what you find. First, find out how to work with what you see on the screen. Four views are available at any time: Map, Satellite, Hybrid, and List. (Refer to Figure 12-2 for a Map view; Figure 12-3 shows the Satellite view.) Select one view by tapping the curling page button in the lower-right corner. The map then curls back and reveals several buttons, as shown in Figure 12-4.

In Map, Satellite, or Hybrid view, you can zoom to see either more or less of the map — or scroll (pan) to see what's above, below, or to the left or right of what's on the screen:

> ✔ **To zoom out:** Pinch the map or *double-tap using two fingers.* To zoom out even more, pinch or double-tap using two fingers again.

Figure 12-3: Satellite view of the map shown in Figure 12-2.

Figure 12-4: The map curls back to reveal these buttons.

Double-tapping with two fingers may be a new concept to you: Merely tap twice in rapid succession with two fingers rather than the usual one finger. That's a total of four taps, input efficiently as two taps per finger.

✔ **To zoom in:** Unpinch the map or double-tap (the usual way — with just one finger) the spot you want to zoom in on. Unpinch or double-tap with one finger again to zoom in even more.

An *unpinch* is the opposite of a pinch. Start with your thumb and a finger together and then flick them apart.

You can also unpinch with two fingers or two thumbs, one from each hand, but you'll probably find that a single-handed pinch and unpinch is handier.

✔ **To scroll:** Flick or drag up, down, left, or right.

Maps and contacts

Maps and contacts go together like peanut butter and jelly. For example, if you want to see a map of a contact's street address, tap the little bookmarks icon in the search field, tap the Contacts button at the bottom of the screen, and then tap the contact's name. Or type the first few letters of the contact's name in the search field and then tap the name in the list that automatically appears below the search field.

After you find a location by typing an address into Maps, you can add that location to one of your contacts. Or you can create a new contact with a location you've found. To do either, tap the location's pushpin on the map, and then tap the little > in a blue circle to the right of the location's name or description (shown for Gullivers in Figures 12-2 and 12-3) to display its Info screen (see Figure 12-5).

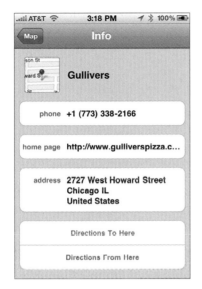

Figure 12-5: The unscrolled Info screen for Gullivers Pizzeria (left), and the same screen when you scroll to the bottom (right).

Now tap the Add to Contacts button on the Info screen. You'll probably have to scroll to the bottom of the Info screen (refer to Figure 12-5, right) to see this button.

You work with your contacts in two ways. One way is to tap the Contacts icon, which is on the second page of icons on the Home screen (swipe from right to left on the Home screen to see this second page). Or two, tap the Phone icon on your Home screen, and then tap the Contacts icon in the Phone screen's dock.

You can also get driving directions from most locations, including a contact's address, to most other locations, including another contact's address. You see how to do that in the "Smart map tricks" section, later in the chapter.

Timesaving map tools: Bookmarks, Recents, and Contacts

Maps offers three tools that can save you from having to type the same locations over and over. All three are in the Bookmarks screen, which appears when you tap the little blue bookmarks icon on the right side of the search field (refer to Figure 12-4).

At the bottom of the Bookmarks screen, you find three buttons: Bookmarks, Recents, and Contacts. The following sections give you the lowdown on these buttons.

Bookmarks

Bookmarks in the Maps app, like bookmarks in Safari, let you return to a location without typing a single character. Simply tap the little > in a blue circle to the right of the location's name or description to display the Info screen for that location. Tap the Add to Bookmarks button on the Info screen. (You may have to scroll down the Info screen to see the Add to Bookmarks button.)

You can also drop a pin anywhere on the map by tapping the curling page button in the lower-right corner, and then tapping the Drop Pin button. After you've dropped a pin, you can press and drag it anywhere on the map. When the pin is where you want it, lift your finger to drop the pin and a banner with the location of the pin (if Maps can figure it out) and a little > in a blue circle appears. Tap the little > and the Info screen for the dropped pin appears. Now tap the Add to Bookmarks button on the Info screen.

The info screen for a dropped pin offers several buttons in addition to Add to Bookmarks, namely Directions to Here, Directions from Here, Add to Contacts, Share Location, and Remove Pin.

After you add a bookmark, you can recall it at any time. To do so, tap the bookmarks icon in the search field, tap the Bookmarks button at the bottom of the screen, and then tap the bookmark name to see it on a map.

The first things you should bookmark are your home and work addresses. These are things you use all the time with Maps, so you might as well bookmark them now to avoid typing them over and over. Also create zip code bookmarks for your home, work, and other locations you frequently visit. Then when you want to find businesses near any of those locations, you can choose the zip code bookmark and type what you're looking for, such as *78729 pizza, 60645 gas station,* or *90201 Starbucks.*

To manage your bookmarks, first tap the Edit button in the top-left corner of the Bookmarks screen. Then:

 ✔ **To move a bookmark up or down in the Bookmarks list:** Drag the little icon with three gray bars that appears to the right of the bookmark upward to move the bookmark higher in the list or downward to move the bookmark lower in the list.

 ✔ **To delete a bookmark from the Bookmarks list:** Tap the – button to the left of the bookmark's name.

When you're finished using bookmarks, tap the Done button in the top-right corner of the Bookmarks screen to return to the map.

Recents

Maps automatically remembers every location you've searched for in its Recents list (unless you've cleared it, as described next). To see this list, tap the bookmarks icon in the search field, and then tap the Recents button at the bottom of the screen. To see a map of a recent item, tap the item's name.

To clear the Recents list, tap the Clear button in the top-left corner of the screen, and then tap the Clear All Recents button.

When you're finished using the Recents list, tap the Done button in the top-right corner of the screen to return to the map.

Contacts

To see a map of a contact's location, tap the bookmarks icon in the search field, and then tap the Contacts button at the bottom of the screen. To see a map of a contact's location, tap the contact's name in the list.

To limit the Contacts list to specific groups (assuming you have some groups in your Contacts list), tap the Groups button in the top-left corner of the screen and then tap the name of the group. Now only contacts in this group are displayed in the list.

When you're finished using the Contacts list, tap the Done button in the top-right corner of the screen to return to the map.

Smart map tricks

The Maps app has more tricks up its sleeve. This section lists a few nifty features you may find useful.

Get route maps and driving directions

You can get route maps and driving directions to any location from any other location in a couple of ways:

- **If a pushpin is already on the screen:** Tap the pushpin and then tap the little > in a blue circle to the right of the name or description. This action displays the item's Info screen. Now tap the Directions to Here or Directions from Here button to get directions to or from that location, respectively.

- **When you're looking at a map screen:** Tap the Directions button at the bottom of the map screen. The Start and End fields appear at the top of the screen. Type the start and end points or select them from your bookmarks, recent maps, or contacts if you prefer. If you want to swap the starting and ending locations, tap the little swirly arrow button to the left of the Start and End fields.

When the start and end locations are correct, tap the Route button in the bottom-right corner of the screen and the route map appears, as shown in Figure 12-6.

If you need to change the start or end location, tap the Edit button in the top-left corner and type a new start or end location.

Weird but true: If you type the end location, you'll have to tap the Route button before you can perform the next step; but if you select the end location from your Bookmarks, Contacts, or Recents list, you won't see the Route button and thus won't have to tap it before you perform the next step.

The next step is to tap the Start button in the top-right corner to receive turn-by-turn driving directions, as shown in Figure 12-7. To see the next step in the directions, tap the right-facing arrow in the top-right corner; to see the preceding step, tap the left-facing arrow in the top-right corner.

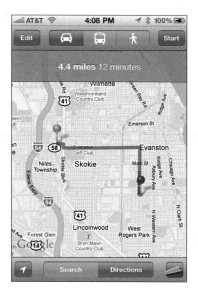

Figure 12-6: The route map from Bob's first house in Skokie to Gullivers Pizza in Chicago.

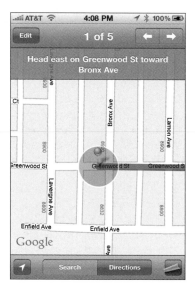

Figure 12-7: The first step in the step-by-step driving directions for the route to Gullivers.

If you prefer your driving directions displayed as a list with all the steps, as shown in Figure 12-8, tap the curling page button in the lower-right corner and then tap the List button.

When you're finished with the step-by-step directions, tap the Search button at the bottom of the screen to return to the regular map screen and single search field, as shown in Figure 12-9.

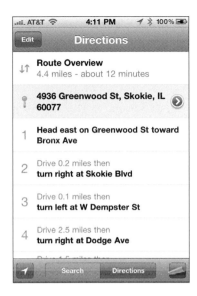

Figure 12-8: Step-by-step driving directions displayed as a list.

Figure 12-9: Tap Search and the map screen and single search field magically reappear.

As well as step-by-step directions work, we wish the iPhone offered the type of audible turn-by-turn directions feature found on some dedicated GPS devices. You know, where some friendly male or female voice states instructions (such as "turn right on Main Street").

TIP

We're in luck. The iPhone can speak directions if you use one of several GPS apps, such as TomTom U. S. A. ($49.99), Navigon MobileNavigator ($79.99), or MotionX GPS Drive ($2.99 plus $2.99 per month or $24.99 per year for Live Voice Guidance), which are all decent. We advise plugging the iPhone into a power outlet if at all possible while driving because such apps can quickly drain the battery.

Get public transportation information and walking directions

After you've provided a starting and ending location and tapped the Route button, the next screen that appears has three icons near the top: a car, a bus, and a person walking. In the preceding example, we showed directions by car, which is the default.

For public transportation information, tap the bus icon instead. When you do, the departure and arrival times for the next bus or train appear, as shown in Figure 12-10. Tap the little clock icon below the Start button (at the top of the screen) to see additional departure and arrival times, as shown in Figure 12-11.

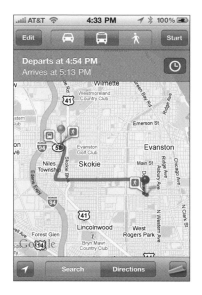

Figure 12-10: A bus route and schedule.

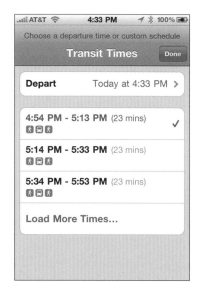

Figure 12-11: Additional departure times for that bus route.

The step-by-step directions for public transportation routes explain where you need to walk to catch the bus or train, where you need to get off that bus or train, and where you have to walk from there to reach your destination, as shown in Figure 12-12.

For step-by-step directions for walking, tap the person walking icon. Walking directions generally look a lot like driving directions except for your travel time. For example, driving time in Figure 12-6 is approximately 12 minutes with traffic; walking time (not shown) is estimated at 1 hour and 24 minutes.

Get traffic info in real time

You can find out the traffic conditions for whatever map you're viewing by tapping the curling page button in the lower-right corner and then tapping the Show Traffic button. When you do this, major roadways are color-coded to inform you of the current traffic speed, as shown in Figure 12-13. Here's the key:

- **Green:** 50 or more miles per hour
- **Yellow:** 25 to 50 miles per hour
- **Red:** Under 25 miles per hour
- **Gray:** No data available at this time

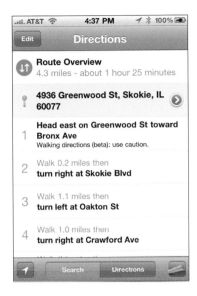

Figure 12-12: Step-by-step directions for public transportation to Gullivers.

Figure 12-13: Traffic is moving really slowly (red), kind of slowly (yellow), and nice and fast (green).

Traffic info isn't available in every location, but the only way to find out is to give it a try. If no color codes appear, assume that traffic information doesn't work for that particular location.

More about the Info screen

If a location has a little > in a blue circle to the right of its name or description (refer to Figure 12-2), you can tap the > to see the location's Info screen.

As we explain earlier in this chapter, you can get directions to or from that location, add the location to your bookmarks or contacts, or create a new contact from it. But you can do three more things with a location from its Info screen:

- Tap the phone number to call it.
- Tap the e-mail address to launch the Mail app and send an e-mail to it.
- Tap the URL to launch Safari and view its Web site.

Contemplating the Compass

The Compass app, available only on the iPhone 3GS and iPhone 4, works like a magnetic needle compass. Launch the Compass app by tapping its icon in the Utilities folder on your Home screen, and it shows you the direction you're facing, as shown in Figure 12-14.

But wait — there's more. If you were to tap the little arrowhead icon in the lower-left corner of the Compass screen, the Maps app launches. Now for the cool part: Tap the little arrowhead icon in the lower-left corner of the Maps app two times and the blue marker grows a little white cone that indicates the direction you're facing, as shown in Figure 12-15.

Figure 12-14: The Compass app says I'm facing north.

Figure 12-15: The map with the cone says I'm facing north, too.

Also note that when the map is in compass mode, the little arrowhead icon in its lower-left corner grows a little white cone as well, letting you know that you're now using the compass mode.

If you rotate to face a different direction while Maps is in compass mode, the map rotates in real time. So the map always displays the direction you're currently facing, even if you've moved around a bit, which is pretty darn cool.

Taking Stock with Stocks

Stocks is another Internet-enabled app on your iPhone. It's kind of a one-trick pony, but if you need its trick — information about specific stocks — it's a winner.

Every time you open the Stocks app by tapping its icon on the Home screen, it displays the latest price for your stocks, with two provisos:

- The quotes may be delayed by up to 20 minutes.
- The quotes are updated only if your iPhone can connect to the Internet via either Wi-Fi or a wireless data network.

So tap that Stocks icon and take a peek. The first time you open Stocks, you see information for a group of default stocks, funds, and indexes. There are more of them than you can see on the screen at once, so flick upward to scroll down.

Adding and deleting stocks, funds, and indexes

Because the chance of you owning that exact group of stocks, funds, and indexes displayed on the screen is slim, this section shows you how to add your own stocks, funds, or indexes and delete any or all default ones if you want.

Here's how to add a stock, a fund, or an index:

1. **Tap the *i* button in the bottom-right corner of the initial Stocks screen.**

   The *i* is for *info.*

2. **Tap the + button in the top-left corner of the Stocks screen.**

3. **Type the stock symbol or the name of the company, index, or fund.**

4. **Tap the Search button.**

   Stocks finds the company or companies that match your search request.

5. **Tap the one you want to add.**

6. **Repeat Steps 4 and 5 until you're through adding stocks, funds, and indexes.**

7. **Tap the Done button in the top-right corner.**

And here's how to delete a stock (the steps for deleting a fund or an index are the same):

1. **Tap the *i* button in the bottom-right corner of the initial Stocks screen.**

2. **Tap the – button to the left of the stock's name.**

3. **Tap the Delete button that appears to the right of the stock's name.**

4. **Repeat Steps 2 and 3 until all unwanted stocks have been deleted.**

5. **Tap the Done button.**

That's all there is to adding and deleting stocks.

 To change the order of the list, tap the *i* button and then drag the three horizontal lines to the right of the stock, fund, or index up or down to its new place in the list.

Details, details, details

To see the details for an item, tap its name to select it and the lower portion of the screen will offer additional information. Note the three small dots under the words *Quotes delayed by 20 minutes*. These dots tell you that there are three screens of information, all shown in Figure 12-16. To switch between these three screens, simply swipe to the left or the right on the lower part of the screen.

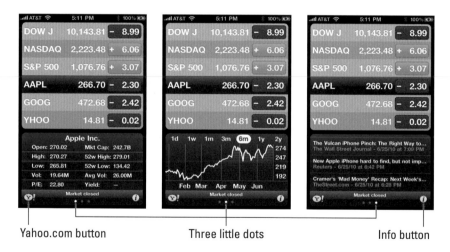

Yahoo.com button   Three little dots   Info button

Figure 12-16: The Stocks screens.

To look up additional information about a stock at Yahoo.com, first tap the stock's name to select it, and then tap the Y! button in the lower-left corner of the screen. Safari launches and displays the Yahoo.com finance page for that stock.

Charting a course

Referring to Figure 12-16, note the chart at the bottom of the middle image. At the top of the chart, you see a bunch of numbers and letters, namely 1d, 1w, 1m, 3m, 6m, 1y, and 2y. They stand for 1 day, 1 week, 1 month, 3 months, 6 months (selected in Figure 12-16), 1 year, and 2 years, respectively. Tap one of them and the chart updates to reflect that period of time.

That's sweet but here's an even sweeter feature: If you rotate your iPhone 90 degrees, the chart appears in full-screen, as shown in Figure 12-17. Here are three cool things you can do with full-screen charts:

- Touch any point in time to see the value for that day.
- Use two fingers to touch any two points in time to see the difference in values between those two days, as shown in Figure 12-17.
- Swipe left or right to see the chart for another stock, fund, or index.

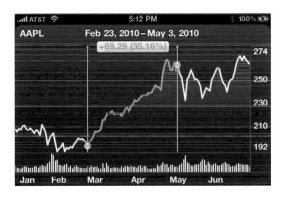

Figure 12-17: Use two fingers to see the difference in values ($69.29, or 35.16%) between two dates (Feb 23, 2010 and May 3, 2010).

By default, the Stocks app displays the change in a stock's price in dollars. You can instead see the change expressed as a percentage or as the stock's market capitalization. Simply tap the number next to any stock (green numbers are positive; red numbers are negative) to toggle the display for all stocks — dollar change, percent change, market cap. So if your stocks, funds, and indexes are currently displayed as dollars, tapping any one of them switches them all to percent — and tapping again switches them to market cap.

Another method requires more steps: Tap the *i* button in the bottom-right corner of the initial Stocks screen. Then tap the %, Price, or Mkt Cap button at the bottom of the screen. The values are then displayed in the manner you chose. Tap the Done button in the top-right corner when you're finished.

Weather Watching

Weather is a simple app that provides you with the current weather forecast for the city or cities of your choice. By default, you see a six-day forecast for the chosen city. If the background for the forecast is blue, as it is in Figure 12-18, it's daytime (between 6:00 a.m. and 6:00 p.m.) in that city; if it's a deep purple, it's nighttime (between 6:00 p.m. and 6:00 a.m.).

To add a city, first tap the *i* button in the bottom-right corner. Next, tap the + button in the upper-left corner, type a city and state or zip code, and tap the Search button in the bottom-right corner of the screen. Finally, tap the name of the found city. Add as many cities as you want this way.

To delete a city, tap the *i* button in the bottom-right corner. Tap the red – button to the left of its name, and then tap the Delete button that appears to the right of its name.

You can also choose between Fahrenheit and Celsius by first tapping the *i* button in the bottom-right corner and then tapping either the °F or °C button near the bottom of the screen. When you're finished, tap the Done button in the top-right corner of the screen.

If you've added more than one city to Weather, you can switch between them by flicking your finger across the screen to the left or the right.

See the three little dots — two gray and one white — at the bottom of the screen in Figure 12-18? They denote the number of cities you have stored (which is three in this case).

Last, but not least, to see detailed weather information about a city at Yahoo. com, tap the Y! button in the lower-left corner of the screen. Safari launches and then displays the Yahoo.com weather page for the current city, as shown in Figure 12-19.

Figure 12-18: The six-day forecast for Austin, TX.

Figure 12-19: Detailed weather on Yahoo.com is just a tap away.

Part V
The Undiscovered iPhone

The 5th Wave   By Rich Tennant

"Hold on, Barbara. I'm pretty sure there's an app for this."

*T*his part is where we show you what's under the hood and how to configure your iPhone to your liking. Then we look at the things to do if your iPhone ever becomes recalcitrant.

In Chapter 13, we explore every single iPhone setting that's not discussed in depth elsewhere in the book. iPhone offers dozens of different preferences and settings to make your iPhone your very own; by the time you finish with Chapter 13, you'll know how to customize every part of your iPhone that *can* be customized.

We love going on a shopping spree as much as the next guy. Chapter 14 is all about shopping in the App Store, an emporium replete with a gaggle of neat little programs and apps (more than 200,000 of them). Best of all, unlike most of the stores you shop in, a good number of the items can be had for free.

iPhones are well-behaved little beasts for the most part, except when they're not. Like the little girl with the little curl, when they're good they're very, very good, but when they're bad, they're horrid. So Chapter 15 is your comprehensive guide to troubleshooting for the iPhone. It details what to do when almost anything goes wrong, offering step-by-step instructions for specific situations as well as a plethora of tips and techniques you can try if something else goes awry. You may never need Chapter 15 (and we hope you won't), but you'll be very glad we put it here if your iPhone ever goes wonky on you.

13

Setting You Straight on Settings

Are you a control freak? The type of person who must have it your way? Boy, have you landed in the right chapter.

Throughout this book, you have occasion to drop in on Settings, which is kind of the makeover factory for the iPhone. For example, we show you how to open Settings (by tapping its Home screen icon) to set ringtones, change the phone's background or wallpaper, and specify Google, Yahoo!, or Bing as the search engine of choice. We also show you how to alter security settings in Safari, tailor e-mail to your liking, and get a handle on how to fetch or push new data.

©PhotoDisc, Inc.

The Settings area on the iPhone is roughly analogous to the Control Panel in Windows and System Preferences on a Mac.

Because we cover some settings elsewhere, we don't dwell on every setting here. But you can still discover plenty to help you make the iPhone your own.

Sky-High Settings

When you first open Settings, you see the scrollable list shown in Figure 13-1. In all but airplane mode (at the top of the list), a greater-than symbol (>) appears to the right of each listing. This symbol tells you that the listing has a bunch of options. Throughout this chapter, you tap the > symbol to check out those options.

Figure 13-1: Presenting your list of settings.

If you scroll down to the bottom of the Settings list, you may see settings that pertain to some of the specific third-party apps you've added to the iPhone, as shown in Figure 13-1, right. (See Chapter 14 for the scoop on third-party apps.)

Airplane mode

Using a cell phone on an airplane is a no-no. But there's nothing verboten about using an iPod on a plane to listen to music, watch videos, and peek at pictures — at least, after the craft has reached cruising altitude.

So how do you take advantage of the iPhone's built-in iPod (among other capabilities) while temporarily turning off its phone, e-mail, and Internet functions? The answer is, by turning on airplane mode.

To do so, merely tap Airplane Mode on the Settings screen to display On (rather than Off).

That act disables each of the iPhone's wireless radios: Wi-Fi, EDGE, 3G (if applicable), and Bluetooth. While your iPhone is in airplane mode, you can't make or receive calls, surf the Web, watch YouTube, or do anything else that requires an Internet connection. The good news is that airplane mode keeps your battery running longer — particularly useful if your flight is taking you halfway around the world.

The appearance of a tiny airplane icon on the status bar in the top-left corner reminds you that airplane mode is turned on. Just remember to turn it off when you're back on the ground.

If you plug the iPhone into an iPod accessory that isn't necessarily compatible because of possible interference from the iPhone's wireless radios, you may see a message like the one shown in Figure 13-2. If you do, consider turning on airplane mode.

Wi-Fi

As we mention in Chapter 10, Wi-Fi is typically the fastest wireless network you can use to surf the Web, send e-mail, and perform other Internet tricks on the iPhone. You use the Wi-Fi setting to determine which Wi-Fi networks are available to you and which one to exploit based on its signal.

Tap Wi-Fi and all Wi-Fi networks in range are displayed, as shown in Figure 13-3. (Alternatively, you can reach this screen by tapping General, tapping Network, and then tapping Wi-Fi.)

Figure 13-2: In this case, airplane mode might be a good idea.

Figure 13-3: Checking out your Wi-Fi options.

A signal-strength indicator can help you choose the network to connect to if more than one is listed; tap the appropriate Wi-Fi network when you reach a decision. If a network is password-protected, you see a lock icon.

You can also turn on or off the Ask to Join Networks setting. Networks that the iPhone is already familiar with are joined automatically, regardless of which one you choose. If the Ask feature is on, you're asked before joining a new network. If it's off, you have to select a network manually.

If you used a particular network automatically in the past but no longer want your iPhone to join it, tap the > symbol next to the network in question (within Wi-Fi settings), and then tap Forget This Network. The iPhone develops a quick case of selective amnesia.

In some instances, you have to supply other technical information about a network you hope to glom on to. You encounter a bunch of nasty-sounding terms: DHCP, BootP, Static, IP address, Subnet Mask, Router, DNS, Search Domains, Client ID, HTTP proxy, and Renew Lease. (At least this last one has nothing to do with real estate or the vehicle you're driving.) Chances are that none of this info is on the tip of your tongue — but that's okay. For one thing, it's a good bet that you'll never need to know this stuff. What's more, even if you *do* have to fill in or adjust these settings, a network administrator or techie friend can probably help.

Sometimes, you may want to connect to a network that's closed and not shown on the Wi-Fi list. If that's the case, tap Other and use the keyboard to enter the network name. Then tap to choose the type of security setting the network is using (if any). Your choices are WEP, WPA, WPA2, WPA Enterprise, and WPA2 Enterprise. Again, it's not exactly the friendliest terminology, but we figure that someone nearby can provide assistance.

If no Wi-Fi network is available, you have to rely on 3G or EDGE. If they aren't available either, you can't rocket into cyberspace until you regain access to a network.

Settings for Your Senses

The next bunch of settings control what the iPhone looks like and sounds like.

Notifications

App developers can send you alerts related to the programs you've installed on your iPhone by exploiting the Apple Push Notification service. Such alerts are typically in text form but may include sounds as well. Or they may appear in a little circle affixed to the app icon as numbered badges. You can receive such alerts even when the app isn't running. If you find alerts intrusive or distracting or merely want to preserve battery life — yep, notifications can sap some juice — turn off all notifications globally by tapping Notifications on the Settings screen and then tapping the switch so that it reads Off.

You can turn off notifications for individual apps. Simply tap an app in the list below the global Notifications setting, as shown in Figure 13-4, and turn on or off the app's sounds, alerts, or badges.

Figure 13-4: Notify the iPhone of your Notifications intentions.

Sounds

Consider the Sounds settings area as the iPhone's soundstage. There, you can turn on or off audio alerts for a variety of functions: new voicemail messages, new text messages, new mail, sent mail, and calendar alerts. And you can set ringtones here.

You can also decide whether you want to hear lock sounds and keyboard clicks. In addition, you can determine whether the iPhone should vibrate when you receive a call. And, you can drag the volume slider to determine the loudness of your ringer and alerts. Note that you can instead use the physical volume buttons on the side of the iPhone to change the volume of the ringer and alerts, as long as you're not already on a call or using the iPod to listen to music or watch video.

Figure 13-5: Sliding this control adjusts screen brightness.

Brightening up your day

Who doesn't want a bright, vibrant screen? Alas, the brightest screens exact a trade-off: Before you drag the brightness slider shown in Figure 13-5 to the max, remember that brighter screens sap the life from your battery more quickly.

We recommend tapping the Auto-Brightness control so that it's on. This control adjusts the screen according to the lighting conditions around the iPhone while being considerate of your battery.

Wallpaper

Choosing wallpaper is a neat way to dress up the iPhone according to your taste. You can sample the pretty patterns and designs that the iPhone has already chosen for you by tapping the thumbnails shown in Figure 13-6. But stunning as they are, these images may not hold a candle to the masterpieces in your own photo albums (more about those in Chapter 9). After making a selection, tap the image, and then tap Set. You can set wallpaper for the Home screen, the Lock screen, or both by tapping the appropriate button.

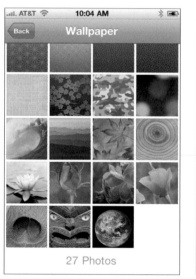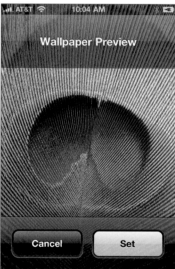

Figure 13-6: Choosing a masterpiece background.

In General

Certain miscellaneous settings are difficult to pigeonhole. Apple wisely lumped these under the General settings moniker. Figure 13-7 gives you a look at them all.

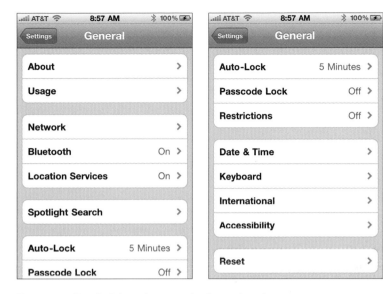

Figure 13-7: You find these items on the General settings screen.

About About

You aren't seeing double. This section is all about the setting known as About. And About is full of trivial (and not-so-trivial) information *about* the device. What you find here is straightforward:

- ✔ **Name of your network**
- ✔ **Number of songs stored on the device**
- ✔ **Number of videos**
- ✔ **Number of photos**
- ✔ **Number of apps**
- ✔ **Storage capacity used and available:** Because of the way the device is formatted, you always have a little less storage than the advertised amount of flash memory.
- ✔ **Software version:** We were up to version 4.0 as this book was being published. But in parentheses next to the version number, you also see a number such as 8A293, which is the build number of the software version you have. The build number changes whenever the iPhone's software is updated.

- **Carrier:** Yep, that's AT&T in the United States.

- **Model and serial numbers**

- **Wi-Fi address**

- **Bluetooth address:** More on Bluetooth shortly.

- **IMEI and ICCID:** Say what? These abbreviations stand for the International Mobile Equipment Identity and Integrated Circuit Card Identifier (or smart card) numbers, respectively. Hey, we warned you some of this was trivial.

- **Modern firmware:** The version of the cellular transmitter.

- **Legal and Regulatory:** You had to know that the lawyers would get their two cents in somehow. All the fine print is here. And *fine print* it is. Although you can flick to scroll these lengthy legal notices, you can't pinch the screen to enlarge the text. (Not that we can imagine more than a handful of you will bother to read this legal mumbo jumbo.)

Using Usage

Think of the Usage setting as one of the places to go on the iPhone for statistics about how you employ the device. You find other information in the About setting (under General on the Settings screen), described in the preceding section.

You can scroll up or down the Usage list to discover the following information:

- **Battery Percentage:** How much of your battery is charged in percentage terms. The percentage appears just to the left of the battery gauge at the upper-right corner of the iPhone. You can display the battery percentage only on the iPhone 3GS and 4 models.

- **The amount of time since you last fully charged your iPhone:** Indicated in days and hours, for the time when the iPhone has been unlocked and in use and also when it has been in standby mode.

- **Call time:** Shown for the current period and for the lifetime of the product.

- **Cellular Network Data:** The amount of network data you sent and received over EDGE or 3G. You can reset these statistics by tapping the Reset Statistics button at the bottom of the screen.

Network

A few major controls appear under the Network setting, one of which, Wi-Fi, we address earlier in this chapter and in Chapter 10. The others are Enable 3G, Cellular Data, Data Roaming, Set Up Internet Tethering, and VPN. We tackle them one by one in this section.

Enable 3G

As you're aware by now, the major benefit of the AT&T 3G network is that it's a lot faster than EDGE (though still not as zippy as Wi-Fi). Regardless, you're not always going to be carrying the iPhone in a 3G area — and even when you are in range, you don't always need to take advantage of faster data speeds. Under these circumstances, tap the Enable 3G button so that Off is showing. Why turn off 3G? The faster network also drains your battery much faster. Tap Enable 3G to turn the network back on when you need to.

The Enable 3G option turns up on only the iPhone 3G, 3GS, and 4 models.

Cellular Data

Turn off the Cellular Data option if you don't want to exhaust your cellular minutes. Of course, turning off this setting means you can access the Internet only through Wi-Fi.

Data Roaming

You may unwittingly rack up lofty roaming fees when using Safari, exchanging e-mails, and engaging in other data-heavy activities while traveling abroad. Turn off data roaming to avoid those excess charges.

Set Up Internet Tethering

When tethering is turned on, you can share the iPhone's Internet connection with a PC via Bluetooth or USB. As of this writing, AT&T was charging $20 a month on top of your regular data plan for this service.

We're sad to report that, as of this writing, you can't use the tethering feature on the iPhone to provide an Internet connection for its close sibling, the iPad.

VPN

A *virtual private network,* or *VPN,* is a way for you to securely access your company's network behind the firewall — using an encrypted Internet connection that acts as a secure "tunnel" for data. The iPhone software supports the protocols *L2TP* (Layer 2 Tunneling Protocol), *PPTP* (Point-to-Point Tunneling Protocol), and Cisco *IPSec VPN,* which apparently provides the kind of security that satisfies network administrators.

You can configure a VPN on the iPhone by tapping VPN under Network, tapping Add VPN Configuration, and then tapping one of the aforementioned protocols. Then, using configuration settings provided by your company, fill in the appropriate server information, account, password, encryption level (if appropriate), and other information. Better yet, lend your iPhone to the techies where you work and let them fill in the blanks on your behalf.

After you configure your iPhone for VPN usage, you can turn that capability on or off by tapping (yep) the VPN On or Off switch under Settings.

Bluetooth

Of all the peculiar terms you may encounter in techdom, *Bluetooth* is one of our favorites. The name is derived from a tenth-century Danish king named Harald Blåtand, who, the story goes, helped unite warring factions. And, we're told, *Blåtand* translates to *Bluetooth* in English. (Bluetooth is all about collaboration between different types of devices — get it?)

Blåtand was obviously ahead of his time. Although he never dialed a cell phone, he now has an entire short-range wireless technology named in his honor. On the iPhone, you can use Bluetooth to communicate wirelessly with a compatible Bluetooth headset or hands-free car kit. These optional headsets and kits are made by Apple and many others. They've become more of a big deal as a number of states and municipalities around the United States make it illegal to hold a phone to your mouth and ear to gab while you're driving. To ensure that the iPhone works with one of these devices, it has to be wirelessly *paired,* or coupled, with the chosen device. With the optional iPhone Bluetooth headset that Apple sells, you can automatically pair the devices by placing the iPhone and headset in a *dual dock* (supplied with the headset), which you connect to your computer.

If you're using a third-party accessory, follow the instructions that came with that headset or car kit so that it becomes *discoverable,* or ready to be paired with your iPhone. Then turn on Bluetooth (under General on the Settings screen) so that the iPhone can find such nearby devices and the device can find the iPhone. Bluetooth works up to a range of about 30 feet.

 You know Bluetooth is turned on when you see the Bluetooth icon on the status bar. If the symbol is blue or white, the iPhone is communicating wirelessly with a connected device. (The color differences provide contrast to whatever is behind the icon.) If it's gray, Bluetooth is turned on in the iPhone *but* a paired device isn't nearby or isn't turned on.

To unpair a device, tap it from the device list shown in Figure 13-8 so that the word Connected becomes Not Connected. Tap the device again to reconnect.

To divorce a Bluetooth device from the iPhone, tap the right arrow in the blue circle to the right of the Bluetooth you're unceremoniously dumping. On the next screen, tap Forget This Device. At least you won't have to pay alimony.

iOS 3 and 4 provide support for *stereo* Bluetooth headphones, car kits, and other accessories, so you can stream stereo audio from the iPhone to those devices. Sadly, stereo Bluetooth still doesn't work on the original iPhone.

The iPhone can tap into Bluetooth in other ways. One is through *peer-to-peer* connectivity, in which you can engage in multiplayer games with other nearby iPhone users. You can also do such things as exchange business cards, share pictures, and send short notes. And, you don't even have to pair the devices, as you do with a headset or car kit.

What's more, you can use an Apple Wireless Keyboard or other Bluetooth keyboard (on the 3GS or 4 models) to more easily type on the iPhone.

 You still can't use Bluetooth to exchange files or sync between an iPhone and a computer. Nor can you use it to print stuff from the iPhone on a Bluetooth printer. That's because the iPhone doesn't support any Bluetooth profiles (or specifications) required to allow such wireless stunts to take place.

Location services

Location, location, location. By using Maps, through (several) apps, and by geotagging photos taken with its camera, the iPhone makes good use of knowing where you are. The iPhone 3G, 3GS, and 4 models exploit built-in GPS, but even the first-generation iPhone can find your general whereabouts (by *triangulating* signals from Wi-Fi base stations and cellular towers).

If that statement creeps you out a little, don't fret. To protect your right to privacy, individual apps pop up quick messages (similar to the one shown in Figure 13-9), asking whether you want them to use your current location. But you can also turn off Location Services right in Settings. Not only is your privacy shielded, but you also keep your iPhone battery juiced a little longer.

You can also allow individual apps to determine your approximate location. Any app that requested your whereabouts within the last 24 hours will display the location services icon next to its name in the Location Services screen in Settings. When an app is using your location, that icon — it resembles a tiny arrowhead — appears in the status bar at the top of the screen.

Figure 13-8: Falling out of love — tap an item so you're no longer connected.

Figure 13-9: The Where app wants to know where you are.

Auto-lock

You can set the amount of time that elapses before the phone automatically locks or turns off the display. Your choices are Five Minutes Before, Four Minutes Before, and so on, all the way down to One Minute. Or, you can choose to have the iPhone never lock automatically.

If you work for a company that insists on a passcode (see the next section), the Never Auto-Lock option isn't on the list your iPhone shows you.

Don't worry if the iPhone is locked. You can still receive calls and text messages and adjust the volume.

Passcode

You can select a passcode to prevent people from unlocking the iPhone. Tap Passcode Lock. Then use the virtual keypad to enter a 4-digit code. During this setup, you have to enter the code a second time before it's accepted.

You can also determine whether a passcode is required immediately, After 1 Minute, After 5 Minutes, or After 15 Minutes. Shorter times are more secure, of course. On the topic of security, the iPhone can be set to automatically erase your data if you (or someone else!) make ten failed passcode attempts.

Your settings will be reset to their defaults and all your media and information might as well be dust.

You can also change the passcode or turn it off later (unless your employer dictates otherwise), but you need to know the present passcode to apply any changes. If you forget the passcode, you have to restore the iPhone software, as described in Chapter 15.

The iPhone has two kinds of passcodes. A simple passcode is a four-digit number. If you require a more stringent password — one that is much harder to guess — turn off the simple passcode and come up with something much more difficult to crack, a longer combination of letters, numbers, punctuation, and special characters.

Under Passcode Lock settings on the 3GS and 4, you have the option to turn on or off voice dialing.

Restrictions

Parents and bosses may love the Restrictions tools, but kids and employees usually think otherwise. You can clamp down, um, provide proper parental guidance to your children by preventing them at least some of the time from using the Safari browser, YouTube, Location Services, the camera, FaceTime, or iTunes. Or, you might not let them install new apps or make purchases in the apps you do allow. When restrictions are in place, icons for off-limit functions can no longer be seen.

For instance, you can allow Junior to watch a movie on the iPhone but prevent him from watching a flick that carries an R or NC-17 rating. You can also restrict access to certain TV shows and apps, based on age-appropriate ratings. Stop feeling guilty: You have your users' best interests at heart.

Home button (3G only)

On the iPhone 3GS and iPhone 4, double-pressing the Home button summons the multitasking tray, which we introduce in Chapter 2. On the iPhone 3G, you can specify what happens when you double-press Home. (Thus, you won't see the Home button setting on newer models.) iPhone 3G owners can set it so that double-pressing the Home button displays the Home screen, Search screen, Phone Favorites, Camera app, or iPod app.

Date and time

In our neck of the woods, the time is reported as 11:32 PM (or whatever time it happens to be). But in some circles, it's reported as 23:32. If you prefer the latter format on the iPhone's status bar, tap the 24-Hour Time setting (under Date & Time) to turn on the setting.

This setting is just one that you can adjust under Date & Time. You can also have the iPhone set the time automatically, using the time reported by the cellular network (and adjusted for your time zone).

If automatic time-setting is turned off, you're asked to select the time zone and then set the date and time manually. Here's how:

1. **Tap Set Automatically so that it's off.**

   You see fields for setting the time zone and the date and time.

2. **Tap the Time Zone field.**

   The current time zone and virtual keyboard are shown.

3. **Tap out the letters of the city or country whose time zone you want to enter until the one you have in mind appears. Then tap the name of that city or country.**

   The Time Zone field is automatically filled in for that city.

4. **Tap the Set Date & Time field so that the time is shown. Then roll the bicycle-lock-like controls until the proper time is displayed.**

5. **Tap the date shown so that the bicycle-lock-like controls pop up for the date. Then roll the wheels for the month, day, and year until the correct date appears.**

6. **Tap the Date & Time button to return to the main Date & Time settings screen.**

Keyboard

Under Keyboard settings, you can turn on or off autocapitalization and turn on or off Enable Caps Lock.

Autocapitalization, which the iPhone turns on by default, means that the first letter of the first word you type after ending the preceding sentence with a period, a question mark, or an exclamation point is capitalized.

If Cap Locks is enabled, all letters are uppercased LIKE THIS if you double-tap the shift key. (The shift key is the one with the arrow pointing north.)

You can also turn on a keyboard setting that inserts a period followed by a space when you double-tap the Space key. Additionally, you can choose to use an international keyboard (as discussed in Chapter 2), which you select from the International setting — the next setting after Keyboard in the General settings area. As you might have surmised, this is also the area where you can turn on or off the keyboard's autocorrection smarts.

International

The iPhone is an international sensation. It's sold and used around the world by people of all nationalities. In the International section, you can set the language you type on (by using a custom virtual keyboard), the language in which the iPhone displays text, and the language in which it speaks through Voice Control. Heck, you can even select a different region format (from among numerous countries) and a different calendar type, among Gregorian, Japanese, Buddhist, and Republic of China.

Accessibility

The Accessibility tools (available on the 3GS and 4 only) are targeted at people with certain disabilities:

- **VoiceOver:** A screen reader describes aloud what's on the screen. The screen reader can read e-mail messages, Web pages, and more.

- **Zoom:** This tool is a screen magnifier for those who are visually challenged. To zoom, double-tap the screen with *three* fingers, and drag three fingers to move around the screen.

- **White on Black:** This tool reverses the colors on the iPhone to provide a higher contrast for people with poor eyesight.

- **Mono Audio:** If you suffer hearing loss in one ear, the iPhone can combine the right and left audio channels so that both can be heard in both earbuds.

- **Speak Auto-Text:** When this setting is on, the iPhone automatically speaks autocorrections and capitalizations.

- **Triple-press the Home Button:** As you know by now, double-pressing the Home button launches multitasking. But you can set up the iPhone so that triple-pressing the button (pressing three times really fast) turns on certain Accessibility features. By doing so, you can turn VoiceOver on or off, Zoom on or off, or White on Black on or off.

Reset

As little kids playing sports, we ended an argument by agreeing to a "do-over." Well, the Reset settings on the iPhone are one big do-over. Now that we're (presumably) grown up, we're wise enough to think long and hard about the consequences before implementing do-over settings. Regardless, you may encounter good reasons for starting over; some of these are addressed in Chapter 15.

Here are your reset options:

- **Reset All Settings:** Resets all settings, but no data or media is deleted.

- **Erase All Content and Settings:** Resets all settings *and* wipes out all your data.

- **Reset Network Settings:** Deletes the current network settings and restores them to their factory defaults.

- **Reset Keyboard Dictionary:** Removes added words from the dictionary. As we point out early on, the iPhone keyboard is intelligent. And one reason it's so smart is that it learns from you. So when you reject words that the iPhone keyboard suggests, it figures that the words you specifically banged out ought to be added to the keyboard dictionary.

  This option deletes *all* the words you've added to the keyboard dictionary, so it will make your keyboard stupider instead of smarter. We suggest that you think twice before you invoke this option.

- **Reset Home Screen Layout:** Reverts all icons to the way they were at the factory.

- **Reset Location Warnings:** Restores factory defaults.

Phoning In More Settings

We cover most of the remaining settings in earlier chapters devoted to e-mail, calendars, the iPod (photos and music), Safari, and e-mail. Still, we didn't get to a few other settings — 'til now.

Sorting and displaying contacts

Do you think of us as Ed and Bob or Baig and LeVitus? The answer to that question will probably determine whether you choose to sort your Contacts list alphabetically by last name or first.

Tap Mail, Contacts, Calendars; scroll down to the Contacts section; and peek at Sort Order. Then tap Last; First; or First, Last.

You can also determine whether you want to display a first name or last name first. Tap Display Order, and then choose First; Last; or Last, First.

While you're at it, check out the Default Account setting under the Contacts settings. If you create new contacts outside a specific account, the default account you select here is the account to which the new contact will be added.

Nothing phone-y about these settings

In Chapter 4, we tip our hand and indicate that we save a few more phone tricks — those found in Phone settings — for this chapter.

Tap Phone now to review some of the choices we don't get to in that chapter. Be aware that you have to scroll down the screen to find Phone settings.

Call forwarding

If you expect to spend time in an area with poor or no cell phone coverage, you may want to temporarily forward calls to a landline or other portable handset. Here are the simple steps:

1. **On the Settings screen, tap Phone and then tap Call Forwarding.**

2. **Tap to turn on Call Forwarding.**

3. **Use the virtual keypad to enter the number where you want incoming calls to ring.**

4. **Tap the Call Forwarding button to return to the main Call Forwarding screen.**

To change the forwarding number, tap the circle with the X in the Phone Number field to get rid of the old number, and then enter a new one.

Remember to turn off Call Forwarding to receive calls directly on your iPhone again.

You must have cellular coverage while setting the Call Forwarding feature.

Call waiting

Tap the Call Waiting button to turn the feature on or off. If Call Waiting is off and you're speaking on the phone, the call is automatically dispatched to voicemail.

Caller ID

Don't want your name or number displayed on the phone you're calling? Make sure to tap Show My Caller ID so that it's off. If privacy isn't a concern, you can leave this setting on.

TTY

Folks who are hearing impaired sometimes rely on a teletype, or TTY, machine, to hold conversations. You can use the iPhone with standard TTY devices by plugging a cable from the TTY device into an optional $19 iPhone TTY adapter, and then plugging the adapter into the iPhone. Make sure the TTY setting on the phone is turned on.

SIM locking

The tiny SIM (Subscriber Identity Module) card inside your iPhone holds your phone number and other important data. Tap to turn on SIM PIN and enter a password with the keypad. Then, if someone gets hold of your SIM, he or she can't use it in another phone without the password.

If you assign a PIN to your SIM, you have to enter it to turn the iPhone off and on again.

AT&T Services

A major difference between the iPhone and all the other Apple products you might buy is that you enter into a relationship with not only Apple but also the phone company when you have an iPhone. Tap AT&T Services and then tap any of the following options for a shortcut phone call:

- **Check Bill Balance:** The phone dials *225# and, if all goes according to plan, you receive a text message with the due date and sum owed. This type of text message isn't counted against your messaging allotment.

- **Call Directory Assistance:** The phone dials 411.

- **Pay My Bill:** The iPhone dials *729 and you're connected to an automated voice system. You can pay your bill with a checking account, debit card, or credit card by following the voice prompts.

You're billed for phone service *from AT&T,* not from Apple. Of course, charges for any music or other content purchased in iTunes from your computer are paid to Apple through whichever credit card you have on file, as with any iPod.

- **View My Minutes:** This time, *646# is called. You again receive a text reply that doesn't count against your messaging allotment.

- **Voice Connect:** The iPhone dials *08 to connect you to automated news, weather, sports, quotes, and more. Just bark out the kind of information you're looking for, such as finance, and follow voice prompts for stock quotes and business news, for example. Or, say "Sports" and follow the voice prompts to see the latest scores of your favorite team.

Not all AT&T Services make a phone call. If you tap the AT&T MyAccount button, Safari opens an AT&T account management page on the Web.

Nike + iPod

You're passionate about fitness. You're equally passionate about music. In the summer of 2006, Apple teamed with the folks at Nike on a $29 wireless sports kit that lets runners place a sensor inside a Nike sneaker that can wirelessly communicate with a receiver connected to an iPod Nano. As runners dash off, they can track time, distance, and calories burned on the Nano, receive vocal feedback, and upload results to a Nike Web site. Runners can even play a select "power song" on the iPod for that last push when they're feeling exhausted.

Apple added the Nike + app to the iPhone 3GS and 4 (but not to earlier models). When you turn on the app in Settings, your iPhone can record every step you make. You don't have to connect a separate receiver, as you do on the Nano. By using Nike + on your iPhone, you can select one of the workout routines shown in Figure 13-10.

Figure 13-10: Born to run with your iPhone.

Find My iPhone

We hope you never have to use the Find My iPhone feature — though we have to say that it's pretty darn cool. If you inadvertently leave your iPhone in a taxi or restaurant, Find My iPhone may just help you retrieve it. The feature requires a MobileMe subscription.

To turn on Find My iPhone, tap Mail, Contacts, Calendars, and then tap the me.com e-mail account you added to the iPhone. (You get a me.com e-mail account when you join MobileMe.) Refer to Chapter 11 to see how to add an e-mail account to the iPhone. Make sure the Find My iPhone setting is turned on.

Now suppose that you lost your phone — and we can only assume that you're beside yourself. Log in to your MobileMe me.com account from any browser on your computer. Click Find My iPhone.

Apple now supplies a free Find My iPhone app in the App Store. So you could use an iPhone loaded with this app to locate another iPhone (or iPad). You still need a MobileMe subscription.

Assuming that your lost phone is turned on and in the coverage area, its general whereabouts should appear on a map, as shown in Figure 13-11. In our tests, Find My iPhone found our iPhones quickly.

Figure 13-11: Locating a lost iPhone.

The truth is that even seeing your iPhone on a map may not help you much, especially if the phone is lost somewhere in midtown Manhattan. Take heart. At the MobileMe site, click Display a Message and then bang out a plea to the Good Samaritan whom you hope picked up your phone. The message appears on the lost iPhone's screen. Don't forget to include in the message a way for the person to reach you, such as the message displayed on the iPhone in Figure 13-12.

Figure 13-12: An appeal to return the phone.

To get someone's attention, you can also sound an alarm that plays for two minutes, even if the phone was in silent mode. Hey, that alarm may come in handy if the phone turns up under a couch in your house.

After all this labor, if the phone is seemingly gone for good, click Remote Wipe at the MobileMe site to delete your personal data from afar and return the iPhone to its factory settings. And, if you ever get your phone back afterward, you can always restore the information with an iTunes backup on your PC or Mac.

We trust that you control freaks are satisfied with all the stuff you can manage in Settings. Still, the iPhone may not always behave as you want. For the times when things get *out* of control, we highly recommend Chapter 15.

Apps-O-Lutely!

*O*ne of the best things about the iPhone these days is that you can download and install apps created by third parties, which is to say not created by Apple (the first party) or you (the second party). At the time of this writing, more than 225,000 apps are available and well over 2,000,000,000 (yes, 2 billion) apps have been downloaded. Some apps are free, other apps cost money; some apps are useful, other apps are lame; some apps are perfectly well-behaved, other apps quit unexpectedly (or worse) The point is that of the many apps out there, some are better than others.

In this chapter, we take a broad look at iPhone apps. Don't worry: We have plenty to say about specific apps in Chapters 16 and 17.

You can obtain and install apps for your iPhone in two ways:

✔ On your computer

✔ On your iPhone

To use the App Store on your iPhone, it must be connected to the Internet. And, if you obtain an app on your computer, it isn't available on your iPhone until you sync it with your computer.

But before you can use the App Store on your iPhone or computer, you need an iTunes Store account. If you don't already have one, we suggest that you launch iTunes on your computer, click Sign In near the upper-right corner of the iTunes window, then click Create New Account, and then follow the on-screen instructions. Or, if you prefer to create your account on your iPhone rather than on your computer, follow the instructions near the end of Chapter 7.

Let's put it this way: If you don't have an iTunes Store account, you can't download a single cool app for your iPhone. 'Nuff said.

Using Your Computer to Find Apps

Okay, start by finding cool iPhone apps using iTunes on your computer. Follow these steps:

1. **Launch iTunes.**

2. **Click the iTunes Store in the source list on the left.**

3. **Click the App Store link.**

   The iTunes App Store appears.

4. **Click the iPhone button at the top of the screen (as opposed to the iPad button).**

   The iPhone App section of the App Store appears, as shown in Figure 14-1.

Looking for apps from your computer

After you have the iTunes App Store on your screen and have clicked the iPhone button so that you're looking at iPhone apps and not iPad apps, you have a couple of options for exploring its virtual aisles. Allow us to introduce you to the various "departments" available from the main screen.

Browsing the iPhone App Store screen

The main departments are featured in the middle of the screen, and ancillary departments appear on either side of them. We start with the ones in the middle:

- The **New and Noteworthy** department has 16 visible icons (starting with NCAA Football to My Photo Album in Figure 14-1), representing apps that are — what else? — new and noteworthy.

  Only 16 icons are visible, but the New and Noteworthy department has more than that. Look to the right of the words *New and Noteworthy*. See the words *See All?* That's a link; if you click it, you'll see *all* apps in this department on a single screen. Or you can drag the scroll bar at the bottom of the New and Noteworthy section to the right to see more icons.

✔ The **What's Hot** department also displays 16 icons (G4 to Duplicam Camera in Figure 14-1), representing apps that are popular with other iPhone users. Note the See All link and scroll bar for this department, either of which you can use to see more apps that are hot.

✔ The **Staff Favorites** department, which appears below the What's Hot department, is not visible in Figure 14-1. The same drill applies to its See All link and scroll bar.

Figure 14-1: The iTunes App Store, in all its glory.

Apple has a habit of redecorating the iTunes Stores every so often, so allow us to apologize in advance if things aren't exactly as described here.

You also see a large display ad at the top of the screen (I Am T-Pain in Figure 14-1) and six featured links between the New and Noteworthy department and the What's Hot department (Hot New Games to iBooks in Figure 14-1). Some of these link to specific apps (such as The Elements); others link to a group of apps with a theme, such as Hot New Games, Soccer, and iBooks.

Three Top Charts departments appear to the right of the main ones: Paid Apps, Free Apps (one of our favorite departments), and Top Grossing Apps, which is not visible in Figure 14-1. The number-one app in each department is displayed as both an icon and its name; the next nine apps show text links only.

Finally, the black App Store button near the top of the screen is also a drop-down menu (as are most of the other department links to its left and right). If you click and hold on most of these department links, a menu with a list of the department's categories appears. For example, if you click and hold on the App Store link, you can choose specific categories such as Books, Business, Education, Entertainment, and others from the drop-down menu, allowing you to bypass the App Store home page and go directly to that category.

Using the Search field

Browsing the screen is helpful, but if you know exactly what you're looking for, we have good news and bad news. The good news is that there's a faster way than browsing: Just type a word or phrase in the Search Store field in the upper-right corner of the main iTunes window, as shown in Figure 14-2, and then press Enter or Return to initiate the search.

The bad news is that you have to search the entire iTunes Store, which includes music, television shows, movies, and other stuff in addition to iPhone apps.

Ah, but we have more good news: Your search results are segregated into categories — one of which is iPhone Apps (refer to Figure 14-2). And, here's even more good news: If you click the See All link to the right of the words *iPhone Apps,* all iPhone apps that match your search word or phrase appear.

Click the little downward-facing triangle to the right of each item's price to display a drop-down menu. The menu for the first Flashlight app in Figure 14-2 lets you add the product to your wish list, send an e-mail with a link to this product, copy the link to this product to the Clipboard so you can paste it elsewhere, or share it on Facebook or Twitter.

Figure 14-2: I want to use my iPhone as a flashlight, so I searched for the word *flashlight.*

Getting more information about an app

Now that you know how to find apps in the App Store, this section delves
a little deeper and shows you how to get additional info about an app that
interests you.

Checking out the detail screen from your computer

To find out more about an app icon, a featured app, or a text link on any of
the iTunes App Store screens, just click it. A detail screen like the one shown
in Figure 14-3 appears.

This screen should tell you most of what you need to know about the app,
such as basic product information and a narrative description, what's new
in this version, the language it's presented in, and the system requirements
to run the app. Click the blue More links to the right of the Description and
What's New sections to expand them and see additional details.

Rating

Free App button

More links

Figure 14-3: The detail screen for Pocket Legends, a nifty free game for your iPhone.

Bear in mind that the app description on this screen was written by the app's developer and may be somewhat biased. Never fear, gentle reader: In the next section, we show you how to find reviews of the app written by people who have used it.

Notice that this app is rated 9+, as you can see below the Free App button shown in Figure 14-3. And just below the rating is the reason for that rating: Frequent/Intense Cartoon or Fantasy Violence.

Following is a list of the ratings as of this writing:

- **4+:** Contains no objectionable material.

- **9+:** May contain mild or infrequent occurrences of cartoon, fantasy, or realistic violence; or infrequent or mild mature, suggestive, or horror-themed content that may not be suitable for children under the age of 9.

- **12+:** May contain infrequent mild language; frequent or intense cartoon, fantasy, or realistic violence; mild or infrequent mature or suggestive themes; or simulated gambling that may not be suitable for children under the age of 12.

- **17+:** May contain frequent and intense offensive language; frequent and intense cartoon, fantasy, or realistic violence; mature, frequent, and intense mature, suggestive, or horror-themed content; sexual content; nudity; depictions of alcohol, tobacco, or drugs that may not be suitable for children under the age of 17. You must be at least 17 years old to purchase games with this rating.

One other feature of the detail pages that's worth mentioning is that most apps include one or more useful links, right below the app description. In Figure 14-3, one link goes to the Web site of the developer (Spacetime Studios), and the other links to the Pocket Legends Support Web pages. We urge you to explore such links at your leisure.

Reading reviews from your computer

If you scroll down the detail screen, near the bottom you find a series of reviews by the app's users. (You can see the summary of customer ratings but not the actual reviews in Figure 14-3.) Each review includes a star rating, from zero to five. If an app is rated four or higher, it is probably well liked by people who own it.

As you can see, Pocket Legends has an average rating of 3½ stars based on 2,091 user reviews (19,405 reviews for all versions of the app). You'll find three or four recent reviews with their star ratings if you scroll down this page a little, and below them a link to even more user reviews.

Downloading an app

Downloading an app is simple. When you find an app you want to try, just click its Get App or Buy App button. At that point, you have to log in to your iTunes Store account, even if the app is free.

After you log in, the app begins downloading. When the app has finished downloading, it appears in the Apps section of your iTunes library, as shown in Figure 14-4.

We are using the Grid view for the apps in Figure 14-4, but you can view your apps in two other ways, namely List view and Cover Flow view. To change views, click one of the three icons just to the left of the search field (labeled in Figure 14-4). Also note the two buttons below the icons, which say Apps (selected in Figure 14-4) and Genres. These provide two additional ways to look at your collection of apps; we suggest you try 'em all.

Figure 14-4: Apps you downloaded appear in the Apps section of your iTunes library.

Downloading an app to your iTunes library from your computer is only the first half of getting it onto your iPhone. After you download an app, you have to sync your iPhone before the app will be available on it.

Updating an app

Every so often, the developer of an iPhone app releases an update. Sometimes these updates add new features to the app, sometimes they squash bugs, and sometimes they do both. In any event, updates are usually a good thing for you and your iPhone, so it makes sense to check for them every so often. To do this on your computer using iTunes, click the Check for Updates link near the lower-right corner of the App screen.

If you click the Get More Apps link at the bottom of the screen, you find your-self back at the main screen of the iTunes App Store (refer to Figure 14-1).

Using Your iPhone to Find Apps

Finding apps with your iPhone is almost as easy as finding them by using iTunes. The only requirement is that you have an Internet connection of some sort — Wi-Fi or wireless data network — to browse, search, download, and install apps.

To get started, tap the App Store icon on your iPhone's Home screen. After you launch the App Store, you see five icons at the bottom of the screen, rep-resenting five ways to interact with the store, as shown in Figure 14-5.

Looking for apps from your iPhone

The first three icons at the bottom of the screen — Featured, Categories, and Top 25 — offer three ways to browse the virtual shelves of the App Store.

Browsing the iPhone App Store

The Featured section has three tabs at the top of the screen: New (refer to Figure 14-5), What's Hot, and Genius. These three tabs represent three differ-ent pages full of apps. Genius is a new feature and perhaps the most interest-ing tab of all — it suggests apps you might enjoy based on the apps currently installed on your iPhone.

The Categories section works a little differently: It has no tabs, and its main page contains no apps. Instead, it offers a list of categories such as Games, Entertainment, Utilities, Social Networking, and Music, to name a few, as shown in Figure 14-6.

Tap a category to see either a page full of apps of that type or a list of sub-categories for that type. For example, the Games category offers subcatego-ries such as Action, Arcade, Kids, Music, and Puzzle. Other categories have no subcategories — you'll go directly to the page full of apps when you tap them. To make your browsing easier, each category or subcategory page has three tabs — Top Paid, Top Free, and Release Date.

The Top 25 section works much the same as the Featured section. Its three tabs — Top Paid, Top Free, and Top Grossing — represent pages of the most popular apps that either cost money (paid and top grossing) or don't (free).

Each page displays roughly 20 to 25 apps, but you see only 4 or 5 at a time on the screen. Remember to flick up or down if you want to see the others.

Figure 14-5: The icons across the bottom represent the five sections of the App Store.

Figure 14-6: The Categories section lets you browse for apps in categories such as these.

Using the Search icon

Know exactly what you're looking for? Instead of simply browsing, you can tap the Search icon and type a word or phrase.

Finding more information about an app

Now that you know how to find apps in the App Store, the following sections show you how to find additional information about a particular app.

Checking out the detail screen from your iPhone

To find out more about any app on any page, tap the app. You see a detail screen like the one shown in Figure 14-7.

Remember that the app description on this screen was written by the developer and may be somewhat biased.

Reading reviews from your iPhone

Scroll down to the bottom of any detail screen, and you find a star rating for that app. It's also the link to that app's reviews; tap it to see a page full of them. At the bottom of that page is another link: More Reviews. Tap it to see (what else?) more reviews.

Downloading an app

To download an app to your iPhone, tap the price button near the top of its detail screen. In Figure 14-7, the price button is the blue rectangle that says Free. You may or may not be asked to type your iTunes Store account password before the App Store disappears and the Home screen, where the new app's icon will reside, appears in its place. The new icon is slightly dimmed, and appears with a blue progress indicator and the word *Loading* or *Installing,* as shown in Figure 14-8.

Progress bar

Figure 14-7: Remote, the free app from Apple, lets you control iTunes or AppleTV from your iPhone.

Figure 14-8: The blue progress bar indicates that the app is more than halfway through downloading.

By the way, if the app is rated 17+, you see a warning screen after you type your password. You have to tap the OK button to confirm that you're over 17 before the app will download.

The app is now on your iPhone, but it isn't copied to your iTunes library on your Mac or PC until your next sync. If your iPhone suddenly loses its memory (unlikely) or you delete the app from your iPhone before you sync (as described later in this chapter), that app is gone forever. That's the bad news.

The good news is that after you've paid for an app, you can download it again if you need to — from iTunes on your computer or the App Store app on your iPhone — and you don't have to pay for it again.

After you download an app to your iPhone, the app Is transferred to your iTunes Apps library the next time you sync your phone.

Updating an app

As mentioned earlier in this chapter, every so often the developer of an iPhone app releases an update. If one of these is waiting for you, a little number in a circle appears on the App Store icon on your Home screen as well as on the Updates icon at the bottom of the screen. Tap the Updates icon if any of your apps need updating.

If you tap the Updates button and see (in the middle of the screen) the message *All Apps are Up-to-Date,* none of the apps on your iPhone requires an update at this time. If an app needs updating, an Update button appears next to the app. Tap the button to update the app. If more than one app needs updating, you can update them all at once by tapping the Update All button in the upper-right corner of the screen.

If you try to update an app purchased from any iTunes Store account except your own, you're prompted for that account's ID and password. If you can't provide them, you can't download the update.

Working with Apps

That's almost everything you need to know about installing third-party apps on your iPhone. However, you might find it helpful to know how to delete and organize apps.

Deleting an app

You can delete an app in two ways: in iTunes on your computer or directly from your iPhone.

To delete an app in iTunes, click Apps in the source list and then do one of the following:

- ✔ Click the app's icon to select it and then choose Edit➪Delete.
- ✔ Right-click (Control+click on a Mac) the app's icon and choose Delete.

Either way, you see a dialog box asking whether you're sure you want to remove the selected app. If you click the Remove button, the app is removed from your iTunes library, as well as from any iPhone that syncs with your iTunes library.

You can't delete any Apple apps that came with your iPhone, but here's how to delete a third-party app on your iPhone:

1. **Press and hold any icon until all the icons begin to jiggle.**

2. **Tap the little x in the upper-left corner of the app you want to delete, as shown in Figure 14-9.**

   A dialog box appears, informing you that deleting this app also deletes all its data, as shown in Figure 14-10.

3. **Tap the Delete button.**

Deleting an app from your iPhone this way doesn't get rid of it permanently. It remains in your iTunes library until you delete it from iTunes, as described earlier in this chapter. Put another way: Even though you deleted the app from your iPhone, it's still in your iTunes library. If you want to get rid of an app for good and for always after you delete it on your iPhone, you also must delete it from your iTunes library.

Little x

Figure 14-9: Tap an app's little x to mark the app for deletion.

Figure 14-10: Tap Delete to remove the app from your iPhone.

Organizing your apps

You can have up to 11 Home screens (or "pages") of apps. And if you're like many iPhone users, you'll soon have a substantial collection of apps in your iTunes library and on your iPhone. So let's look at a few ways to organize those apps for easy access.

On your computer (in iTunes)

First things first: On your computer, make sure you've selected your iPhone in the Devices section below the iTunes Store on the left side of the iTunes window. Then, click the Apps tab near the top of the window (shown in Figure 14-11).

Scrolling list of Home screens with 9 selected

Sync Apps section   iPhone section displaying Home screen 9

Figure 14-11: Ten screens of apps with screen 9 selected.

You can organize your apps in the following ways:

- ✔ In the iPhone section, you can click and drag an app icon to a new location on the same screen.

- ✔ You can drag an app from the Sync Apps section on the left to any of the 11 screens in the Home screen list on the right, as long as the screen has no empty screens before it. In other words, you can drag an app to screen 7 as long as at least one app each is on screens 1 through 6.

- ✔ You can change the order of screens in the Home screen list by clicking and dragging a screen upward or downward in the list and dropping it in its new location. After you have a few pages worth of apps, give it a try — it's easy and kind of fun.

On your iPhone

To rearrange apps on your iPhone, first press and hold on any app until all the apps begin to jiggle and dance, and the little black "delete me" x's appear. Figure 14-12 shows the screen before (left) and after (right) moving an app. The app you press and hold doesn't have to be the one you want to move — any app will do.

- ✔ To move an app after the jiggling starts, press it, drag it to its new location (other apps on the screen will politely move out of its way to make space for it), and release it, as shown on the right of Figure 14-12.

- ✔ To move an app to a different Home screen after the jiggling starts, press the app and drag it all the way to the left or right edge of the screen. The preceding or next Home screen, respectively, will appear. Keep dragging the app to the left or right edge of each successive Home screen until you reach the screen you want. Then drop the app in its new location on that screen. If the screen already holds 16 apps, the last icon on the page will be pushed to the next Home screen. Be persistent — sometimes it takes a few tries to make the screens switch.

All these techniques for iTunes and iPhones work with apps in the dock: by default, Phone, Safari, Mail, and iPod. In Figure 14-12, we've replaced the Mail app with the Messages app and changed the positions of the iPod and Safari icons, so our dock probably looks different than yours.

You can add apps beyond the Home screen 11. To do so, just keep selecting check boxes for apps in the Sync Apps section after all 11 screens are filled. You won't be able to see the icons for these apps on any Home screen, so you'll have to access them via Spotlight search. On the other hand, because iOS 4 supports up to 2,112 apps on the 11 available Home pages (16 folders per page x 12 apps per folder x 11 available pages = 2,112 apps), you'll probably never need this tip. (If you've forgotten how to create folders, refer to the section on organizing icons into folders in Chapter 2.)

Figure 14-12: The way things were (left), and what happens when we drag the Dr. Bob icon from the bottom row to the top row.

You use the same technique — drag one app on top of another app — to create folders in both iTunes and on your iPhone. And to place an app into an existing folder, you drag that app on top of the folder.

A few more facts about Home screens. We mention this elsewhere, but in case you missed it: The little dots above the four apps in the dock indicate how many Home screens you have. The white dot denotes the Home screen you're currently looking at. So, for example, the dots in Figure 14-12 tell us we're looking at screen 9 of 10 Home screens.

And last but not least, we'd be remiss if we didn't at least provide the following reminders. You can create folders that hold up to 12 apps each, put Spotlight to work to quickly find and launch apps no matter which Home screen they're on, and take advantage of multitasking to quickly switch between recently used apps. If you're hazy on any of these three concepts, we suggest that you flip back to Chapter 2, where they are expounded upon in full and loving detail.

There you have it — you now know everything you need to know to find, install, delete, and organize iPhone apps!

As Steve Jobs is so fond of saying in his keynotes, there is one last thing: In a few pages (Chapters 16 and 17, to be precise), to kick off the famous Part of Tens, we tell you about ten of our favorite free iPhone apps and ten that cost dough.

When Good iPhones Go Bad

*I*n our experience, iPhones are usually reliable devices. And, most users we talk to report trouble-free operation. Notice our use of the word *most*. That's because every so often, a good iPhone goes bad. It's not a common occurrence, but it does happen. So in this chapter, we look at the types of bad things that can happen, along with suggestions for fixing them.

What kind of bad things are we talking about? Well, we're referring to problems involving

- ✔ The phone itself

- ✔ Making or receiving calls

- ✔ Wireless networks

- ✔ Sync, computers (both Mac and PC), or iTunes

After all the troubleshooting, we tell you how to get even more help if nothing we suggest does the trick. Finally, if your iPhone is so badly hosed that it needs to go back to the mother ship for repairs, we offer ways to survive the experience with a minimum of stress or fuss.

©PhotoDisc, Inc.

iPhone Issues

Our first category of troubleshooting techniques applies to an iPhone that's frozen or otherwise acting up. The recommended procedure when this happens is to perform the six *Rs* in sequence:

- ✔ Recharge
- ✔ Restart
- ✔ Reset your iPhone
- ✔ Remove your content
- ✔ Reset settings and content
- ✔ Restore

If your iPhone acts up on you — if it freezes, doesn't wake up from sleep, doesn't do something it used to do, or in any other way acts improperly — don't panic; this section describes the things you should try, in the order that we (and Apple) recommend.

If the first technique doesn't do the trick, go on to the second. If the second one doesn't work, try the third. And so on.

Recharge

If your iPhone acts up in any way, shape, or form, the first thing you should try is to give its battery a full recharge.

Don't plug the iPhone's dock connector–to–USB cable into a USB port on your keyboard, monitor, or USB hub. You need to plug the cable into one of the USB ports on your computer itself, because the USB ports on your computer supply more power than the other ports.

Note that you can use the included USB power adapter to recharge your iPhone from an AC outlet rather than from a computer. So if your iPhone isn't charging when you connect it to your computer, try charging it from a wall outlet instead.

Restart

If you recharge your iPhone and it still misbehaves, the next thing to try is restarting it. Just as restarting a computer often fixes problems, restarting your iPhone sometimes works wonders.

Here's how to restart:

1. **Press and hold the sleep/wake button.**

2. **Slide the red slider to turn off the iPhone, and then wait a few seconds.**

3. **Press and hold the sleep/wake button again until the Apple logo appears on the screen.**

4. **If your phone is still frozen, misbehaves, or doesn't start, do a force-quit as follows, and then try Steps 1–3 again.**

   • If you have a first-generation iPhone or iPhone 3G, force-quit by pressing and holding the Home button for 6 to 10 seconds.

   • If you have an iPhone 3GS or 4, force-quit as follows: Press and hold the sleep/wake button until the red Slide to Power Off button appears, and then release the sleep/wake button. Don't drag the red slider. Instead, with the red slider still on the screen, press and hold the Home button for 6 to 15 seconds.

If these steps don't get your iPhone back up and running, move on to the third *R,* resetting your iPhone.

Reset your iPhone

To reset your iPhone, merely press and hold the sleep/wake button while pressing and holding the Home button on the front. When you see the Apple logo, you can release both buttons.

Resetting your iPhone is like forcing your computer to restart after a crash. Your data shouldn't be affected by a reset. So don't be shy about giving this technique a try. In many cases, your iPhone goes back to normal after you reset it this way.

Remember to press *and hold* both the sleep/wake button and the Home button. If you press both and then release them, you create a *screen shot* — a picture of whatever is on your screen at the time — rather than reset your iPhone. (This type of screen picture, by the way, is stored in the Photos app's Camera Roll. Find out more about this feature at the end of Chapter 18.)

Unfortunately, sometimes resetting *doesn't* do the trick. When that's the case, you have to take stronger measures.

Remove content

If you've been reading along in this chapter, nothing you've done should have taken more than a minute or two. We hate to tell you, but that's about to change because the next thing you should try is removing some or all of your data, to see whether it's the cause of your troubles.

To do so, you need to sync your iPhone and reconfigure it so that some or all of your files are removed from the phone. The problem could be contacts, calendar data, songs, photos, videos, or podcasts. If you suspect a particular data type — for example, you suspect your photos because whenever you tap the Photos icon on the Home screen, your iPhone freezes — try removing that type of data first.

Or, if you have no suspicions, deselect every item on every tab in iTunes (Info, Apps, Music, Movies, Photos, and so on) and then sync. When you're finished, your iPhone should have no data on it.

If that method fixed the problem, try restoring your data, one type at a time. If the problem returns, you have to keep experimenting to determine which particular data type or file is causing the problem.

If you're still having problems, the next step is to reset your iPhone's settings.

Reset settings and content

Resetting involves two steps: The first one, resetting your iPhone settings, resets every iPhone *setting* to its default — the way it was when you took it out of the box. Resetting the iPhone's settings doesn't erase any of your data or media. The only downside is that you may have to go back and change some settings afterward, so you can try this step without trepidation. Tap the Settings icon on your Home screen, tap General, tap Reset, and then tap Reset All Settings.

Be careful *not* to tap Erase All Content and Settings, at least not yet. Erasing all content takes more time to recover from (because your next sync takes a long time), so try Reset All Settings first.

At this point, you could try resetting some of the other options available on the Reset screen, such as Reset Network Settings, Reset Keyboard Dictionary, Reset Home Screen Layout, or Reset Location Warnings. It's not likely to help but might be worth a try before you resort to erasing all content and settings, as we're about to describe.

Now, if resetting all settings didn't cure your iPhone, you have to try Erase All Content and Settings. (Read the next Warning first.) You find that option in the same place as Reset All Settings (tap Settings, General, and Reset).

This strategy deletes everything from your iPhone — all your data, media, and settings. Because all these items are stored on your computer — at least in theory — you should be able to put things back the way they were during your next sync. But you lose any photos you've taken, as well as contacts, calendar events, and any playlists you've created or modified since your last sync.

After using Erase All Content and Settings, check to see whether your iPhone works properly. If it doesn't cure what ails your iPhone, the final *R,* restoring your iPhone using iTunes, can help.

Restore

Before you give up the ghost on your poor, sick iPhone, you can try one more thing. Connect your iPhone to your computer as though you were about to sync. But when the iPhone appears in the iTunes source list, click the Restore button on the Summary tab. This action erases all your data and media and resets all your settings.

Because all your data and media still exist on your computer (except for photos you've taken, contacts, calendar events, notes, and playlists you've created or modified since your last sync, or iTunes or App Store content you've purchased or downloaded since your last sync, as noted previously), you shouldn't lose anything by restoring. Your next sync will take longer than usual, and you may have to reset settings you've changed since you got your iPhone. But other than those inconveniences, restoring shouldn't cause you any trouble.

Okay. So that's the gamut of things you can do when your iPhone acts up. If you tried all this and none of it worked, skim through the rest of this chapter to see whether anything else we recommend looks like it might help. If not, your iPhone probably needs to go into the shop for repairs.

Never fear, gentle reader. Be sure to read the last section in this chapter, "If Nothing We Suggest Works." Your iPhone may be quite sick, but we help ease the pain by sharing some tips on how to minimize the discomfort.

Problems with Calling or Networks

If you're having problems making or receiving calls, problems sending or receiving SMS text messages, or problems with Wi-Fi or your wireless carrier's data network, this section may help. The techniques here are short and sweet — except for the last one, restore. Restore, which we describe in the preceding section, is still inconvenient and time consuming, and it still entails erasing all your data and media and then restoring it.

First, here are some simple steps that may help. Once again, we suggest that you try them in this order (and so does Apple):

1. **Check the cell signal icon in the upper-left corner of the screen.**

   If you don't have at least one or two bars, you may not be able to use the phone or messaging function.

2. **Make sure you haven't left your iPhone in airplane mode, as described in Chapter 13.**

   In airplane mode, all network-dependent features are disabled, so you can't make or receive phone calls, send or receive messages, or use any apps that require a Wi-Fi or data network connection (that is, Mail, Safari, Stocks, Maps, and Weather).

3. **Try moving around.**

   Changing your location by as little as a few feet can sometimes mean the difference between four bars and zero bars or being able to use a Wi-Fi or wireless data network or not. If you're inside, try going outside. If you're outside, try moving 10 or 20 paces in any direction. Keep an eye on the cell signal or Wi-Fi icon as you move around, and stop when you see more bars than you saw before.

4. **Try changing your grip on the phone (or if it's an iPhone 4, try using a case).**

   Apple says, "Gripping any mobile phone will result in some attenuation of its antenna performance, with certain places being worse than others depending on the placement of the antennas. This is a fact of life for every wireless phone. If you ever experience this on your iPhone 4, avoid gripping it in the lower-left corner in a way that covers both sides of the black strip in the metal band, or simply use one of many available cases."

5. **Turn on airplane mode by tapping Settings on the Home screen, and then tapping the airplane mode On/Off switch to turn it on. Wait 15 or 20 seconds, and then turn it off again.**

   Toggling airplane mode on and off like this resets both the Wi-Fi and wireless data-network connections. If your network connection was the problem, toggling airplane mode on and off may correct it.

6. **Restart your iPhone.**

   If you've forgotten how, refer to the "Restart" section, a few pages back. Restarting your iPhone is often all it takes to fix whatever was wrong.

7. **Make sure your SIM card is firmly seated.**

   A *SIM* (Subscriber Identity Module) card is a removable smart card used to identify mobile phones. Users can change phones by moving the SIM card from one phone to another.

   To remove the SIM card, use the included SIM-eject tool (if you have an iPhone 3G or 3GS), or find a fine-gauge paper clip and straighten one end, and then stick the straight end *gently* into the hole on the SIM tray, as shown in Figure 15-1 for the iPhone 3G and 3GS and Figure 15-2 for the iPhone 4.

When the SIM tray slides out, carefully lift out the SIM card and then reinsert it, making sure it's firmly situated in the tray before you *gently* push the tray back in until it locks.

If none of the preceding suggestions fixes your network issues, try restoring your iPhone as described previously, in the "Restore" section.

Performing a restore deletes everything on your iPhone — all your data, media, and settings. You should be able to put things back the way they were with your next sync. If that doesn't happen, for whatever reason, you can't say we didn't warn you.

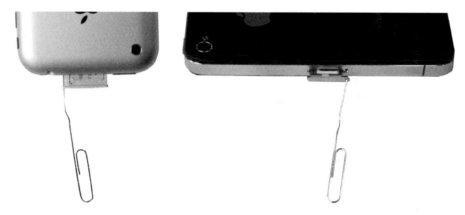

Figure 15-1: Removing the SIM tray on an iPhone 3G or 3GS.

Figure 15-2: Removing the SIM tray on an iPhone 4.

Sync, Computer, or iTunes Issues

The last category of troubleshooting techniques in this chapter applies to issues that involve synchronization and computer-iPhone relations. If you're having problems syncing or your computer doesn't recognize your iPhone when you connect it, here are some things to try.

Once again, we suggest that you try these procedures in the order they're presented here:

1. **Recharge your iPhone.**

   If you didn't try it previously, try it now. Go back to the "iPhone Issues" section, at the beginning of this chapter, and read what we say about recharging your iPhone. Every word there applies here.

2. **Try a different USB port or a different cable if you have one available.**

It doesn't happen often, but occasionally USB ports and cables go bad. When they do, they invariably cause sync and connection problems. Always make sure that a bad USB port or cable isn't to blame.

If you don't remember what we said about using USB ports on your computer rather than the ones on your keyboard, monitor, or hub, we suggest that you reread the "Recharge" section, earlier in this chapter.

Apple has used the same USB cable for iPods and iPhones for many years and also uses that same cable for iPads, so if you happen to have one of those cables handy, give it a try.

3. **Restart your iPhone and try to sync again.**

We describe restarting in full and loving detail in the "Restart" section, earlier in this chapter.

4. **Restart your computer.**

We have found that restarting your computer often fixes issues with syncing your iPhone.

Restarting your computer can fix non-iPhone issues as well. It's a good idea to reboot your computer before you do any kind of troubleshooting, be it with your iPhone or your computer.

5. **Reinstall iTunes.**

Even if you have an iTunes installer handy, you probably should visit the Apple Web site and download the latest-and-greatest version, just in case. You'll always find the latest version of iTunes at `www.apple.com/itunes/download`.

More Help on the Apple Web Site

If you try everything we suggest earlier in this chapter and still have problems, don't give up just yet. This section describes a few places you may find helpful. We recommend that you check out some or all of them before you throw in the towel and smash your iPhone into tiny little pieces (or ship it back to Apple for repairs, as described in the next section).

First, Apple offers an excellent set of support resources on its Web site at `www.apple.com/support/iphone`. You can browse support issues by category, search for a problem by keyword, or even get personalized help by phone, as shown in Figure 15-3.

Get personalized help

Browse by category   Discussion forums   Search by keyword

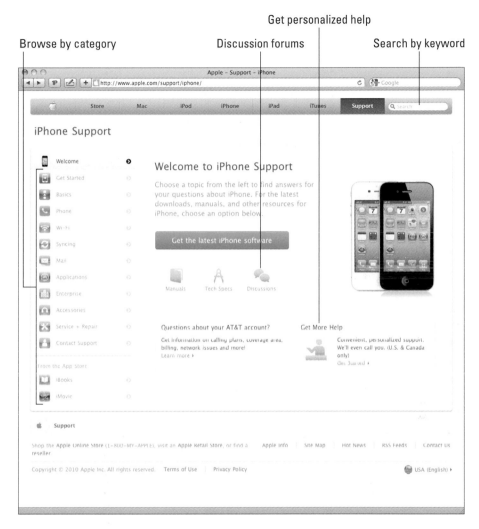

Figure 15-3: The Apple iPhone support pages offer several kinds of helpful information.

While you're visiting the Apple support pages, another section could be helpful: the discussion forums. You find them at `http://discussions.apple.com`, and they're chock-full of questions and answers from other iPhone users. Our experience has been that if you can't find an answer to a support question elsewhere, you can often find something helpful in these forums. You can browse by category, such as "Integrating iPhone into Your Digital Life" (part of the "Using iPhone" category), as shown in Figure 15-4, or search by keyword.

Figure 15-4: Page 1 of 276 pages of discussions about integrating the iPhone into your digital life.

Either way, you find thousands of discussions about almost every aspect of using your iPhone. Better still, frequently you can find the answer to your question or a helpful suggestion.

Now for the best part: If you can't find a solution by browsing or searching, you can post your question in the appropriate Apple discussion forum. Check back in a few days (or even in a few hours), and some helpful iPhone user may well have replied with the answer. If you've never tried this fabulous tool, you're missing out on one of the greatest support resources available anywhere.

Last, but certainly not least, before you give up the ghost, you might want to try a carefully worded Google search. It couldn't hurt, and you might just find the solution you spent hours searching for.

If Nothing We Suggest Helps

If you tried every trick in the book (this one) and still have a malfunctioning iPhone, it's time to consider shipping it off to the iPhone hospital (better known as Apple, Inc.). The repair is free if your iPhone is still under its one-year limited warranty.

You can extend your warranty as long as two years from the original purchase date. To do so, you need to buy the AppleCare Protection Plan for your iPhone. You don't have to do it when you buy the phone, but you must buy it before your one-year limited warranty expires. The cost is $69.

Here are a few things you should know before you take your phone in to be repaired:

- *Your iPhone is erased during its repair,* so you should sync your iPhone with iTunes before you take it in, if you can. If you can't and you entered data on the phone since your last sync, such as a contact or an appointment, the data won't be there when you restore your iPhone upon its return.

- Remove any third-party accessories, such as a case or screen protector.

- Remove the SIM card from your iPhone (as described in the earlier section "Problems with Calling or Networks") and keep it in a safe place.

  Do not, under any circumstances, forget to remove your SIM card. Apple doesn't guarantee that your SIM card will be returned to you after a repair. If you forget this step, Apple suggests that you contact your local AT&T store and obtain a new SIM card with the proper account information. Ouch.

Although you may be able to get your iPhone serviced by AT&T or by mail, we recommend that you take it to your nearest Apple Store, for two reasons:

- **No one knows your iPhone like Apple.** One of the geniuses at the Apple Store may be able to fix whatever is wrong without sending your iPhone away for repairs.

- **Only the Apple Store offers an Advance Replacement Service (ARS) for iPhones needing repairs.** The AppleCare Advance Replacement Service costs $29 when your iPhone is under warranty or covered by the AppleCare Protection Plan. This service provides you with a new iPhone before you have to send in your old one for service.

If your iPhone *isn't* under warranty or AppleCare, you can still take advantage of the Advance Replacement Service — it costs you a lot more, though. See Figure 15-5 for the costs at press time or visit `www.apple.com/support/iphone/service/exchange` for current pricing or more information on the ARS service.

iPhone 4	ARS Charge	Replacement Value	Out-of-Warranty Service Fee	Late Fee
16GB	$29	$599	$199	$200
32GB	$29	$699	$199	$250
iPhone 3GS	ARS Charge	Replacement Value	Out-of-Warranty Service Fee	Late Fee
8GB	$29	$499	$199	$150
16GB	$29	$599	$199	$200
32GB	$29	$699	$199	$250
iPhone 3G	ARS Charge	Replacement Value	Out-of-Warranty Service Fee	Late Fee
8GB	$29	$499	$199	$150
16GB	$29	$499	$199	$150
Original iPhone	ARS Charge	Replacement Value	Out-of-Warranty Service Fee	Late Fee
4GB & 8GB	$29	$399	$199	$100
16GB	$29	$499	$199	$150

A $6.95 shipping fee will be added to the Out-of-Warranty Service fee if you arrange service online or by calling Apple Technical Support. All fees are in US dollars and are subject to local tax.

Figure 15-5: Prices for Advance Replacement Service at press time.

If visiting an Apple or AT&T store isn't possible, call Apple at 1-800-MY-IPHONE (1-800-694-7466) in the United States or visit www.apple.com/contact to find the number to call in other countries.

If you choose the AppleCare Advance Replacement Service, you don't have to activate the new phone and it has the same phone number as the phone it replaces. All you need to do is pop your old SIM card into the new phone, sync it with iTunes to fill it with the data and media files that were on your sick iPhone, and you're good to go.

Part VI
The Part of Tens

*1*t's written in stone somewhere at Wiley world headquarters that we *For Dummies* authors must include a Part of Tens in every single *For Dummies* book we write. It's a duty we take quite seriously. So in this part, you find not just one but two lists of our favorite apps plucked from the iPhone App Store — ten apps that are free and ten that are not. These include programs to turn your iPhone into a grocery list, a baseball reference, and a capable Internet radio. Plus you find a couple of addictive games, and even an app to let you control your Mac or PC remotely from your iPhone.

We close the show with one of our favorite topics: hints, tips, and shortcuts that make life with your iPhone even better. Among the ten, you find out how to share Web pages and pick up another trick or two on using iPhone's virtual keyboard.

Ten Appetizing Apps

*K*iller app is familiar jargon to anyone who has spent any time around computers. The term refers to an app so sweet or so useful that just about everybody wants or must have it.

You could make the argument that the most compelling killer app on the iPhone is the very App Store we expound on in Chapter 14. This online emporium has an abundance of splendid programs — dare we say killer apps in their own right? — many of which are free. These apps cover everything from social networking tools to entertainment. Okay, so some rotten apples are in the bunch too. But we're here to accentuate the positive.

©PhotoDisc, Inc.

With that in mind, in this chapter we offer ten of our favorite free iPhone apps. In Chapter 17, you see ten iPhone apps that aren't free but are worth every penny.

We're showing you ours and we encourage you to show us yours. If you discover your own killer iPhone apps, by all means, let us know so we can check them out.

Shazam

Ever heard a song on the radio or television, in a store, or at a club, and wondered what it was called or who was singing it? With the Shazam app, you may never wonder again. Just launch Shazam and point your iPhone's microphone at the source of the music. In a few seconds, the song title and artist's name magically appear on your iPhone screen, as shown in Figure 16-1.

Figure 16-1: Point your phone at the music (left) and Shazam tells you the artist, title, and more (right).

In Shazam parlance, that song has been *tagged.* Now, if tagging were all Shazam could do, that would surely be enough. But wait, there's more. After Shazam tags a song you can

- ✔ Buy the song at the iTunes store
- ✔ Watch related videos on YouTube
- ✔ Tweet the song on Twitter
- ✔ Read a biography, a discography, or lyrics
- ✔ Take a photo and attach it to the tagged item in Shazam
- ✔ E-mail a tag to a friend

Shazam isn't great at identifying classical music, jazz, or opera, nor is it adept at identifying obscure indie bands. But if you use it primarily to identify popular music, it rocks (pun intended).

The free version of Shazam limits you to five tags a month. If that's enough for you, you're all set. But if you're like us, five tags a month just won't cut it. In that case, we recommend Shazam Encore, which offers unlimited tagging and several other exclusive features. We've tried other apps that claim to do what Shazam does. Although some others cost less, we've yet to find one as good as Shazam or Shazam Encore.

Shazam is amazing. It has worked for us in noisy airport terminals, crowded shopping malls, and even once at a wedding ceremony. Heck, Shazam is so good we gladly coughed up $4.99 for the premium version (Shazam Encore).

Wolfgang's Concert Vault

Wolfgang's Concert Vault is an app that provides you with free access to the largest collection of concert recordings in the world. Some of our favorites include The Who, Led Zeppelin, King Crimson, Neil Young, Pink Floyd, Creedence Clearwater Revival, Elvis Costello, and David Bowie. And if those particular artists don't appeal to you, check out concert recordings by hundreds upon hundreds of other artists.

What's cool is that these offerings are exclusive recordings you probably haven't heard before and probably won't hear elsewhere. You can find master recordings from the archives of Bill Graham Presents, the King Biscuit Flower Hour, and many others.

Before it appeared as an iPhone app, Wolfgang's Concert Vault was a superb Web site (www.wolfgangsvault.com), as shown in Figure 16-2.

The Wolfgang's Concert Vault iPhone app offers a clean, uncluttered interface (see Figure 16-3), and provides many of the Web site's best features, including playlists (see Figure 16-4). And, of course, after you create a free account, you can access your playlists and favorite songs on either the Web site or the iPhone app.

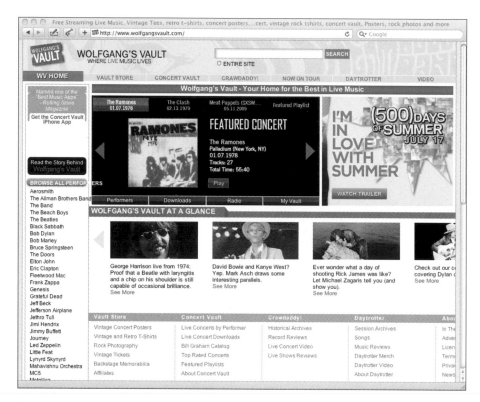

Figure 16-2: The Wolfgang's Vault Web site is more graphical than the iPhone app, but the latter delivers most of the same free goodies.

Both app and Web site let you tag a concert as a favorite, search for songs or artists, and listen to complete concert recordings at no charge. On the Web site, you can also create playlists by culling songs from different concert recordings. We wish the app allowed you to create playlists on your iPhone, but it does let you *listen* to the playlists you've created.

If you love music and want to hear unique live performances of songs you know and love, Wolfgang's Concert Vault is the app for you.

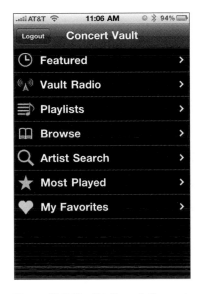

Figure 16-3: The Wolfgang's Concert Vault iPhone app has a simple, clean interface.

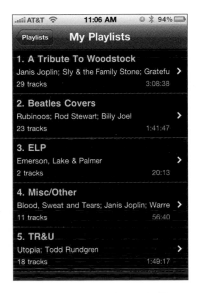

Figure 16-4: Some of Bob's playlists. (Can you tell the kind of music he likes?)

Instapaper

Do you ever come across a Web page you'd like to read later, when you have the time? Sure, you can bookmark those pages, but wouldn't it be nice if you could somehow save them to your iPhone and read them at your convenience? And wouldn't it be even nicer if you could read them without Internet access, such as when you're on an airplane?

We're happy to inform you that you can if you just download the Instapaper iPhone app from Marco Arment. Then, when you're surfing the Web on your Mac, PC, iPhone, iPad, or iPod touch and see a page you want to read later, select the special Instapaper Read Later *bookmarklet* (a special bookmark that uses JavaScript). From then on, you can read the page whenever you choose with the Instapaper iPhone app.

Figure 16-5 shows the Instapaper app displaying some of the Web pages we've saved with the Read Later bookmarklet. And Figure 16-6 shows what one of the articles looks like when you read it with the Instapaper app.

Instapaper is particularly good for long airplane trips. The week before Bob travels, he makes a point of grabbing lots of Web pages with his Read Later bookmarklet to ensure that he doesn't run out of good stuff to peruse during his flight. In fact, Bob likes it so much he's upgraded to the Pro version ($4.99), which adds useful features such as folders for storing your articles, the amazing tilt-scrolling, and automatic updating.

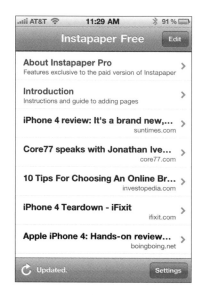

Figure 16-5: Instapaper displaying some Web pages we saved for our future reading pleasure.

Figure 16-6: The iPhone 4 review in the *Chicago Sun Times* on an iPhone.

reQall

reQall is much more than just an iPhone app. It's a complete and feature-packed system that captures information that's important to you and makes it easy for you to remember that info at the appropriate time.

The cool part is the unique way reQall works. You speak to the reQall app (see Figure 16-7). Shortly thereafter, your words are converted into text and sent to you by e-mail, text message, or instant message (or any combination of those three) as well as saved right in the reQall iPhone app, as shown in Figure 16-8).

And reQall's voice-to-text translations are surprisingly accurate, with better than 95 percent accuracy. In fact, the only mistake in the example in Figure 16-8 is that I (Bob) said to send the chapters to *Ed,* not *add.*

Now, that feature alone would be worth more than the price of admission (which, may we remind you, is free), but there's more: reQall understands certain words and can use them to route your reminder to the right place at the proper time. For example, it understands dates and times, so you can have reminders that include a time or a date or both. The reminders show up in all the places mentioned previously on the appropriate date and at the appropriate time. reQall also understands the word *buy,* and will put reminders that use that word on your shopping list. And it understands other words, including *note, ask, tell, remind, meet,* and *meeting.* And if you care to share reminders with others, you can do that, too.

We've been using reQall for more than a year and have seen several free updates and upgrades that just keep making it better and better.

How can you not love a free iPhone app that is elegant, useful, helpful, easy to use, and fun? We recommend reQall without hesitation. In fact, we think you'd be crazy not to try it.

Figure 16-7: Tap this screen and speak for up to 30 seconds.

Figure 16-8: Your speech is converted to text and, among other things, displayed in the reQall app.

IMDb

We like movies, so we both use the IMDb (Internet Movie Database) app a lot. In a nutshell, it knows everything there is to know about almost every movie ever made and many TV shows as well. For example, let's say you want to know something (anything) about the 1997 classic *The Fifth Element.*

Just type *Fifth Element,* tap the Search button, and everything (and we mean everything) about the movie appears — release date, original theatrical trailer, a plot summary, synopsis, the entire cast, the entire crew, critic's reviews, user reviews, trivia, goofs, and more (some of which are shown in Figure 16-9).

But that's not all. IMDb also includes all movies playing in theaters nearby (or near any zip code), showtimes for movies playing nearby, shows on TV tonight, lists such as STARmeter (most-viewed stars on IMDb this week), star birthdays, DVD and Blu-ray discs released recently or to be released soon, and U.S. box office results, all accessible from a well-organized and customizable home screen, shown in Figure 16-10.

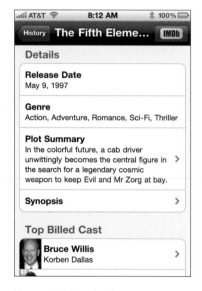

Figure 16-9: Details like these are available for almost every movie.

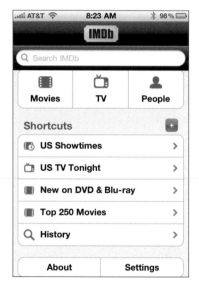

Figure 16-10: The IMDb home screen can be customized to your liking.

We appreciate that we can read reviews, play movie trailers, and e-mail movie listings to others with a single tap. We also enjoy perusing information and movie trailers for soon-to-be-released films and DVDs.

You won't find a more comprehensive guide to films and you can't beat the price!

Pandora Radio

We've long been fans of Pandora on the computer. So we're practically deliri-ous that this custom Internet radio service is available *gratis* on the iPhone.

And Pandora is better than ever, at least on the multitasking iPhone 3GS and iPhone 4 models, because you can listen to music in the background while doing other stuff. But we're getting ahead of ourselves.

Pandora works on the iPhone in much the same way it does on a PC or a Mac. You type the name of a favorite musician or song title and Pandora cre-ates an instant personalized radio station with selections that exemplify the style you chose. Figure 16-11 shows some of the eclectic stations we created. Tapping QuickMix plays musical selections across all your stations. Tapping the New Station button, at the bottom of the screen, displays the iPhone keyboard so that you can add a new station built around an artist, a song title, or a composer. You can also select from stations Pandora has packaged together around a particular genre.

In Figure 16-12, we typed *Beatles* and Pandora created a Beatles station that includes performances from John, Paul, George, and Ringo, as well as tunes from other artists whose songs are similar to songs by the Beatles both col-lectively and individually.

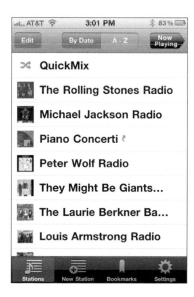

Figure 16-11: Eclectic online radio stations from Pandora.

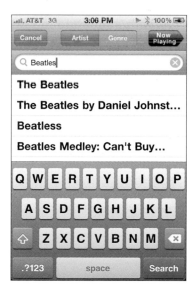

Figure 16-12: Creating a new station couldn't be easier.

And say you type in a song title, such as *Have I Told You Lately.* Pandora constructs a station with similar music after you tell it whether to base tunes on the Van Morrison, Rod Stewart, or other rendition.

Pandora comes out of the Music Genome Project, an organization of musicians and technologists who analyze music according to hundreds of attributes (such as melody, harmony, and vocal performances).

You can help fine-tune the music Pandora plays by tapping the thumbs-up or thumbs-down icon below the album cover of the song being played, as shown in Figure 16-13.

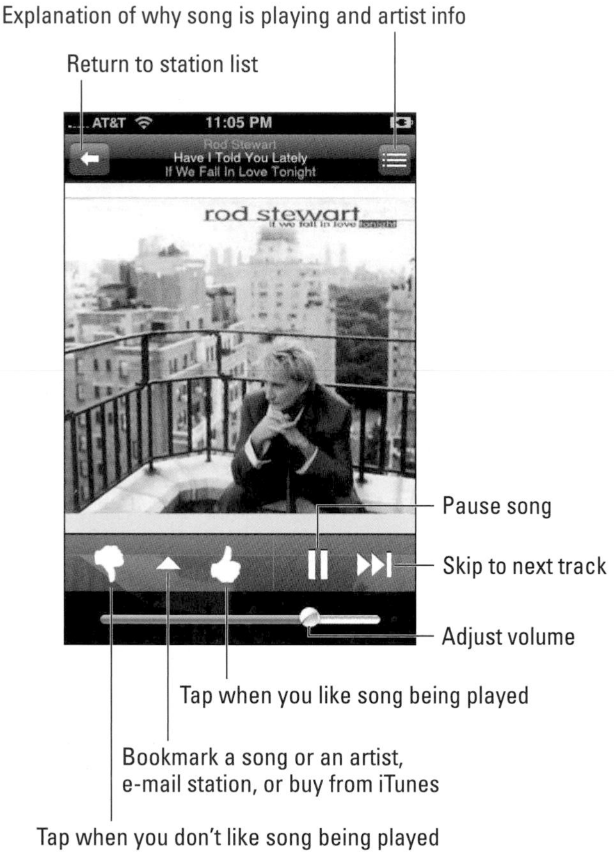
Explanation of why song is playing and artist info
Return to station list
AT&T
11:05 PM
Rod Stewart
Have I Told You Lately
If We Fall In Love Tonight
rod stewart
Pause song
Skip to next track
Adjust volume
Tap when you like song being played
Bookmark a song or an artist,
e-mail station, or buy from iTunes
Tap when you don't like song being played

Figure 16-13: Have we told you lately how much we like Pandora?

If you tap the triangular icon, you can bookmark the song or artist being played, e-mail to a friend the station that the song is playing on, or head to iTunes to purchase the song directly on the iPhone (if available).

Apple iBooks

"Did people once read books on paper?"

Don't be surprised if you have to answer this query from a curious kid some-day. Although we figure that time is still a ways off, the idea behind the question no longer seems so far off or farfetched. For proof, check out Apple's own iBooks (as well as the next app on our freebie list, Amazon's Kindle).

The beauty of electronic books, or e-books (or iBooks according to the Apple lexicon), is that you can schlep a boatload of reading material with you when you travel without breaking your back. And e-books can enhance your reading experience with a bevy of nifty tricks: You can look up the meaning of a word on the spot, change fonts and type sizes, and easily add highlights or bookmarks. Moreover, you can search for every mention of a particular term or subject in a book. Heck, with the iPhone, you can even read in the dark.

Apple introduced its iBooks app and the companion iBookstore online book-seller with the iPad tablet. With iOS 4, Apple brought both app and book-seller to the iPhone (though you still have to go to the App Store to download the iBooks app). As a result, electronic reading will never be the same.

The covers for the books you buy in iBookstore — about 60,000 titles were available as our own book went to press — land on the handsome virtual wooden bookshelf shown in Figure 16-14. You can stash Adobe PDF-formatted documents on the bookshelf too.

Tap a book cover to start reading the book. When you tap a page or drag its corner edge, the page changes, curling like a real book. We think that bit of razzle-dazzle is very cool. Check out Figure 16-15 to sample the controls that make virtual reading a veritable pleasure.

Shopping in iBookstore — to enter, tap the Store button from the bookshelf or "library" view — is an equal pleasure, with numerous ways to browse or search books you want to read, including from the *New York Times* bestseller lists.

Figure 16-16 shows one of the storefront views in the joint. Explore the various buttons for other views and to uncover books of interest.

Remove or change the order of books on the shelf

Display PDFs   Tap book to open it

Display books   Enter iBookstore

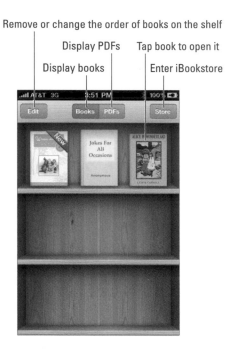

Figure 16-14: Your virtual bookshelf.

Change display brightness   Change fonts and font sizes

Contents or bookmarks   Search

Return to Library   Add bookmark

Figure 16-15: Handy reading tools.

Browse by category　　Return to Library

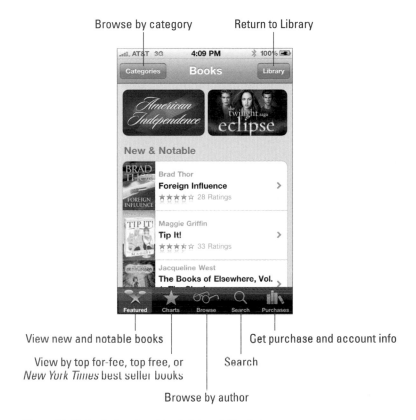

View new and notable books

View by top for-fee, top free, or
New York Times best seller books

Get purchase and account info

Search

Browse by author

Figure 16-16: Exploring the virtual aisles of iBookstore.

Tap any of the books that intrigue you to read reviews, get a free sample, and make a purchase. Pricing for iBooks varies, but the $12.99 sum for Brad Thor's *Foreign Influence,* the title shown in Figure 16-17, is typical for a new work. And the good news that is prices are almost always less expensive than their hardcover counterparts.

And, assuming you sync your iPhone and other devices with your computer regularly, your bookmarks, highlights, notes, and last location in a book will remain in sync with copies of the same book on an iPad or an iPod touch.

See other books in store

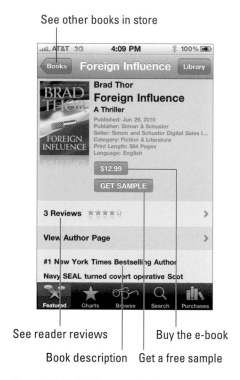

See reader reviews   Buy the e-book

Book description   Get a free sample

Figure 16-17: Buying an e-book is almost always cheaper than a hardcover work.

Amazon Kindle

The folks over at Amazon made a splash with the company's Kindle electronic readers. (When it comes to introducing high-profile products, we think the folks at Apple know a little something about making a splash too.) But although Ed is a fan of the Kindle reader, even he thinks they're expensive — $189 and up at the time this book was in production.

Kindle for the iPhone, on the other hand, is free, though of course you're still on the hook for buying electronic versions of books. You can buy e-books from a PC or a Mac and wirelessly transfer them to the Kindle app. Or within the app, you can tap Get Books, which transports you to Safari on the iPhone. From there, you can purchase titles in the online Kindle Store and send them wirelessly to the iPhone.

One huge advantage for the Kindle Store over the iBookstore: The Kindle Store, with more than 620,000 titles, has a lot more books than iBookstore's approximately 60,000 titles.

As with iBooks in Apple's iBookstore, e-books for Kindle are deeply discounted compared to their physical books. In the past, Amazon sold most new release bestsellers for just $9.99. But when this book was being published, prices were in a state of flux (and generally on the rise). Thor's *Foreign Influence* e-book cost $12.99 in the Kindle store (as well as in iBookstore). Figure 16-18 shows the Kindle Store on the iPhone, which you get to by tapping the Get Books button in the list of books in your library.

The books you own show up in a list like the one in Figure 16-19. Tap the title you want to read.

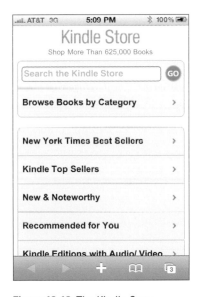

Figure 16-18: The Kindle Store.

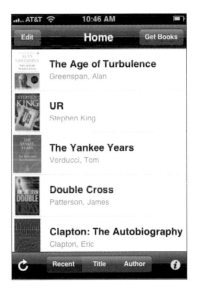

Figure 16-19: Tap to read a book in your Kindle library.

The Kindle app doesn't have nearly as large a screen as you find on a dedicated Kindle reader (and that goes, obviously, for the iBooks app compared to Apple's iPad). But the reading experience on the iPhone is surprisingly good, plus you can perform such tricks as adjusting the font size and text color (black, white, sepia), adding bookmarks, and reading in portrait or landscape mode by rotating the device. Controls for customizing your reading are shown in Figure 16-20. And with true iPhone flair, you can pinch to zoom in on what you're reading. The iPhone can even show off Kindle book covers in color, which not even the Kindle itself can do.

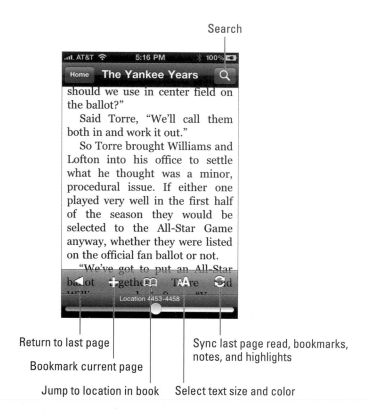

Search

Return to last page

Bookmark current page

Jump to location in book

Sync last page read, bookmarks, notes, and highlights

Select text size and color

Figure 16-20: Controls to make reading more pleasurable.

If you own a Kindle reader, you can switch back and forth between it and the iPhone Kindle app, without losing your place in whatever you're reading, a feature Amazon calls Whispersync. Bookmarks and such are synced. And that's downright novel.

WhitePages Mobile

Yea, yea, we know: Plenty of phone directories are on the Internet. But WhitePages Mobile is an incredibly handy resource for finding home and business numbers on the fly or doing a reverse phone lookup (you have the number but have no clue whose number it is). Figure 16-21 shows the different types of searches you can make.

When new listings pop up, you can add them to your contacts or update existing contacts. You can also get maps and directions to where folks live or work. In some cases, WhitePages Mobile provides other information, including the age range of the person and some of the other people living in the person's household. And WhitePages Mobile uses GPS to detect your current whereabouts.

Skype

You're probably thinking, "Why in goodness' sake do you need an app that makes phone calls when you're already carrying a cell phone?" Well, Skype calls are routed over the Internet through what geeks refer to as *VOIP* (Voice over Internet Protocol). And if you frequently call friends, colleagues, or relatives who are overseas, you can save money by not paying AT&T's lofty international rates. As with Skype on a PC or a Mac, direct calls made to other Skype members are free, and you can also instant message them for free (though they may incur a per-message charge). Through Skype, you can also call landline or mobile phones in the United States and around the world at low rates while not exhausting your monthly AT&T allowance. Furthermore, you can communicate with people using Skype on a computer, an iPad, an iPod touch, or (of course) an iPhone.

If a person is in your Skype contacts, just tap his or her name to call and begin a chat. You can display all your contacts or only those presently online. The app is conveniently integrated with your iPhone contacts too; if you tap a phone number there, the number is prepopulated in Skype's on-screen dial pad, shown in Figure 16-22.

Figure 16-21: Finding a number through WhitePages Mobile.

Figure 16-22: You can tap out a real phone number on Skype.

While you're on a call, you can summon the on-screen dial pad, mute a call, place a call on hold, and turn on or off the speakerphone.

Even better, you can make Skype-to-Skype calls and call other phones over 3G from your phone. When the Skype app first appeared, you had to have Wi-Fi access to make Skype calls. Skype-to-Skype calls over 3G are free, at least until the end of 2010, after which you'll likely be charged a small fee. Making calls over Wi-Fi will remain free.

As this book went to press, some Skype users were clamoring for FaceTime video chat support as well as the capability to get calls in the background over Skype while they do other stuff. The latter feature is promised through multitasking (for 3GS and 4 owners) and may be in place by the time you read this book. (Other VOIP apps already take advantage of multitasking in this way, albeit for a service fee. One to try is Line2.) We're less sanguine about FaceTime calling for Skype, at least right away.

17

Ten Apps Worth Paying For

If you read Chapter 16, you know that lots of great free apps are available for your iPhone. But as the old cliché goes, some things are worth paying for. Still, none of the ten for-pay apps we've chosen as some of our favorites are likely to break the bank. As you're about to discover, some of the apps on this list are practical and others are downright silly. The common theme? We think you'll like carrying these apps around on your iPhone.

©iStockphoto.com/Helder Almeida

Tiger Woods PGA Tour ($4.99)

Bob loved Electronic Arts' Mac version of Tiger Woods PGA Tour and played it until his fingers bled. Now he's enjoying the iPhone version almost as much. The graphics and level of detail are incredible, as shown in Figure 17-1, and the user interface is among the best we've seen for an iPhone game. And the touch-and-drag swing meter, shown in Figure 17-2, is one of the best touchscreen game controls either of us has tried.

Figure 17-1: The graphics and detail in Tiger Woods PGA Tour are outstanding.

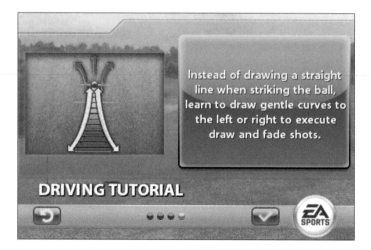

Figure 17-2: Drag your finger to the left or right as shown to execute draw and fade shots.

With your choice of seven world-famous golf courses and top golfers such as Annika Sorenstam, Vijay Singh, and of course, Tiger Woods, along with real-time play-by-play commentary by Sam Torrance and Kelly Tilghman, you can play over and over and over without repetition.

Say what you will about Tiger Woods, but if you like golf or just enjoy a beautifully designed iPhone game, Tiger Woods PGA Tour is a bargain at $4.99.

Zosh ($2.99)

It's a common scenario for a busy executive. You're on a business trip when a client e-mails paperwork that requires your signature — pronto. You search the town trying to locate both a printer so you can print and sign the document and a fax machine to send it off.

Or you can put Zosh on the case. The app lets you sign documents on the iPhone with your finger. Here's how: To access a PDF document in Zosh, you attach the item to an e-mail and send it to `mydocs@zosh.com`. Then open the Zosh app on the iPhone, tap the document you just e-mailed from the Home screen, and position the document so that the area that requires your signature is at or near the center of the screen.

Tap Insert to add your signature (or text, date, or image), as shown in Figure 17-3. Figure 17-4 shows the blank screen where you scribble your signature, right next to the X. If you don't like what your signature looks like — believe us, scribbling on the iPhone takes practice — tap Erase and try again.

Figure 17-3: The first step to inserting your John Hancock or other info.

Figure 17-4: Scribble your signature on this screen.

TIP

If you're having trouble getting your signature right, try signing with the iPhone in landscape mode.

When you've finished filling out the item on your iPhone, Zosh sends it back to your e-mail address. Tap the Transmit button to e-mail the document to yourself or to other e-mail recipients.

Zosh includes tools to help smooth this process A built-in algorithm lets you resize and fit a fat signature. You can also change the ink color and font type. In addition, Zosh is compatible with a variety of popular file formats, including PDF, Word, Excel, PPT and JPG.

OldBooth Premium ($1.99)

OldBooth Premium is just plain fun. It lets you take any full-face photo and apply wonderfully goofy transformations to it. A picture is worth a thousand words, so we'll start this description with Figure 17-5, which clearly demonstrates just what it is that OldBooth Premium does.

Figure 17-5: The original photos of Bob and his wife Lisa are on the far left; the three OldBooth images of each appear to the right of them.

You get the picture, don't you? (Pun completely intended.)

Using OldBooth Premium is as easy as 1-2-3:

1. **Select a gender and then select one of the 20 mask styles available for each gender.**

2. **Select a picture.**

   You can either take a new photo with your iPhone's camera or select a picture from your iPhone's Photo Library.

3. **Resize the picture by pinching or unpinching, rotate the picture by pressing and dragging, and adjust the brightness of the picture, the mask, or both.**

   When you're happy with the image, save it to your iPhone's camera roll, where you can use it as wallpaper, e-mail it to a friend, assign it to a contact, or send it to MobileMe. The picture will be exported to your Mac or PC the next time you sync.

OldBooth is easy and lots of fun for less than two bucks.

If two bucks sounds like too much to pay, you can get a free version called OldBooth Lite, which has a limited number of masks. We predict that once you've tried the free version, you'll gladly shell out $1.99 for the real deal.

GottaGo ($1.99)

If you've ever wanted a perfect excuse to leave a meeting (or anywhere else, for that matter), you'll love GottaGo. This clever little app lets you create a bogus phone call or text message and have it appear on your iPhone at any time you choose. At the appropriate moment, your iPhone rings or chimes and you receive what looks and sounds just like a real phone call or text message.

The GottaGo unlock screen is animated just like the real thing. You can attach an image to your GottaGo call so it truly looks like you're receiving a real phone call. You can record custom audio that you hear when you answer the fake call. And you can select your own wallpaper and ringtone to make the effect even more realistic. The call settings screen is shown in Figure 17-6, and the resulting fake call appears in Figure 17-7.

When you gotta go, nothing gets you out of there faster than the GottaGo iPhone app. Isn't two bucks a tiny price to pay for your freedom?

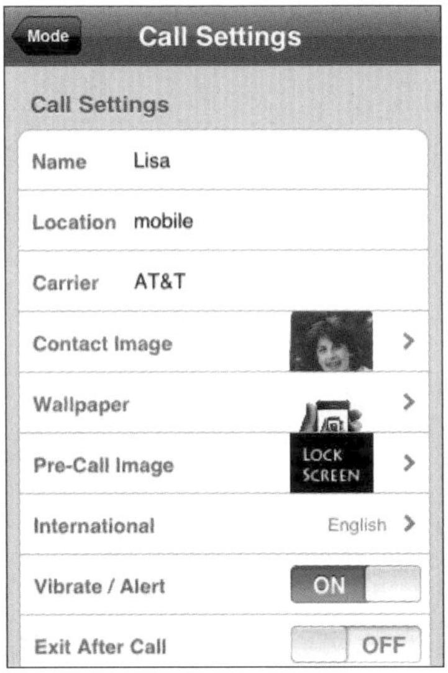

Figure 17-6: GottaGo has a myriad of settings to make your fake call (or text message) look like the real thing.

Figure 17-7: Even you might be fooled by GottaGo.

WordsWorth ($1.99)

Being writers ourselves, we love a good word game, and one of our favorites so far is WordsWorth. You form words by tapping letters on the screen. Longer words using rarer letters (such as *J, Z,* and *Qu,* for example) score more points than shorter words with more common letters.

To make things interesting, the app includes certain special tiles, such as blue wild cards, green bonuses, and red timers, all shown in Figure 17-8. A gold tile (see Figure 17-9) helps you grow your score. The timer tiles are the most insidious; if their time runs out before you've used the letter, the game is over.

WordsWorth doesn't have a fixed time limit per game. Instead, it's level-based — each time you achieve the prescribed number of points, you advance to the next level. And, of course, the levels grow increasingly harder with more and rarer timed tiles, fewer vowels, and rarer consonants.

If you can't find any more words on the screen, you can shuffle the tiles by shaking your iPhone. But be careful: A limited number of shuffles are available for each level.

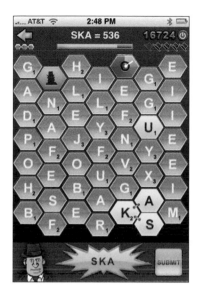

Figure 17-8: Special tiles make WordsWorth a challenge.

Figure 17-9: Going for the gold in WordsWorth.

Although WordsWorth is simple, it's engaging and addictive. And you can even compete against other players over Bluetooth or Wi-Fi, or challenge your friends on the Facebook social network.

Lots of terrific word-based games are available for the iPhone. Another favorite worth checking out is a Boggle-like game called Wurdle from Semi Secret Software, which will also set you back only $1.99.

iTeleport ($24.99)

We admit that iTeleport isn't cheap and is more than a little geeky, but it's so cool and potentially useful that we would have been remiss had we not included it.

iTeleport is technically a VNC (Virtual Network Computing, also known as remote screen control) client. Put another way, it's an iPhone app for controlling your Mac, Windows, or Linux computer "from a few feet away or from halfway around the world."

Yes, you can actually see your computer screen and control its keyboard and mouse from anywhere in the world (as long as your iPhone can connect to the Internet through Wi-Fi, 3G, EDGE, or whatever).

Figure 17-10 shows an iPhone running iTeleport, which is controlling a Mac in another room (though the Mac could just as easily be in a different city, state, or country).

Disconnect   Settings   Modifier keys   Shortcuts   Keyboard

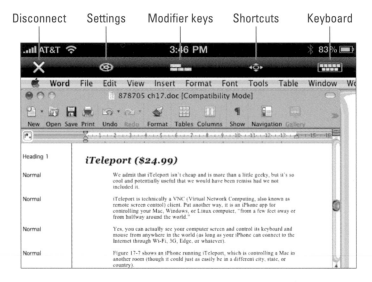

Figure 17-10: I'm editing this chapter with Microsoft Word while controlling my Mac remotely with iTeleport.

iTeleport is an iPhone app, so you pinch and unpinch to zoom in and out. In Figure 17-10, we zoomed in on the upper-left corner of the Mac screen, where this very chapter is being edited in Microsoft Word.

There's little you can do on your Mac, PC, or Linux computer that you can't control remotely with iTeleport — though of course you're dealing with a smaller screen on the iPhone. We use iTeleport to check mail accounts other than the ones on our iPhones, to grab files from our hard drive and e-mail them to ourselves (at our iPhone e-mail addresses) or others, and to make sure backups are running when scheduled.

Another cool use for the app is as a spy cam. This feature requires that you have a computer with a built-in camera, such as an iMac, a MacBook, or a MacBook Pro. Open an app that uses the built-in camera (for example, Photo Booth on the Mac or a Webcam program under Windows), and you'll be able to watch what's happening in front of that computer on your iPhone no matter where in the world you happen to be.

Several free or less expensive VNC apps are available in the iTunes Store, but iTeleport is the only one we've found that is robust and reliable enough to recommend.

Baseball Statistics 2010 Edition ($2.99)

Consider Baseball Statistics 2010 Edition a dream app for a passionate baseball fan. One of the things that makes baseball such a great game is the statistics that have defined the sport since, well, the 19th century. (We won't add a steroids comment — oops, just did.) Baseball Statistics from Bulbous Ventures puts all those stats at your fingertips, so you can settle barroom bets or just relive memories of favorite ballplayers from when you were a kid.

The app has easily accessible yearly stats for every Major League player and team since 1871 — nope, we weren't around — from batting, fielding, and pitching statistics to team wins, losses, and attendance.

The 2010 Edition adds a baseball card feature that displays a player's career stats, as if it were the back of a baseball card, when you rotate the iPhone to its side. We only wish we also could get a front baseball-card view with a picture of a uniform-clad player, but we're quibbling.

Poking around is fun. We found stats for outfielder Cherokee Fisher of the 1872 Baltimore Canaries. (Check out Figure 17-11 for evidence that the Canaries existed.) And to help decide one of those classic "who-was-better" barroom debates, we compared Mickey Mantle's career stats to Willie Mays's.

About the only bad thing we can say about Baseball Statistics (which used to be called just Baseball) is that the app was once free. But Ed, a passionate New York Mets junkie, would gladly spring for the $2.99 tab. Heck, that sum would have bought an awfully good seat at the ballpark when Tom Seaver was pitching brilliantly for the 1969 Miracle Mets. His stats from that season are shown in Figure 17-12.

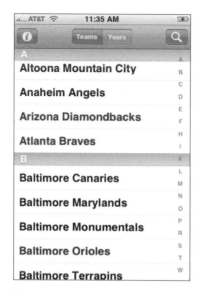

Figure 17-11: And you thought the Orioles were the only Major League team in Baltimore.

Figure 17-12: An amazing year for Tom Terrific and the Miracle Mets of 1969.

Ocarina ($0.99)

Almost overnight, Ocarina, Smule's addictive app, became one of the most popular in the App Store. It can transform your iPhone into an ancient flute-light instrument. You gently blow into the iPhone's microphone and play notes by pressing and holding your fingers over any of four virtual on-screen holes, shown in Figure 17-13. There are 16 possible combinations.

At Smule's Web site, you can learn how to play and even find Ocarina sheet music for everything from *I've Grown Accustomed to Her Face* to *Yellow Submarine.*

Tap the Globe menu icon (not shown in Figure 17-13) to hear other people play around the world. The sound waves depicted in Figure 17-14 are coming from the Middle East. You can tap a heart to show other people you think highly of their performances, and they in turn can show you the love.

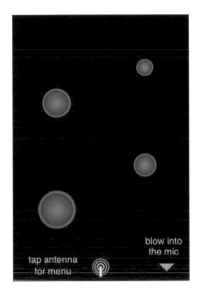

Figure 17-13: Turning the iPhone into an ancient flute-like instrument.

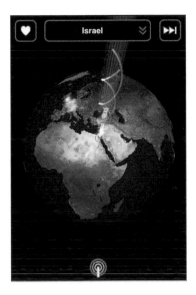

Figure 17-14: Some lovely notes from Israel.

Air Video ($2.99)

We both have more than 100GB of movies and TV shows in our iTunes Library, so an iPhone with 16GB or even 32GB of storage just doesn't cut it. Having to decide which movies and TV shows to sync to our iPhone makes us crazy — we want all of our movies and TV shows available on our iPhones all of the time.

Well, with Air Video, we can. Air Video lets you stream video from your Mac or PC to your iPhone. It works over a 3G or Wi-Fi connection. You can use it with almost all common video formats, and you can convert most formats on the fly, so you can usually start watching your video immediately after you select it.

After you've purchased the Air Video iPhone app, the first step is to download the free Air Video server and launch it on your Mac or PC. The second step is to tell the server which folder contains the video you want to access remotely. That's all there is to it — there is no step 3!

What Bob loves most about Air Video is that he can carry around an entire season of his son's high school football games without them using up a single megabyte of precious storage on his 32GB iPhone. Figure 17-15 shows the Air Video movie selection screen; remember that these huge movie files are stored on a computer in a remote location, not on his iPhone.

The only thing that makes Air Video less than perfect is that it doesn't work with DRM (digital rights management) protected video. So it won't work with video content you purchase from the iTunes Store, though it works fine with free video podcasts and iTunes U courseware that you download from the iTunes Store.

Even so, for a mere $2.99, we can access any and all of our personal video collection without using a single bit (or byte) of space on our iPhone. (You can even try a free version with a limited number of movies.) And that, friends, is a wonderful thing.

Zagat to Go ($9.99)

Hey, you have to eat sometime. Zagat to Go, the newly updated app from Handmark, lets you access the popular Zagat ratings for restaurants, hotels, nightspots, and other destinations around the world — there are in excess of 40,000 listings from 45-plus Zagat guides.

You can search; filter results by food, décor, cost, and service; and read Zagat's famous thumbnail commentaries, as shown in Figure 17-16. Foodies can tap into GPS to find decent restaurants when they're traveling. You can even use Zagat in an offline mode when you don't have access to the Internet. And if you have an iPad as well as an iPhone, you can use the app on both devices.

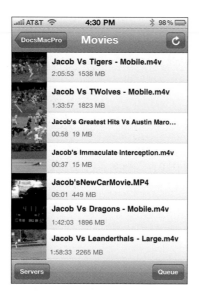

Figure 17-15: We can watch any of these movies on our iPhone.

Figure 17-16: Finding a swanky place to eat.

18

Ten Helpful Hints, Tips, and Shortcuts

*A*fter spending a lot of quality time with our iPhones, it's only natural that we've discovered more than a few helpful hints, tips, and shortcuts. In this chapter, we share some of our faves.

Do the Slide for Accuracy and Punctuation

Our first tip can help you type faster in two ways: by helping you type more accurately and by enabling you to type punctuation and numerals faster than ever before.

While reading this book, you find out how to tap, double-tap, and even double-tap with two fingers. Now we want to introduce you to a new gesture we like to call the *slide*.

To do the slide, you start by performing the first half of a tap. That is, you touch your finger to the keyboard screen but don't lift it up. Now, without lifting your finger, slide it onto the key you want to type. You'll know you're on the right key because it pop ups and enlarges.

First, try the slide during normal typing. Stab at a key. If you miss, rather than lifting your finger, backspacing, and trying again, do the slide onto the proper key. After you get the hang of the slide, you'll see that it saves a lot of time and improves your accuracy as well.

Now here's the best part: You can use the slide to save time with punctuation and numerals, too. The next time you need to type a punctuation mark or number, try this technique:

1. **Start a slide action with your finger on the 123 key.**

   The 123 key is to the left of the Space key when the alphabetical keyboard is active. This is a slide, not a tap, so don't lift your finger just yet.

2. **When the punctuation and numeric keyboard appears on-screen, slide your finger onto the punctuation mark or number you want to type.**

3. **Lift your finger.**

The cool thing is that the punctuation and numeric keyboard disappears and the alphabetical keyboard reappears — all without tapping the 123 key to display the punctuation and numeric keyboard and without tapping the ABC key (the key to the left of the Space key when the punctuation and numeric keyboard is active).

Practice the slide for typing letters, punctuation, and numerals, and we guarantee that in a few days you'll be typing faster and more accurately.

Autocorrect Is Your Friend

In this section, we describe two related tips about autocorrection that can also help you type faster and more accurately.

Auto apostrophes are good for you

First, before moving on from the subject of punctuation, you should know that you can type *dont* to get to *don't*, and *cant* to get to *can't*. We told you to put some faith in the iPhone's autocorrection software. And that applies to contractions. In other words, save time by letting the iPhone's intelligent keyboard insert the apostrophes on your behalf for these and other common words.

We're aware of a few exceptions. The iPhone cannot distinguish between *it's,* the contraction of *it is,* and *its,* the possessive adjective and possessive pronoun. It has the same issue with other contractions such as won't (wont) and can't (cant).

Make rejection work for you

If the autocorrect suggestion isn't the word you want, reject it instead of ignoring it. Finish typing the word and then tap the x to reject the suggestion before you type another word. Doing so makes your iPhone more likely to accept your word the next time you type it (or less likely to make the same incorrect suggestion the next time you type the word).

Here you thought you were buying a tech book, and you get grammar and typing lessons thrown in at no extra charge. Just think of us as full-service authors.

The Way-Cool Hidden iTunes Scrub Speed Tip

Here's the situation: You're listening to a podcast or audiobook and trying to find the beginning of a specific segment by moving the scrubber left and right. The only problem is that the scrubber isn't very precise and your fat finger keeps moving it too far one way or the other. Never fear — your iPhone has a wonderful (albeit somewhat hidden) fix. Just press your finger on the scrubber (that little round dot on the scrubber bar), but instead of sliding your finger to the left or right, slide it downward toward the bottom of the screen (see Figure 18-1). As you slide, the scrubbing speed changes like magic and the amount of change is displayed above the scrubber bar. The default (normal) speed is called high-speed scrubbing; when you slide your finger downward, the speed changes to half-speed scrubbing, then to quarter-speed scrubbing, and finally to fine scrubbing. This scrub trick is easier to do than to explain, so give it a try.

While you're sliding, keep an eye on the elapsed time and remaining time indicators because they provide useful feedback on the current scrubbing speed.

Scrubber

Elapsed time   Remaining time

Slide finger

Figure 18-1: Press on the scrubber and slide your finger downward to change the scrubbing rate.

Tricks with Links and Phone Numbers

The iPhone does something special when it encounters a phone number or URL in e-mail and SMS text messages. The iPhone interprets as a phone number any sequence of numbers that looks like a phone number: 1-123-555-4567, 555-4567, 1.123.555.4567, and so on. The same goes for sequences of characters that look like a Web address (URL), such as `http://www.WebSiteName.com` or `www.WebSiteName.com`. When the iPhone sees what it assumes to be a URL, it appears as a blue link on your screen.

If you tap a phone number or URL sequence like the ones just shown, the iPhone does the right thing. It launches the Phone app and dials the number for a phone number, or it launches Safari and takes you to the appropriate Web page for a URL. That's useful but somewhat expected. What's more useful and not so expected is the way Safari handles phone numbers and URLs.

Assault on batteries

Because this is a chapter of tips and hints, we'd be remiss if we didn't include some ways that you can extend your battery life. First and foremost: If you use a carrying case, charging the iPhone while it's in that case may generate more heat than is healthy. Overheating is bad for both battery capacity and battery life. So take the iPhone out of the case before you charge it.

If you're not using a 3G or Wi-Fi network, or a Bluetooth device (such as a headset or car kit), consider turning off the features you don't need in Settings. Doing so could mean the difference between running out of juice and being able to make that important call later in the day.

Activate Auto-Brightness to enable the screen brightness to adjust based on current lighting conditions, which can be easier on your battery. Tap Settings on the Home screen, tap Brightness, and then tap the On/Off switch, if necessary, to turn it on.

Turning off Location Services (tap Settings, tap General, and then tap the On/Off switch to turn off Location Services) and Push (tap Settings, tap Fetch New Data, and then tap the On/Off switch to turn off Push) can also help to conserve battery life.

Finally, turning on EQ (see Chapter 7) when you listen to music can make it sound better, but it also uses more processing power. If you've added EQ to tracks in iTunes using the Track Info window, and you want to retain the EQ from iTunes, set the EQ on your iPhone to flat. Because you're not turning off EQ, your battery life will be slightly worse but your songs will sound just the way you expect them to sound. Either way, to alter your EQ settings, tap Settings on the Home screen, tap iPod, and then tap EQ.

Apple says a properly maintained iPhone battery will retain up to 80 percent of its original capacity after 400 full charge and discharge cycles. You can replace the battery at any time if it no longer holds sufficient charge. Your one-year limited warranty includes the replacement of a defective battery. Coverage jumps to two years with the AppleCare Protection Plan. Apple will replace the battery if it drops below 50 percent of its original capacity.

If your iPhone is out of warranty, Apple will replace the battery for $79.00 plus $6.95 shipping, plus local tax, and will also dispose of your old battery in an environmentally friendly manner.

Let's start with phone numbers. When you encounter a phone number on a Web page, give it a tap. A little dialog box appears on the screen displaying that phone number and offering you a choice of two buttons: Call or Cancel. Tap Call to switch to the Phone app and dial the number; tap Cancel to return to the Web page.

Here's another cool Safari trick, this time with links. If you press and hold on a link rather than tapping it, a little floating text bubble appears and shows you the underlying URL.

You also see the underlying URL if you press and hold on a URL in Mail or Messages. Having this information in Mail or Messages is even more useful because it enables you to spot bogus links without switching to Safari or actually visiting the URL.

Finally, here's one last Safari trick. If you press and hold on most graphic images, a Save Image button appears. Tap it and the picture is saved to the camera roll in the Photos app.

Share the Love

Ever stumble on a Web page you just have to share with a buddy? The iPhone makes it dead simple. From the site in question, tap the + button at the bottom of the browser. Then tap the Mail Link to This Page button that appears on-screen. A mail message appears with the Subject line prepopulated with the name of the Web site you're visiting, and the body of the message prepopulated with the URL. Just type something in the message body (or don't), supply your pal's e-mail address, and then tap the Send button.

Choosing a Home Page for Safari

You may have noticed that there's no home page Web site on the iPhone version of Safari, as there is in the Mac and PC versions of the browser (and for that matter, every other Web browser we know of). Instead, when you tap the Safari icon, you return to the last site you visited.

The trick is to create an icon for the page you want to use as your home page. This technique is called creating a *Web clip* of a Web page. Here's how to do it:

1. **Open the Web page you want to use as your home page and tap the + button.**

2. **Tap the Add to Home Screen button.**

   An icon that will open this page appears on your Home screen (or one of your Home screens if you have more than one).

3. **Tap this new Web clip icon instead of the Safari icon, and Safari opens to your home page instead of to the last page you visited.**

You can even rearrange the icons so that your home page icon, instead of the Safari icon, appears in the dock (the bottom row that appears on every Home screen), as shown in Figure 18-2. See the tip in Chapter 1 for rearranging icons if you've forgotten how.

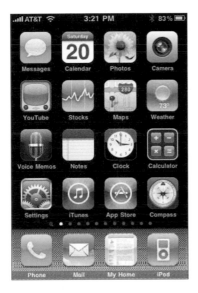

Figure 18-2: The My Home icon appears where Safari usually appears in the dock.

Don't forget that you can create folders by dragging one icon onto another. This trick works for Web clip icons as well as for app icons, and you're free to mix and match clips and apps in the same folder!

Storing Files

A tiny Massachusetts software company known as Ecamm Network is selling an inexpensive piece of Mac OS X software that lets you copy files from your computer to your iPhone and copy files from the iPhone to a computer. (There's no Windows version.) Better still, you can try the $19.95 program called PhoneView for a week before deciding whether you want to buy it. Go to www.ecamm.com to fetch the free demo.

In a nutshell, here's how it works. After downloading the software onto your Mac, double-click the program's icon to start it. To transfer files and folders to the iPhone (assuming there's room on the device), click the Copy to iPhone button on the toolbar, and then select the files you want to copy. The files are copied into the appropriate folder on the iPhone. Alternatively, you can drag files and folders from the Mac desktop or a folder into the PhoneView browser.

To go the other way and copy files from your iPhone to your computer, highlight the files or folders you want copied, and click the Copy from iPhone button on the toolbar. Select the destination on your Mac where you want to store the files, and then click Save. You can also drag files and folders from the PhoneView file browser onto the Mac desktop or folder. Or you can double-click a file in the PhoneView browser to download it to your Mac's Documents folder.

If you need access to the files on your iPhone, or if you want to use your iPhone as a pseudo hard disk, PhoneView is a bargain.

Create Ringtones for Free in GarageBand

The capability to create free iPhone ringtones with Apple's GarageBand application (which is bundled with every Mac) was beyond the purview of the ringtone discussions in previous chapters. Creating those ringtones, however, is relatively easy. Start by launching GarageBand and creating a new Music project. Then:

1. **Click the Media Browser button to reveal the media browser pane.**

2. **Click the disclosure triangle to reveal the contents of your iTunes library.**

3. **Click your iTunes music library to reveal its contents.**

4. **Select the song you want to turn into a ringtone and drag it onto the timeline (*Hello Muddah, Hello Faddah!* in Figure 18-3).**

   You can't use songs purchased from the iTunes store for ringtones if they are protected by Apple's digital rights management copy protection. GarageBand won't let you drag a protected song onto its timeline.

   Apple stopped using copy protection for music files in April 2009. If you purchased the song after that, you're good to go. If you purchased the song before then, you can pay a small upgrade fee (30 cents at press time) to convert the song to iTunes Plus, Apple's new higher-quality, non-copy-protected format.

   The bottom line is that you can make ringtones only from songs you've ripped yourself from CD or downloaded without rights management or other copy protection (such as MP3s from Amazon.com or files in Apple's iTunes Plus format).

5. **Click the cycle region button to enable the cycle region.**

6. **Click in the middle of the cycle region and drag it to the portion of the song you want to use as your ringtone.**

Disclosure triangle for iTunes   Media Browser pane

Timeline   iTunes music libary

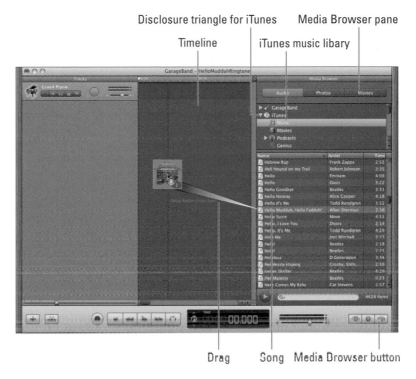

Drag   Song   Media Browser button

Figure 18-3: Creating a custom ringtone, part I.

7. **Fine-tune the start and end points by clicking and dragging the cycle region's left and right edges, as shown in Figure 18-4.**

   For best results, keep your ringtones under 30 seconds.

8. **Click the play button to hear your work. When you're satisfied with it, choose Share⇨Send Ringtone to iTunes.**

The next time you sync, your new ringtone becomes available on your iPhone. To use it as your ringtone, tap Settings, Sounds, Ringtone, and then tap the ringtone in the list of available sounds. To associate the ringtone with a specific contact or contacts, find the contact in either the Contacts app or the Phone app's Contacts tab, tap Ringtone, and then tap the ringtone in the list of available sounds.

If you have a microphone, you can record ringtones featuring voice recordings such as the following. "Yo! It's your bro!" "This is your mother. Pick up the phone right this moment." "Ed Baig calling." "Incoming! Incoming!" "This is your iPhone and I'm ringing." And so on. You get the picture.

Cycle region

Cycle region start   Cycle region end

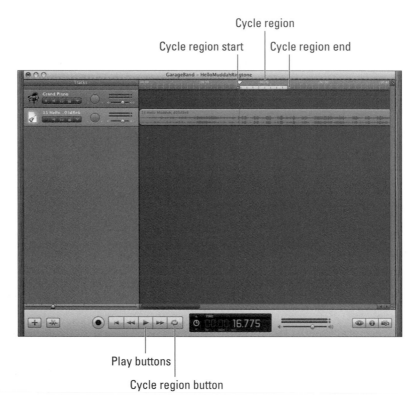

Play buttons

Cycle region button

Figure 18-4: Creating a custom ringtone, part II.

Taking a Snapshot of the Screen

True confession: We threw in this final tip because, well, it helps people like *us*.

Permit us to explain. We hope you've admired the pictures of the iPhone screens that are sprinkled throughout this book. We also secretly hope that you're thinking what marvelous photographers we must be.

Well, the fact is, we couldn't take a blurry picture of the iPhone using its built-in (and only recently documented by Apple) screen-grab feature if we wanted to.

Press the sleep/wake button at the same time you press the Home button, but just for an instant. The iPhone grabs a snapshot of whatever is on the screen. The picture lands in the iPhone's camera roll; from there, you can synchronize it with your PC or Mac, along with all your other pictures. And from there, the possibilities are endless. Why, your picture could wind up just about anywhere, including in a *For Dummies* book.

Getting Apps Out of the Multitasking Tray

iOS 4's multitasking is great, but sometimes you don't want to see an app's icon in the multitasking tray. Don't worry — it's easy to remove any app that's cluttering up your tray.

To get rid of an app icon in the multitasking tray, here's what you do:

1. **Double-press the Home button.**

   The multitasking tray appears.

2. **Press any icon in the tray until all of the icons begin to wiggle and display a little red – symbol, as shown in Figure 18-5.**

3. **Tap the little red – symbol for the app (or apps) you want to remove from the tray.**

   The app disappears from the multitasking tray. (We tapped the Comic Touch app in Figure 18-5.) To fill the gap in the tray, apps slide to the left. (Icons from the group of apps you'd see if you swiped from right to left on the tray slide onto the screen as needed.)

4. **Press the Home button to end the wiggling and hide the red – symbols.**

5. **Press the Home button again to dismiss the multitasking tray.**

Figure 18-5: Press any icon in the multitasking tray until the icons wiggle and grow little red – symbols.

Figure 18-6: After removing Comic Touch, the Photos and Camera icons slide to the left to fill the space.

You can use this trick to stop an app that's running in the background, too. For example, if Pandora Radio is playing in the background and you decide you've had enough Pandora for now, just follow the preceding steps and Pandora will shut the heck up. Without this trick, you'd have to open Pandora, tap the Pause button, then press the Home button to close Pandora. Using the tip is easier and often faster.

Index

• *U* •

• *V* •

• W •

• Y •